Moral Wages

Moral Wages

The Emotional Dilemmas of
Victim Advocacy and Counseling

KENNETH H. KOLB

UNIVERSITY OF CALIFORNIA PRESS

University of California Press, one of the most
distinguished university presses in the United
States, enriches lives around the world by
advancing scholarship in the humanities, social
sciences, and natural sciences. Its activities are
supported by the UC Press Foundation and by
philanthropic contributions from individuals
and institutions. For more information, visit
www.ucpress.edu.

University of California Press
Oakland, California

Library of Congress Cataloging-in-Publication Data

Kolb, Kenneth H., 1975-
   Moral wages : the emotional dilemmas of victim
advocacy and counseling / Kenneth H. Kolb.
      pages cm
   Includes bibliographical references and index.
   ISBN 978-0-520-28270-4 (cloth : alk. paper)—
ISBN 978-0-520-28272-8 (pbk. : alk. paper)—
ISBN 978-0-520-95866-1 (e-book)
   1. Human services.   2. Social advocacy.   3. Social
work administration.   4. Counseling.   I. Title.
   HV40.K643 2014
   363.82'9253--dc23

                              2013049807

Manufactured in the United States of America

23 22 21 20 19 18 17 16 15 14
10 9 8 7 6 5 4 3 2 1

In keeping with a commitment to support
environmentally responsible and sustainable
printing practices, UC Press has printed this book
on Natures Natural, a fiber that contains 30%
post-consumer waste and meets the minimum
requirements of ANSI/NISO Z39.48-1992 (R 1997)
(Permanence of Paper).

CONTENTS

Acknowledgments *vii*

1. Emotional Dilemmas *1*

2. Moral Wages *21*

3. Empowerment in Practice *53*

4. Difficult Clients *85*

5. The Allure of Legal Work *113*

6. Men at Work *142*

7. Managing Dilemmas and Retooling *169*

Appendix: Fieldwork Methods *187*

Notes *193*

References *203*

Index *213*

ACKNOWLEDGMENTS

This book would not have been possible were it not for the openness and enthusiasm of the entire staff at SAFE (Stopping Abuse in Family Environments). They opened their doors to me, answered my questions, and let me document their stories. Without their participation, I would have no findings to share. For that, I am truly grateful.

Many of the ideas in this book were developed during long and thoughtful conversations with a number of really smart people over the years. I offer all of them my most sincere thanks. This includes (but is not limited to) my colleagues in the Sociology Department at Furman University, especially Allison Hurst and Kyle Longest, who read and commented on complete chapters of previous versions of the book. Kelly Besecke read a complete draft manuscript early in the process and offered a number of helpful suggestions. Emily Kane and Shamus Khan graciously offered invaluable advice on how to put together a prospectus. I owe a debt of gratitude to my editor, Maura Roessner—and her colleague Jack Young—at the University of California Press for their professionalism and enthusiasm about my project. I also thank my symbolic interactions friends, Jen Dunn, Sinikka Elliot, Nancy Berns, Jen Lois, Kerry Ferris, Joel Best, David Franks, Doni Loseke, Melinda Milligan, Chuck Edgley, Robert Dingwall, Natalia Ruiz Junco, and Michael Borer, for offering ample intellectual inspiration every August at our annual meetings.

I acknowledge the following for their generous permission to incorporate some of my previously published materials in this book. Many of the ideas and concepts used in chapter 3 appear in the articles "Claiming Competence: Biographical Work among Victim-Advocates and Counselors," in *Symbolic Interaction* 34(1) (2011) and "Traps on the Path to Analysis" in *Symbolic Interaction* 34(4) (2011) and are reprinted with permission from Wiley Blackwell and Sons. Some of the material in chapter 4 appears in "Sympathy Work: Identity and Emotion Management among Victim-Advocates and Counselors" in *Qualitative Sociology* 34(1) (2011) and is reprinted with permission from Springer Science Business. An earlier version of chapter 4 was published previously in "Victim Advocates' Perceptions of Legal Work," *Violence against Women* 17(12) (2011) and is reprinted with permission from Sage Publications.

For their help, and friendship, I am eternally grateful to my sociological siblings, Matt Ezzell, Krista McQueeney, and Heather Kane, who read and commented on my first set of field notes as well as offered last minute suggestions all the way up to final publication; I also thank my qualitative cousins in the UNC, NC State fieldworker diaspora, Martha Copp, Amanda Gengler, Jessica Fields, Michelle Wolkomir, and Doug Schrock. For helping me establish these connections—and friendships—I thank Michael Schwalbe, whose work has had a profound influence on my teaching and scholarship. I owe all my merit as a fieldworker to Sherryl Kleinman, who taught me first how to ask the right questions and then what to make of people's answers. She also valued good writing—which convinced me that I should listen to what she had to say.

Outside of the academic world, my parents, Ken Kolb and Carolyn Kolb, and my sister, Pherabe Kolb, have been consistent sources of support and encouragement. And my daughter, Vivian, who arrived halfway through this project, has been a ceaseless source of inspiration. Children are the best field-workers because they do not take anything for granted. Her energy and curiosity are continual reminders of how I *should* approach my work every day.

Most of all, I thank my spouse, Sarah, for her endless patience from the fieldwork to the writing phase of this work. Her social work and public health perspectives were invaluable as I developed the various arguments in the book. She read my drafts, listened as I practiced my conference presentations, and provided insightful feedback over the years. Her love and understanding helped me get through the most challenging phases. I dedicate this book to her.

CHAPTER ONE

Emotional Dilemmas

[handwritten margin note: • Meg ⟩ part time / • Jesse ⟩ / • Cathleen — only full time advocate]

Staff meetings at SAFE (Stopping Abuse in Family Environments) were typically dry affairs—an agenda of items to cover, a list of tasks to be divvied up,
various reports from different offices—but this one felt different. Kelly, a codirector at SAFE, had just introduced a new topic—"service gaps"—and
posed a question to the group: "What can we do to keep clients from falling
through the cracks?" Cathleen, a victim advocate, spoke first: "I've been
having nightmares about not helping women out. I wish the other staff [in
the office] knew we were operating at a bare minimum." The counselors who
worked upstairs responded with sympathy to Cathleen's plea but did not
have an answer to her problem. SAFE had just had 20 percent of its annual
budget cut because a source of state funding had dried up. As a result, two of
the three advocates on staff had been reduced to part time—leaving Cathleen
as the only full-time advocate. "If I'm the only one who is full time, if no one
else is around, I feel like it is all my responsibility, and that sucks." Com-
pounding the problem, even though SAFE staffing had been reduced, the
incoming flow of calls and walk-in clients continued unabated. Jesse, one of
the advocates whose hours had been cut, explained that less time in the
office only meant more stress: "I don't have enough time to do all my
work. . . . It takes a toll."

Meg, another advocate, was also worried. She paused for a moment and
then started to cry. She apologized for her tears and explained, "I still feel
responsible for Shelly." She was referring to a SAFE client who had been
murdered the year before. This case occurred long before the recent budget
cuts and was seemingly unrelated to the recent staffing problems, but everyone at the meeting understood the connection.

Shelly's case was well known in the SAFE office. Jesse and Meg worked
with her and remembered the details well (including the date of Shelly's first

1

visit to SAFE the year before: October 13). Over the past months, I had heard the timeline of her case countless times. Shelly had come to SAFE because her relationship with her husband had steadily deteriorated. He had stopped working because of an injury and was waiting for disability checks to start arriving. He had become abusive with their daughter (pinning her against a wall when she would not turn down her radio), and Shelly did not know what to do.

Meg was the first advocate to work with Shelly. They discussed the benefits and risks associated with a "protective order"—a type of restraining order. Contrary to popular belief, the SAFE advocates were trained to be skeptical of legal solutions and spent a great deal of time warning clients about the potential downsides of bringing in cops and lawyers to help. In plain language, Meg laid out the risks to Shelly: "You could try for a protective order, that is certainly an option to you, but I just want to warn you, it's possible [a judge] could drop it, and he'd be able to come back to the home." Knowing all too well what her husband might do if enraged and emboldened, Shelly decided against a legal strategy. Instead, she went back home to see whether he would calm down. She rested her hopes on his earlier claim that he would leave the relationship once his disability payments started arriving.

Two weeks later, Shelly returned to the SAFE office. Her husband had grabbed her wrist and twisted her arm behind her back. Again, the subject of his rage was mundane: the TV remote control. Shelly walked into Meg's office, exhausted. "She was dressed in sweats and had her hair pulled back and no makeup. She seemed very tired . . . very tired . . . like she had just had enough." This time, she wanted a protective order. As an advocate, Meg was careful not to fill out the forms for Shelly; she did not have a license to practice law and pointed out the limits of her legal abilities to all of her clients. Meg handed Shelly a clipboard with the protective order paperwork and sat down next to her. She answered Shelly's questions about legal jargon and what a judge might say. Because Shelly expected that her husband would challenge the protective order in court, Meg arranged for a local lawyer to represent her pro bono. A year later, Meg could still recall who was in court that day, where they were sitting, and what they were wearing (for example, Shelly's father wore snakeskin boots). Shelly won her case and was granted the protective order for a year, meaning that her husband could not come near her, her home, or try to contact her. "I remember her being very relieved it was over and smiling. It was the first time I had seen her smile." They talked over the phone a few times over the next week, but Meg never saw her again.

Over the next week, Shelly's husband violated the terms of the order (and was arrested) twice: the first time for entering her home when no one was home and repeatedly firing a gun into the walls and ceiling; the second time, for contacting Shelly by phone. On both occasions, he posted bail ($10,000 for the second violation). At this point, Meg was trying to keep in continual contact with law enforcement and Shelly's lawyer, but there were gaps in communication. Shelly had stayed one night in SAFE's emergency shelter, but she had not told Meg. The shelter was located only a few miles from the main SAFE office, but staff members in the two locations often went days without seeing or speaking to each other. Unfamiliar with her case history, Christina, the shelter director, respected Shelly's decision to leave after one night. She thought it would be "disempowering" to force her to stay (even though she admitted she was tempted to tell Shelly not to leave).

A day later, the husband approached Shelly outside her workplace, killed her, and then turned the gun on himself. Meg learned of the news while in court helping another client obtain a protective order. They were before the same judge who had presided over Shelly's hearing.

In their private interviews with me, Meg and Christina speculated what they might have done differently had they known more details at the time. They knew that Shelly's husband's first arrest had been for firing a gun inside the home, but they did not know that he had been on the phone with her at the time when the shots rang out. They later learned that he had been trying to scare Shelly into believing that he had just killed himself while she was on the line. Additionally, local law enforcement suspected that he was suicidal, but they were unsure and thus did not place him under forced supervision. Had they known about the phone episode, they might have acted differently. Finally, while law enforcement officers in a different county were monitoring his whereabouts—they knew that he had moved into a hotel—they did not realize that he was staying in a room only a few hundred yards from Shelly's job.

In the staff meeting, Meg's tears about the year-old case had brought the discussion to a halt, and Kelly—her boss—quickly interjected to soothe her: "It was not your fault. . . . She was offered a lot of services. . . . Don't claim responsibility for something he did." Meg stopped crying, but more from fatigue than because of the words of comfort. In the previous year, she had heard all these lines before. In private, Meg told me that she still felt guilty. She wanted to believe that she had done everything she could have for this client, "but I can't do that in this case." To the rest of the staff at the meeting, she looked up from her tissue and apologized for bringing up Shelly's case once again: "I probably couldn't have prevented her death, and I know that . . . and I know I keep bringing her name up, but this week is the anniversary of when she came in." It was October 12.

Jesse was not ready to move on to the next topic on the meeting agenda, either. She had also worked on Shelly's case. Her part-time status was partly because of the budget cuts, but not entirely. She was still in college. Fifteen years younger than Meg, she offered the same services as the other advocates: she answered the hotline, met with walk-in clients, and accompanied clients to court as they interacted with the assistant district attorney's office. Yet, she complained that her on-the-job training did not prepare her for the pressure she felt when dealing with such a vulnerable clientele: "Every client who has come in since . . . I worry is going to be another Shelly. I worry whenever a client comes in with the same stalking history or tells you where to look for their body if they are killed." Tears started to well in Jesse's eyes, too. I saw that the tissue box on the table was empty and felt like I should do something to help her. Just a few weeks earlier, I had been joking with Jesse in this same room. Upon hearing about my plan to conduct research at SAFE, Jesse teased me that because I was a man I must be scared to be around a bunch of "man-hating feminazis." We had laughed a lot that afternoon. But now, sitting in the same chair, Jesse's mood was starkly different. I quietly got up from the table, grabbed a roll of toilet paper from the bathroom, and handed it to her. She smiled for a moment, continued to sob, and stared blankly at the floor.

Kelly offered Jesse roughly the same words of encouragement that she had to Meg, but she was also aware of the time and wanted to move through the meeting agenda. Shelly had not been the first SAFE client to be murdered. Kelly had been in this line of work for nearly three decades and remembered when legal, medical, and social service institutions were indifferent (at best) and hostile (at worst) to the needs of victims.[1] She knew what Meg, Jesse, and Cathleen were going through. She prompted the rest of the staff to brainstorm possible solutions. "What can we do?" she asked the group.

Answers included diverting other staff (from the shelter or the counselors' office) to help the advocates or reducing the number of hours the agency was open to the public. Within moments after each suggestion, it became clear that each solution would have created another problem. The advocates welcomed more help to greet and process new clients but worried that those unfamiliar with their special duties might miss subtle clues that clients leave for the well-trained eye. They argued that a simple phone call to SAFE requesting the address for free legal services might be a subtle cry for help that the counselors or shelter staff members might not recognize. Additionally, even if they could process all the clients in their caseloads, where would they meet with them? The SAFE office had only a few private rooms for use at any given time. Kelly mentioned the possibility of changing its message to clients: "If we can't offer all of these services, should we be advertising them?" Despite being offered a way to reduce their workload, the advocates quickly said "No"; turning clients away was not an option. To them, shutting the door on women who need help was unthinkable. They wanted a different solution, but they did not know what it was. Meg asked bluntly, "Is there a light at the end of the tunnel?" to which Kelly responded, "Not any time soon."

This meeting said a lot about the emotional dilemmas of advocacy and counseling at SAFE. At every turn, it seemed like the staff faced impossible predicaments. They felt overwhelmed by their workloads, but they did not want to limit their availability to clients. They secretly wished that their clients would sometimes make different decisions (like stay in the shelter one more night), but telling them what to do would mean abandoning the "empowerment" philosophy in which they believed so strongly. They were leery of legal remedies, but they also saw courtrooms as one of the few places where they could help their clients in what they called "concrete" and "tangible" ways. They needed the help of (mostly) men in law enforcement and other organizations to assist their clients, but they also worried that opening their doors to any and all men might invite trouble.

Despite the remarkable ingenuity and problem-solving skills of the staff, these quandaries kept popping up, time after time. By the end of the meeting, the advocates reported feeling a little better; they felt relieved that at least others in the office now understood what they were going through. Yet, in the coming days and weeks, their anxieties would eventually return. Cognitive solutions—"Think about it this way"—or emotional ones—"Don't feel bad"—may work in the short term, but neither added new staff or more hours for existing staff. The reason for this was simple: the agency could not afford them.

WHY STUDY ADVOCATES AND COUNSELORS?

The current scholarship on domestic violence (DV) and sexual assault (SA) offers plenty of answers regarding how and why women like Shelly are abused, raped, and murdered every day, but it does so by focusing primarily on victims and their abusers.[2] These studies typically ask questions such as, "Why is there so much abuse? How can it be stopped? Which policies deter violence better than others?" These questions are important. We need to know which services work better than others. However, this line of research largely sidesteps the workplace experiences of the people who deliver them: victim advocates and counselors. If we want to understand why some forms of help are more effective than others, then we should probably know more about those doing the helping.

The stories of advocates and counselors offer insight into DV and SA from a different perspective. In what ways do advocates and counselors find their work rewarding? In what ways do they find it disheartening? What kinds of relationships do they have with their clients? What challenges do they face at work, and how might their jobs set them up for these experiences? In this book, I relay events from their perspectives and put their experiences into a wider, sociological context.

Victim-service providers are often depicted as especially caring and compassionate—somehow different from the rest of us. But, in many ways, their experiences are typical and ordinary: the result of a group of people claiming a common identity, working under similar conditions, seeking to solve routine puzzles with limited tools. They interpreted their successes as individual achievements (which made them feel good), but this meant they also saw their failures as a product of their personal shortcomings (which had the opposite effect). My analysis focuses on the bigger picture. I argue that their self-doubts, worry, guilt, and confusion were not because they had somehow failed to learn how "to cope." I also refute the notion that their stress and tears were signs that they should have somehow worked harder or studied their training manuals even more thoroughly. The real reason they kept facing the same dilemmas again and again is that they worked in an emotionally risky arena, often with few and ineffective solutions for their clients and themselves. Their experiences were unique, because SAFE was its own place, but they were also patterned, because they were fighting the same fight as hundreds of other agencies like it. By focusing on the experiences of victim-service providers, I can show how emotional dilemmas can be structured into particular kinds of work.

This book is not the first to study battered women's shelters or victim support agencies (Loseke 1992; Dunn 2002; Martin 2005), but it is unique in that it captures how the inner lives (emotional experiences and identity) of those who work there are shaped by wider forces beyond their control. The jobs of victim advocates and counselors—as we know them today—did not exist fifty years ago. They were an outgrowth of a second-wave feminist movement concern that women who had been abused were being mistreated by the primary institutions (legal, medical, and social service) that have traditionally served their needs. The women who founded places like SAFE decades ago believed there was a better way, and they set out to design and administer a qualitatively different kind of help. This meant different services and different standards. This had consequences for the people receiving services (the victims) as well as those providing them. The questions I ask focus on how those decisions and patterns set in motion long ago intersect with the individual lives of advocates and counselors today. For example, how might the policies put in place to ensure that victims are not told what to do unintentionally make the job of the service provider both easier and harder? I observed a wide range of emotional experiences among staff members at SAFE (sympathy, guilt, frustration, compassion, and elation); how might those feelings be built into the demands of their jobs?

To accomplish this task, I rely primarily on evidence gathered from their experiences at the micro level. This means that while I make note of some broad-scale (macro) changes in how abuse has been treated over the years, I largely focus on how those shifts shape the subjective experiences of individuals within one particular agency (SAFE). My claims are based on observations and in-depth interviews of staff over a period of fourteen months, as well as my time training and volunteering at a neighboring agency over a period of four months. I conducted fieldwork in places where DV and SA work "officially" takes place, including the SAFE office, courtroom hallways, hospital rooms, emergency shelters, and sheriff's department lobbies, as well as the everyday venues where coworkers "hang out" together—restaurants, car trips, coffee shops.[3] At the very least, I hope to offer readers a revealing snapshot of a job that can be simultaneously challenging, frustrating, and gratifying.

THE EVOLUTION OF DV AND SA AGENCIES IN THE UNITED STATES

To understand the emotional dilemmas of victim advocates and counselors, it is helpful to put the workplace where I conducted research into perspective. SAFE helps victims of DV and SA. At the time of my research, June 2005 to August 2006, the agency had an annual budget of nearly $1 million (with 80 percent from municipal, state, and federal grants and 20 percent from private donations) and served a local population of roughly sixty thousand people within a seven-hundred-square-mile area in the southeastern United States. Compared to its peers, SAFE offered a more comprehensive menu of services (see table 1). In the main office, staff members offered a crisis hotline, walk-in support services, court advocacy, individual counseling, and support groups. SAFE's emergency shelter was located off-site in an unpublished location where staff also held support groups and helped residents solve immediate problems. Additionally, some SAFE staff members spent most of their time away from the office: these programs included a "batterers' intervention program" for abusers;[4] in-home family counseling, community awareness projects, and a youth educational program operated in coordination with the local school system. In this book, I focus primarily

TABLE 1

Victim services offered at SAFE during research period

Service provided	Frequency/year
Crisis-hotline calls (new clients)	36
Walk-in client consultations	1,930
Counseling appointments	112
In-home family counseling appointments	79
Emergency shelter residents	45
Victims' support group participants	69
Abuser intervention program participants	46
Court advocacy contacts	853
Domestic violence protective orders processed	198

on the work of the victim advocates and counselors who were housed in the main office and the shelter.

Although outsiders might view advocates and counselors together, insiders at SAFE knew the difference. The counselors had ample training (they either had professional degrees or were working toward them) and met with clients by appointment, making their work schedules largely predictable. In contrast, the advocates were largely trained on the job and had no control over when the crisis hotline would ring or a walk-in would arrive at SAFE's door. Unlike the counselors, the advocates did not know whether a call or a doorbell meant a familiar client checking in with a routine question or a new person with a graphic history of abuse to learn and investigate.[5] Despite the unpredictability of their work, they had to quickly assess whether a client was past the crisis stage. If so, the client was referred upstairs, where counselors helped her through the later stages of the healing and recovery process. If a client's wounds (physical and emotional) were still too raw, she stayed with the advocates downstairs.[6]

SAFE was held in high regard in the local social service community. This was no small accomplishment. SAFE was located in a conservative part of a conservative state that was slowly becoming more progressive with the influx of residents from larger cities located nearby. As a result, staff members had to negotiate with outsiders whose opinions of DV and SA varied widely—from the conservative "old guard" to the more liberal "transplants." This posed challenges for outreach and fund-raising activities, but they managed it very well. SAFE won a regional award for outstanding service the year I conducted research. This was especially significant considering the budget cuts previously noted.

Despite improvements since the mid-1990s, DV and SA remain persistent social problems nationwide. Even though the frequency of reports of these crimes has declined (albeit at a slower pace than the reduction of the overall crime rate), roughly one in four women will experience some form of violence from an intimate partner in her lifetime (Tjaden and Thoennes 2000). According to police reports analyzed by the Bureau of Justice Statistics in 2005, 1,181 women in the United States were murdered by their intimate male partners (Catalano 2007). Also, between 2009 and 2010, based on a two-year rolling average, 775,650 women were victims of rape, attempted rape, sexual assault, robbery, aggravated assault, or simple assault by their current or former intimate partners (Catalano 2012). Yet, because of the high number of unreported or misclassified incidents, these figures do not tell the whole story. According to a survey conducted by the National Center for Injury and Prevention Control (which includes unreported crimes), the problem is much worse. Of all women alive in the year 2010, an estimated 21.84 million had been raped in their lifetimes, with 1.27 million of those instances occurring in the year 2009 alone (Black et al. 2011:18). Additionally, in that same year, an estimated 4.74 million women had suffered physical violence (not including rape) at the hand of intimate partners, with 39.17 million similarly victimized at some point in the past (Black et al. 2011:38). As a result, there is no evidence to suggest that places like SAFE will suffer from lack of demand any time soon.[7]

Places like SAFE began springing up across the United States alongside the second-wave feminist movement of the 1960s and '70s (Martin 2005). In 1964, one of the first such agencies, Haven House, was established in California (Schecter 1982). By 1974, the first reference to "wife abuse" appeared in the *Reader's Guide to Periodical Literature* (Loseke 1992:14). Also in 1974, the National Organization for Women established its first anti-rape task forces (Martin

2005:97). Although these organizations have been growing steadily, identifying exactly how many there are presents some methodological challenges. On the one hand, they want to advertise their services to victims in need, but on the other hand, too much visibility can attract attention from unwanted visitors—such as abusers seeking the location of emergency shelters. As a result, an adequate census of places like SAFE has not been conducted.[8]

Despite these limitations in measurement, past scholarship has estimated that between 1975 and 1978, up to three hundred such organizations existed (Tierney 1982). Since then, their numbers have grown. By 1996, there were more than twelve hundred rape crisis centers (Martin 2005:99), and according to the *National Directory of Domestic Violence Programs*, there were 2,031 DV-related programs and shelters in the United States in 2008 (National Coalition Against Domestic Violence 2008). The growth among agencies like SAFE will likely continue as long as victim advocates and counselors continue to disagree with the wider public over the root causes of abuse and the best strategies to help victims.

In contrast to the ways abuse is typically treated in popular discourse, places like SAFE see abuse as a social—not an individual—problem. First and foremost, victim advocates and counselors blame the general devaluation of women in society today. They recognize that some abusers are psychotic or pathological, but they view those as exceptions rather than the norm. For the most part, they believe that violence against women "is a particular form of domination based on social relationships of unequal power" and a mechanism for men's social control of women (Schechter 1982:34). Without changing the culture, advocates and counselors argue, abuse will always exist. From their perspective, arresting all the abusers in the world would be a futile endeavor: the deep-seated patriarchal assumptions in our culture would only produce another generation to take their place. As a result, they often complain that hospitals, law enforcement agencies, and departments of social services (DSS) only address abuse in superficial ways. They believe that—no matter how well-intentioned—these institutions cannot tackle a pervasive social problem as long as they treat the symptoms of the problem rather than cure the underlying disease.

To do this, the founders of places like SAFE set about to create an entirely new approach. They developed "coordinated-community response" plans

(Pence and Paymar 1993) to educate the public and create intervention programs to reform abusers. They fought to change the ways victims were treated by doctors, police officers, lawyers, judges, and social workers. They also adopted a supportive, nondirective approach to helping individual victims. For example, advocates and counselors do not always tell their clients to call the police. Rather, they prefer a wait-and-see approach (like Meg did in Shelly's case), gently guiding their clients to identify all the potential consequences of bringing in the criminal justice system. Once police and district attorneys get involved, victims may have little or no say in how their cases will proceed. Because places like SAFE define abuse as the denial of power and control over one's life, all their services are geared toward helping clients make their own decisions according to what *the client* sees as the best path to safety and recovery.[9] They argue that this approach, what they call their "empowerment philosophy," is what makes their services different—and better.

Casting themselves as an alternative to traditional institutions has also meant creating new types of workplaces. In the beginnings of the movement, the first DV and SA organizations adopted different policies and management styles, in contrast to intimidating police departments, sterile emergency rooms, and hectic DSS waiting rooms. For clients, they created places that felt safe and secure. For staff, they devised policies that made the workplace more egalitarian, "collectivist, nonhierarchical, nonbureaucratic, and free of professional and technical elitism" (Martin 2005:96–97).

However, for all their efforts to create a *different* type of workplace, DV and SA agencies have a mixed record when attending to the needs of women of color. SAFE employed a predominately all-white staff, and this is still the norm for most agencies like it (Martin 2005). As a result, they are still susceptible to accusations that feminist organizations are primarily the domain of middle-class heterosexual women who have the economic and social resources to engage in social movements (Matthews 1989). This is a persistent criticism: throughout the civil rights movement, poor women and women of color often felt excluded from feminist struggles (Cole and Guy-Sheftall 2003). Also, because past campaigns against violence against women disproportionately targeted men of color, "incidents that linked race and rape caused further disjuncture between white feminists and blacks in the current feminist movement" (Matthews 1989:520). As a result, racial diversity within places like SAFE has been elusive: "Women of color had reason to distrust both the campaign against rape and the larger women's movement. . . . Significant shortcomings mar the movement's successes, especially as it claims to represent all women" (Bevacqua 2000:200). In general, the victim advocates and counselors at SAFE were aware of this critique of the history of their movement, and the codirectors made specific efforts in hiring to increase the ethnic and racial diversity of its workforce; but still, in the agency where I conducted research, most of the staff in the main office and most of their clients were white or (less frequently) Latina.[10]

One of the most notable changes to occur over time is that places like SAFE have become increasingly reliant on funding from federal, state, and municipal granting agencies. These funding opportunities, while attractive, also come with many strings attached. As political scientist and legal scholar Kristin Bumiller has argued (2009), the neoliberal reforms that took hold in the United States in the late 1970s and early '80s have had a profound effect on the ways places like SAFE operate.[11] During this time, state and federal governments simultaneously shrank public budgets devoted to solving social problems while also tightening the regulations and conditions necessary for those in need of help to receive welfare assistance. These reforms also ushered in an explosive growth in the criminal justice and penal system. Since then, agencies like SAFE have started to reconsider their long-standing "ambiguous stance toward the state" (Matthews 1994:xii). By accepting these monies, previously small-scale, grass-roots efforts had to agree to make changes to the way they delivered services, reported outcomes, and coordinated with other organizations.

Rather than force places like SAFE to make "compromises and structural changes," under duress, Bumiller (2009:4) argues that public funding entities achieved the same result via the guidelines written into their grant opportunities. Today, to establish their credibility with clients and the community, they are now more likely to cite their "law enforcement-friendly attitudes and practices" (Corrigan 2013:30) as well as their academic credentials, professional licenses, and organizational efficiency (Barner and Carney 2011). The codirectors at SAFE were aware of this general trend and tried their best to stay true to their second-wave feminist roots. However, they perceived that some changes were inevitable. As one member of SAFE's board described this historical evolution to me, "This agency is a movement type agency, and [we] haven't lost that focus. . . . But it's not like the old days when we just had bake sales." In sum, those who managed and ran SAFE understood the risks of partnering with people (police, lawyers, judges) whom "the movement" had before characterized as potential adversaries, but they believed that if the money could be used to help their clients, it was worth it.

The cooperative stance that agencies like SAFE have since adopted toward the criminal justice system has yielded both costs and benefits. As women's studies scholar Maria Bevacqua (2000) has argued, the movement was able to capitalize on the "tough on crime" political rhetoric of the past few decades to pass tougher legislation to combat DV and SA. In this sense, the politics of law and order that oversaw a massive expansion of the prison population in the United States in the 1980s and '90s served to help the battered women's and anti-rape movement achieve some of its goals. The irony of this unlikely political alliance has not gone unnoticed. "The paradox of the law-and-order approach as both bane and boon to anti-rape organizing was not lost on movement activists . . . who view rape as the symbolic and real domination of women by men" and not "just another crime" (Bevacqua 2000:121). Legislators and policy makers who might have been otherwise disinterested in violence against women suddenly came to see rape crisis centers and battered women's shelters as potential collaborators in identifying and incarcerating lawbreakers. To this day, agencies that assist victims of DV and SA still grapple with the implications of their partnership with the criminal justice system.

Another notable change during the past three decades is that those who work inside places like SAFE have slowly distanced themselves from second-wave feminist language and identity. Even though elements of second-wave feminism can be found in their policies and procedures (such as their emphasis on restoring women's power and control within intimate relationships), staff members are less likely to identify themselves or label their services as explicitly feminist (Corrigan 2013). This rhetorical shift is not a new phenomenon. Past research has shown that advocates and counselors have long been drawn to the idea of "individualism and personal growth as the proper step toward eliminating" violence against women rather than spending all their energy "calling for collective action" (Andersen and Renzetti 1980:336). This was generally the case at SAFE. Although the advocates and counselors were able to articulate the relationship between gender inequality and violence against women on a societal level, they still understood their primary purpose as helping individual clients solve immediate problems. Sociologist Amanda Gengler reported similar findings in her recent study of a battered women's shelter: "While the language of feminism is still frequently invoked, much of the political activism inherent in the goals and operating principles of these early organizations has faded as staff focus on short-term individual change rather than long-term social change" (Gengler 2012:501).

Places like SAFE have not been the only ones to change, though. The institutions that battered women's shelters and rape crisis centers were created to replace (or offer an alternative to) have also undergone a significant transformation. Although the criminal justice system is far from perfect, advocates and counselors at SAFE often pointed to local task forces and advisory boards as examples of newfound communication and cooperation. For each story about misinformed sheriff's deputies, unfeeling doctors, and unnecessarily rigid caseworkers at the office of Child Protective Services, staff members could also offer counterexamples of contacts in these institutions who "got it"—such as sympathetic lawyers or local nurses. Although this does not mean that those who work in places like SAFE now see hospitals, courtrooms, police stations, or the DSS as safe spaces for their clients, the advocates and counselors I studied did believe that things were changing—slowly—for the better. Despite the litany of abuses their clients had suffered in these other institutions in the past, SAFE advocates and counselors voiced a qualified optimism that future reforms will enable these counterparts to one day effectively cater to the special needs of DV and SA victims.

For all the changes and transformations that agencies like SAFE have gone through over the past three decades, though, some things have remained the same. Victim advocates and counselors still see themselves as people who help others in need. They know their task is difficult, but in exchange for their hard work they earn the right to reap a special kind of reward: they get to feel good about themselves and the wider mission of the organization. What their job lacks in regard to offering extrinsic rewards like pay, power, and prestige, it offers in abundance a form of symbolic compensation I call *moral wages*. This benefit—the positive feelings and sense of satisfaction that come with seeing oneself as a caring and compassionate person—is not as readily available in all lines of work. However, as I show, sometimes seeing oneself as a good person—even when helping victims—is not as easy as it would seem. To earn this reward, they first must overcome a number of emotional dilemmas.

MORAL IDENTITY WORK

To understand why it might be hard for advocates and counselors sometimes to see themselves as caring and compassionate people, it is helpful to know some of my assumptions about how identities work—or, more precisely, how and why people work on their identities. In everyday life, most people take their identities for granted. That is, people understand themselves to be particular kinds of individuals who may act differently in different situations, but whose beliefs, ideals, and behaviors are generally stable. This point of view assumes that identities are "things" that we possess. Sociologists see identity in a different light. Rather than assuming that identities just happen, we see them as accomplishments—something people have to put effort into in order to achieve.

To understand this point, consider the example of someone who sees himself or herself as generally funny or amusing. If being funny just came naturally, then his or her days would simply be filled with amusement and laughter. There would never be occasion for others to remind that person to tell jokes or try to make people laugh, because there would be no need. She or he would just go about telling stories, smiling, and making fun—taking advantage of every appropriate opportunity. Yet, we can easily see one flaw in this example: no one is like that. No matter how consistent we perceive our identity to be, we can usually think of times when we have asked ourselves, "Why am I acting this way? I just don't feel like myself." Or we can remember moments when others—sensing something was off—prodded us to act "like we really are." These reminders, questions, and doubts happen all the time, and they have important implications; they tell us that identities are not as passive and stable as many people assume. If identities just expressed themselves no matter what, there would be no need to tend to them. There would be no need to remind ourselves—or be reminded of—how we *should* be feeling or behaving.

This perspective on identities focuses on the processes involved in their production. Our identities do not automatically speak for themselves. Instead, we communicate them (through words, gestures, and actions) in ways that make sense to ourselves and others. This theoretical approach also assumes that accomplishing an identity is never a given, either: even if we see ourselves as particular kinds of people, there is no guarantee that others will share our views. As a result, we continually gauge how others see us and incorporate their reflected appraisals into our own conception of self. Charles Horton Cooley called this process of seeing ourselves through the eyes of others the "looking glass self" (1902:164); others' reactions serve as a "mirror" through which we observe ourselves to see who we "really" are. This does not mean that flubbing the punch line of a joke can shatter our entire sense of self, but if we fail to live up to our self-imposed expectations enough times, it can cause us to consider others' reactions carefully—and the context in which they are delivered. For example, we do not weigh all appraisals the same (Shibutani 1955). A friend's opinion matters more than a stranger's, so her or his reaction will have a greater impact on how we think about ourselves; but the general point remains: for all their appearance of stability and permanence, identities still require a considerable amount of attention, interpretation, and maintenance (Snow and Anderson 1987).

This understanding of identities as projects under perpetual construction is also a symbolic interactionist one (Blumer 1969). According to this perspective, any given identity is dynamic and fluid; its meaning is continually being revised and reconsidered. Changes and inconsistencies can provoke confusion, but—like a fuzzy image on a television screen—an identity can also be brought back into focus. As sociologist Karen Stein puts it, the goal is to make our identity "internally coherent and externally discernable" (2011:291). Luckily, even though this involves a lot of upkeep, coherency does not require perfection. When there is a rip, we can mend it. If we act in ways that run counter to our identities—and we do not want to abandon them—we can explain away our actions. If our justifications fall short, we can try again.

Eventually, with enough work, ruptures in our identity can usually be restored or modified. Over time, once we've built up a history with others, it becomes a little easier to maintain. People generally expect identities to be stable. When we take something for granted, we often miss inconsistencies because we are not looking for them. This is why identities appear as permanent and passive possessions—even though they are not. Just because we miss the work going on does not mean that none is taking place.

Much of the effort involved in claiming an identity is subtle. It does not require explicit self-directed talk, like loudly proclaiming "I am this kind of person" or holding up bold placards that announce "I am that kind of person." Instead, we often communicate our identities via the impressions we give off (Goffman 1959) during our daily actions and interactions. In short, our behaviors follow a pattern that signifies the kind of person we are—or want to be. Symbolic interactionists refer to these kinds of behavioral conventions as elements of one's "identity code" (Schwalbe and Mason-Schrock 1996:123). This approach assumes that we enact them as a way to signal our "intentions, abilities, and expectations so that others can adjust their behavior toward us" (122). Although we largely take this work for granted, it is a vitally important process: it is through our identities that we gain "a sense of belonging, personal significance, a sense of location relative to others . . . and feelings of worth" (122). As I show throughout the book, accomplishing the identity of caring and compassionate victim advocates or counselors was incredibly important to the women who worked at SAFE. It was through this identity that they were able to define their relationship to a cause larger than themselves (against DV and SA), find meaning in their interactions with clients (which were not always pleasant), and make sense of their sacrifices for the organization.

To put their identity in context, I argue that to be a victim advocate or counselor is to claim a "moral identity." Sociologist Sherryl Kleinman defines a moral identity as "an identity that people invest with moral significance . . . that testifies to a person's good character . . . such as mother, Christian, breadwinner, or feminist" (1996:5).[12] Accomplishing this identity was not easy. It meant never turning away clients who needed help. It meant allowing clients to make their own decisions and not telling them what to do. It meant sympathizing with—not judging—victims. It meant valuing the power of care and emotional sentiment as a means of healing. It meant protecting the organization from hostile outsiders and scrutinizing the intentions of those who offered to help. Adhering to this code may have been difficult, but the payoff was worth it. Accomplishing their shared moral identity enabled them to feel secure in the notion that they did—and were—good; in my terms, it earned them moral wages.

OUTLINE OF THE BOOK

Before the SAFE advocates and counselors could earn their moral wages, they had to first overcome a series of emotional dilemmas that form the basic structure of the book. In chapter 2, I show how not turning away clients sounds good in theory, but what should advocates and counselors do when budget cuts slash staff hours and make their caseloads impossible to finish? They wanted relief, but they did not want to reduce their hours or services, either. In chapter 3, I outline how letting clients make their own decisions was incredibly important at SAFE; they saw their job as empowering their clients to choose their own paths. But what if a client was about to make a risky decision? Should they just stand by and watch disaster unfold, or should they intervene? For most people, intervening and rescuing others is a sign of virtue—but not for victim advocates and counselors. Their identity code was critical of overly directive advice. In chapter 4, I examine how even when sympathizing with clients, there were no easy answers. They were supposed to offer a steady stream of emotional support; however, some clients yelled at them, consistently broke rules, and brazenly lied to them. They saw their sympathy, sentiment, and capacity to care as fundamental indicators of what made their services special. What should they do when their sympathies ran out?

In the second half of the book, I shift the focus from staff members' relationships with clients inside the office to their interactions with outsiders and their respective institutions. In chapter 5, I pay close attention to staff members' tenuous relationship with the criminal justice system. They believed that their quiet and private interactions with clients meant something; they were trained to prioritize these services. Yet, they found themselves drawn to the excitement of helping their clients in and around courtrooms. Did that mean they were compromising their values? In chapter 6,

I focus on an issue that directly involved me—a man conducting research in a place many presume to be hostile to men. I show how staff members were torn about how they should interact with men who offered to help the agency. Nearly all of SAFE clients were women abused by men. Yet, shutting men out of SAFE could have serious downsides. They already suffered from a "man-hater" stereotype that they believed harmed their reputation in court and the wider community. Not letting men help would just exacerbate this image problem. Pragmatically, they needed to include men to improve their public image, but they also worried that some men were a threat to SAFE's clients, staff, and overall reputation.

In the final chapter, I summarize the book and argue how it contributes to current scholarly discussions on emotions, identity, and inequality. However, I finish the book on a much more practical level by offering five suggestions that can be enacted today with a minimal amount of investment by DV and SA agencies. These recommendations are drawn from "tricks of the trade" that savvy advocates and counselors at places like SAFE already do (to varying degrees). My hope is that they can be written into training manuals and policies as a means to help advocates and counselors preempt and manage the emotional dilemmas of their risky—but potentially rewarding—work.

Overall, the purpose of this book is to shed light on the workplace struggles of those fighting on the front lines of a persistent social problem. Any one of the challenges I describe in the following chapters would be enough to make some think twice about signing up for—or keep coming back to— this line of work. When seen as a whole (their burdensome caseloads, the unpredictability of their clients' choices, their clients' sometimes difficult behavior, the devaluation of their care services, the "man-hater" stereotype they face), their perseverance becomes all the more admirable. My job is to show how their struggles are not isolated events. They are not random or unique. Instead, they are effectively structured into this line of work. If readers and practitioners take away only one lesson from this book, it should be this: The emotional dilemmas of victim advocates and counselors are the by-product of a job that calls upon workers to aid and feel for vulnerable clients yet gives them few and feeble tools to do so.

CHAPTER TWO

Moral Wages

Although there is a wealth of research on victims, their experiences, and the causes of abuse, less scholarship focuses on those whose job it is to help them. This is understandable. Victims elicit public sympathy, and we should devote our attention to them so that we can learn how to help them. We should also look to the people causing their pain—the abusers—and ask how or why they continue to harm people with whom they often have intimate relationships. However, by focusing solely on victims and abusers, we often forget to ask questions about the service providers in the middle. What is their work like? Why do they do what they do?

In this chapter, I show how victim advocates and counselors are sustained by something more than just their paychecks. During my research at Stopping Abuse in Family Environments (SAFE), when overhearing and participating in everyday conversations, I never heard workers talk about their work as something they did "just to pay the bills." Instead, their words and deeds indicated that their positions at SAFE meant something more to them. Rather than avoid or sidestep challenging cases, they embraced them.

Fighting for their clients was rarely easy. This was because recent budget cuts and a perpetual lack of resources meant they never had as much staff to help their clients as they would have liked. This wore on them. Yet, when offered the chance to reduce their workloads and limit the services they offered to clients, they refused. Given the pressures they faced, why not make things easier on themselves? They wanted relief from their overwhelming caseloads, but they did not want to turn away clients who needed help. How could they solve this dilemma? Neither option was desirable. Continuing unabated with diminished staff was incredibly difficult, and shutting their doors on women who needed help was anathema to their moral identity. In the end, the advocates and counselors found a way to make the best of a bad situation, and their solution can offer insight into how other people in different jobs manage the risks and rewards that come with helping others.

The trauma that victims of domestic violence and sexual assault (DV and SA) experience can be unimaginable. Helping them exposes advocates and counselors to considerable emotional stress and strain. In many cases, women's lives are on the line. However, the elements that made work at SAFE so challenging—witnessing firsthand the effects of horrible acts—also presented staff members with a special opportunity. By helping women in need, they were able to see themselves as caring and compassionate people; and this was a special feeling. It earned them a sense of pride that they were doing the right thing, at the right place, and at the right time. This sense of satisfaction that they were living up to the demands of their moral identity code, and the positive feelings that come with it, added up to something that not all jobs offer: *moral wages*. At SAFE, these symbolic rewards were the solution to the advocates' and counselors' dilemma. As long as they could feel good about their work and their mission, they could withstand the stress and fatigue.

This idea that people can look inside to make sense of why they put up with undesirable conditions outside (in the everyday world) is not new. Past studies have documented this process by examining the ways that veterinary technicians highlight the "affectional rewards of the job as compensation for its low pay, odious tasks, and other disadvantages" (Sanders 2010:260) and child care providers accept the conditions of their low-wage, low-prestige jobs so long as they can reap the "emotional wages" that come "each time a child smiles at [them]" (Murray 2000:154). However, I trace my usage of the concept of moral wages back to a much older study conducted in an even more unlikely setting.

In his study of post–Civil War race relations in the American South, W. E. B. DuBois analyzed the ways that intrinsic rewards can soften individuals' frustrations with their relative material deprivation. To summarize this phenomenon, he used the term "psychological wage" ([1935]1998:700) to describe the symbolic compensation that working-class whites derived from their ability to see themselves as superior to blacks of all class categories. Thus, during the era of Reconstruction, the psychological wage afforded to poor whites—their sense of supremacy on the basis of their whiteness—served to ameliorate any frustrations they may have had regarding their impoverished conditions relative to more affluent whites. Although the context of DuBois's argument is in stark contrast to the caring and compassionate environment of SAFE, both cases follow the same abstract process: in the absence of extrinsic rewards, people can find ways to elicit and cultivate intrinsic ones as a means to make sense of their current situation.[1]

As I use the term, moral wages are a subset of DuBois's concept. This is because they are reserved exclusively for those who can claim to be caring and compassionate toward others in need. This means that moral wages are not exclusive to work with victims of DV and SA; far from it. They are offered (and earned) in any job that provides employees with ample opportunities to feel good about "doing good." This is not the case in all jobs. Some jobs—bad jobs—offer little in return for hard work; if employees do not like it, they are told to take it or leave it. Other jobs—better jobs—offer extrinsic rewards to do hard work, such as greater pay, power, or prestige. In those two kinds of settings, it is easy to see how and why people keep coming back to work when the going gets tough. My purpose here is to explain why workers stay (and even flourish) in jobs that fall into a different category: workplaces that ask employees to put up with difficult and emotionally trying conditions in exchange for the right to believe that they are good, virtuous, and moral beings.

To explain why moral wages are so important at places like SAFE, I first show what it was like to earn them. This was the payoff; reuniting a client with her kids, watching a victim speak up for herself for the first time—these were the moments they savored. Next, I explain the conditions that foster this kind of symbolic reward: in a broader sense, victim advocacy and counseling is a form of moral "dirty work." Their job is to clean up the mess caused by a systemic social problem. Then I examine two features of jobs that affect the rate at which moral wages are available to workers. Whether occupations require professional credentials or encourage employees to take a sympathetic stance toward others affects the extent to which workers can earn moral wages.

To determine the rate at which victim advocates and counselors at SAFE earned them, I compare their jobs along these two dimensions (credentials and sympathetic stance) and situate them relative to a select group of occupations featured in past scholarship on the topics of identity and emotions that offer either ample moral wages (clergy, volunteers) or barely any at all (industrial managers, bill collectors, paralegals). The purpose of these comparisons is to show how moral wages are not an incidental feature of work at SAFE, but rather what it takes to recruit and retain advocates and counselors to do such challenging work.

In the conclusion of this chapter, I argue that the idea of moral wages helps explain how workers make sense of their decision to help those who suffer the consequences of persistent social problems. At SAFE, and places like it, workers like their work, and even during the times when they do not, they still *want* to like it. Consequently, people can thrive in this kind of work—society's "moral dirty work"—as long as they can overcome the emotional dilemmas in their path and believe they are doing the right thing. Yet, as a society, we should not mistake their ability to persevere as a justification for the budget cuts that force them to do so. Just because agencies like SAFE largely run on moral wages to sustain their workforce does not mean they should; relying on the power of intrinsic rewards to tackle systemic social problems is also a solution fraught with consequences.

EARNING MORAL WAGES

What motivates workers? Extrinsic rewards—like pay, power, and prestige— are important, but people also want meaningful work. If given the chance, workers will find ways to extract positive experiences from even the dreariest of jobs (Burawoy 1979). At SAFE, whenever I brought up their pay as a form of motivation, staff members usually laughed. The idea that they would choose this line of work for a lucrative paycheck seemed silly to them. Instead, they framed their work in moralistic terms. This was a wise choice, because even though they were not working class or poor, they were not especially well paid. More important, they believed that the amount they earned would never match the emotional costs of their work. They also did not see their work as offering them an opportunity to wield power or earn public prestige. In sum, extrinsic rewards cannot explain why the advocates and counselors wanted to work at SAFE. I argue they were in it for a different reason: moral wages.

What does it mean to earn moral wages? In simple terms, to earn moral wages is to experience the positive feelings and sense of satisfaction that come from seeing oneself as a caring and compassionate person who helps others in need. Moral wages are the symbolic rewards that accompany the ongoing accomplishment of a moral identity. This is because achieving one's identity at SAFE was not merely a cognitive experience: the advocates' and counselors' sense that they had lived up to their identity code was affirmed affectually. Put simply, it felt good.

To understand how it felt at SAFE, consider an example of a time I observed Jesse enjoy a bounty of moral wages in the advocates' office. Just moments before, she was visibly exhausted and frustrated. She was at her wit's end trying to process a stack of case files. The database at SAFE was accessed through an outdated software program that the advocates found slow and burdensome. On top of that, because of budget cuts, Jesse's hours at SAFE had recently been cut from full to part time. All the while, the heap of manila folders on her desk continued to grow. She had hoped the extra time off would allow her to focus more on her schoolwork (she was enrolled in a nearby college), but she explained that splitting time between the two meant that neither got the attention it deserved. As she was talking to me— she called it "ranting"—about her caseload, a client walked in. Jesse looked relieved to have an excuse to put her paperwork away. She heaved the bundle of folders off her lap and onto one of the few bare spots on her desk and quickly spun around in her chair to face the client. The woman had good news. She had just found a job. The client talked in almost a whisper, but Jesse boomed in response, "Well, it sounds like you are doing great! You are just what I needed. I've had a hard day." For Jesse, moments like this were the ones that made all the tough times seem worthwhile. She signed up for this job to help others, and her client's success indicated that she had done just that. Others might interpret this victory—a job—as small, but to Jesse it was huge. She was transformed for the rest of the day. The effect was visible. Her face lit up and her posture straightened; for the rest of the day, she went from room to room in the office to share the news with everyone else in the building.

Staff members at SAFE believed that their work, although difficult, was worth it. Things could get tough—very tough—while watching clients recover from being raped or abused, but even the smallest "wins" were enough to keep them going. During a private interview, Emily, a counselor, explained how valuable it was to her to know that she had a positive impact on another's life: "That is one of the things that keeps me coming back. I've had that experience. I know. I've heard from people firsthand, 'You've helped me, you've helped the kids.'" These kinds of interactions with past and current clients were crucially important at SAFE. Staff members were able to squeeze every tiny detail from them to fill up their emotional reserves for the inevitable downtimes ahead.

Stories of clients "helping themselves" served as the most enduring source of moral wages. For example, to help clients, they would provide them with some information—job listings, phone numbers of other social service agencies, apartment addresses—but ask the clients to make their own calls and set up their own appointments. Even when clients asked for more help, staff members tried very hard to get them to be as independent as possible. This is what made their moral identity code such a difficult standard to live up to: it meant sometimes resisting the urge to help their clients as much as possible (make calls on their behalf, drive them around). This was harder than outsiders might presume. It could be painful for staff members to watch their clients go through the growing pains of self-sufficiency. Yet, despite their temptation to "rescue" clients at times, they tried to stand back as much as possible. Staff members at SAFE saw their hands-off approach as precisely what made their services different—and better—than the legal, medical, and social service institutions that have traditionally served the needs of victims. As long as staff members could believe their clients were benefiting from their gentle guidance, they could earn ample moral wages.

Stories of clients' burgeoning "empowerment" typically followed a "tipping-point" narrative whereby staff members described how they nudged clients just enough to get them going on their own. These narratives cast clients as hesitant at first and initially disappointed by the lack of explicit direction at SAFE; however, eventually they would see the benefits of accomplishing their goals themselves. For example, Lisa used the metaphors of a light switch and a kindled flame to describe her clients' transformation from dependent to independent:

> They see it turn on, and you see them doing the stuff that you were trying to do, and you don't have to do anything anymore because they start doing it for themselves. And when I first saw that happen . . . I was like, "Okay, I know this is the right thing to do and taking this moment with them is the right thing to do." And time, and time again, if I could get to that place, they did the work. And they made changes and their fire was stronger, stronger than mine. . . . It was beautiful to watch, and I loved that.

At SAFE, watching clients succeed through their own efforts confirmed staff members' vision of themselves as caring and compassionate people who put their clients on a sustainable path to recovery. By citing her clients' own initiative ("They did the work"), Lisa indicated the value of SAFE's empowerment philosophy; and, by extension, her moral worth as a proponent of this approach to help victims. This does not mean that Lisa believed that her clients could or should do *all* the work of repairing their lives; rather, she thought that prodding her clients in the right direction made them more self-sufficient in the long run. Thus, when clients returned to SAFE with success stories like the client who reported to Jesse she had found a job, staff members showered them with phrases like "Look, you did all the work yourself!"

Although it was sometimes strange to hear, staff members bragged about how much they had helped their clients by pointing out how much their clients had achieved *without* their help. When one resident emerged from her bedroom in the shelter to walk unassisted for the first time after a series of painful surgeries, Rebecca (an advocate in the shelter) stood back and watched in amazement: "She had been practicing by herself in her room, but when she came into the kitchen and was walking by herself . . . I'll always remember that. . . . She never gave up; she would just roll with the punches." Had Rebecca pestered her client to keep up with her physical therapy, or pushed her to practice against her will, the victory would not have been as sweet. It was because the shelter resident had taken the initiative on her own that made Rebecca so proud. By pouring all her praise onto someone other than herself, Rebecca signified her selflessness and her work with residents as virtuous.

These examples show how Jesse, Emily, Lisa, and Rebecca were able to point to clear and unambiguous interactions with clients to affirm their moral identity. Yet, not all cases were cut-and-dried indications of success. Sometimes, to feel good about their services, staff members had to work a bit to make sense of their services as beneficial and effective. This was especially the case when staff members lost all contact with their clients. For example, when Heather mentioned that one of her clients had stopped returning her calls, I asked her how this made her feel. At first, she expressed worry and concern. However, by putting this client's case into more general terms, she was able to frame it as a possible indication of success. In her words, some clients' "thank yous . . . never make it back to the office." When I asked her what she meant, she explained that it was likely too difficult for her client to call or return to SAFE: seeing the office again could dredge up hurtful memories. Thus, victories at SAFE were not always self-evident or immediate; a lack of evidence did not prevent them from earning moral wages. These positive feelings could also be extracted from their work by constructing new meanings from limited information.

The advocates and counselors at SAFE saw helping victims as a slow process that often yielded measured, indirect returns on their emotional investments. When I asked Nora, who ran the educational outreach program in the schools, the same question I asked Heather about how to interpret a client never coming back, she also framed these cases in abstract, positive terms: "You never know how many losses have been prevented." Of course, not hearing from clients could also mean that they were dissatisfied, or worse; but at SAFE, the absence of feedback from clients was cited as evidence that they were still "on their journey to recovery" or as a reminder that advocates might not see the positive results of their services for some time. Although the waiting was difficult, it also amplified the potential payoff. It was because clients' wounds (physical and emotional) could not heal quickly that they came to SAFE for help in the first place. Continuing to work on these cases—even in the absence of immediate good news—yielded moral wages in slow and steady doses.

For all their ability to savor any sign of progress, however, big wins were still a big deal; they could sustain staff members for months. In one case, a client's ex-husband had abducted her children (she had full custody) and taken them out of state. When the advocates learned where he had taken them, they repeatedly called law enforcement in that jurisdiction to enforce the existing custody arrangement. After days of frustrating phone calls, Meg and Jesse finally learned that the local authorities had picked up the client's children. The advocates called the mother immediately to tell her that she could retrieve them right away. Overnight, she drove nonstop to pick them up and bring them back—a five-hundred-mile round-trip journey. The first stop upon their return: the SAFE office. Jesse and Meg gave the children some ice cream and then brought them to a room filled with toys. The client was exhausted and euphoric: "I was going 85 miles an hour the whole way!" The case was a topic of conversation all day and the next. The victory was clear and definable: the ex-husband was arrested on an outstanding warrant, and the mother regained custody of her children. Meg's elation was palpable: "Moments like that keep me going. . . . Did you see her? She was just glowing!" To the advocates, this was what made everything worth it.

However, because of the way work was structured in the SAFE office, some staff members received positive feedback more than others—not because they offered more effective services, but because some jobs involved serving as the public face of SAFE. This meant that different positions at SAFE earned moral wages in different ways. Upstairs, in the codirectors' office, when I asked Kelly about victories at work that made the job meaningful, she described many more examples of positive encounters with past clients and strangers than the advocates or counselors did in response to the same question. This is partly because she had been in the line of work longer, but also because she now spent more time outside the office, interacting with public officials, professional colleagues, and community members. Soliciting and receiving praise (and donations) were part of her job description:

> I run into clients in the community, and they remind me what a difference [SAFE] has made in their lives. And how they are so much better off now, and "Thanks for being there." There is plenty of reward. There needs to be. There needs to be plenty of reward because this is hard work and there's times when there isn't any reward and you're tired. And there are times when clients treat you terribly. And there are times when clients die. So it is good that there are also rewards. And they're not that rare.

Consequently, Kelly and those she supervised had different perceptions of how often clients and outsiders appreciated their work. Kelly knew the difficulties the advocates and counselors faced—she had done similar work earlier in her career—but she no longer engaged in the same draining and stressful work as they did. In the custody case described earlier, Kelly did not spend hours on the phone with sheriff's deputies in another state. She did not have to answer the mother's phone calls before there was good news to report. Kelly did, however, greet the client upon her return with her children. Consequently, as I explore throughout the rest of this chapter, the advocates and counselors took different paths to earn moral wages—different from Kelly, different from each other, and different from workers in other occupations.

MORAL "DIRTY WORK"

The previous section described how it felt to earn moral wages at SAFE. These symbolic rewards were important because they helped solve the primary dilemma that is the subject of this chapter: although staff members wanted to reduce the pressure of their work, they were also unwilling to reduce their caseloads by turning clients away. I argue that they managed this dilemma by pointing to the feelings of satisfaction that came with believing they were helping people in need. These feelings did not reduce their workloads, but they did help them redefine their struggle as worthwhile and good. In other words, their moral wages explain why they chose not make things easier on themselves.

I also argue that the emotional costs and benefits of victim advocacy and counseling are inextricably linked. What made their work hard also made their work meaningful. To better understand why workers would make this bargain, we should look to the fundamental features of jobs that recruit and retain workers based on their desire to accomplish a moral identity. Not all jobs do this. As I mentioned earlier, some jobs tell their workers to "take it or leave it"; others offer things like pay, power, and prestige. But not SAFE, nor other workplaces that "run" on moral wages. These jobs are different because they attract people interested in more than "just a job."

In an essay entitled, "Work and Self," sociologist Everett C. Hughes (1971) used the term "dirty work" to describe jobs that fulfill a crucial and pressing need, but that most people avoid because of the marks they leave behind. Although Hughes originally analyzed work that was physically dirty, it is worth expanding this concept to include jobs that leave different kinds of stains. I build upon Hughes's conceptualization to create a category for work that leaves a mark, but that also can be seen as good and virtuous by the people doing it. I label these kinds of jobs "moral dirty work." Although victim advocacy and counseling are not visibly messy, they can still leave indelible psychological wounds. To keep staff members at SAFE—and other places where society's moral dirty work is done—motivated and engaged, I argue that there needs to be some kind of intrinsic reward to make the hard parts seem virtuous.

To find out which jobs constitute moral dirty work, we must first look to the meanings their workers attach to them. From their point of view, why do they apply for this line of work? Why do they stay? Not all work is done *solely* for the money. SAFE staff members cashed their paychecks every month, but they believed their work meant more than that: it was an opportunity to "do good." Past research on shelter advocates has found that "they are not motivated by money, but passion or love of the job" (Bemiller and Williams 2011:97). Places like SAFE are not alone in this regard. Women who work in abortion clinics have also indicated similar kinds of motivation. From their perspective, they do a type of moral dirty work, too; and their association with these clinics also leaves a stain. They report having trouble finding anyone willing to talk to about their jobs (Wolkomir and Powers 2007), and they lament that even those most likely to support them—people who support women's right to choose—still may not want to discuss what goes on inside the clinic. Instead, most staff in abortion clinics (mostly women) report entering into this line of work because of their "sympathetic pose" toward their clients: women seeking abortions (Joffe 1978:113).[2] Aware of the hostility and unease directed toward their work, they interpret their services through a positive lens—seeing themselves as helping others who are clearly in need. Despite the challenges associated with their moral dirty work, the satisfaction they derive from positive interactions with clients keeps them going.

Advocates and counselors at SAFE may have worked with a different clientele, but they similarly reported that their friends and family rarely wanted to talk about their work with victims of DV and SA, too. Consequently, advocates and counselors—like abortion clinic workers—suffer a certain degree of stigma by association with their clients. To be clear, the stigma suffered by victims—as well as women seeking abortion—is unfair. The "blemishes of individual character" (Goffman 1963:4) these women bear are largely due to sexist assumptions that blame them for their own abuse— or unwanted pregnancy. But these stains exist, nonetheless. For victims, evidence of them can be found in the accusatory questions victims are often called on to answer (What were you wearing? Why where you there? Why didn't you leave?). It can also be seen in the ways that people sidestep the topic of abuse, even those who claim to be supportive of the cause. Thus, the advocates and counselors knew that while many people valued their jobs, they also knew that not all were willing to do them, or even talk about them.

To make things worse, the cases that others did not want to hear about were precisely the ones that best showcased staff members' selflessness and virtuosity. Had others put aside their discomfort and uneasiness, the SAFE advocates and counselors could have impressed upon them just how hard they worked for their clients. Instead, the most trying and challenging cases—the ones that would have garnered the most respect and admiration— were often left unsaid, invisible.

For a clear example of this kind of moral dirty work that often went unspoken, consider the first time Heather helped a client through the "rape kit" process. The night it occurred, Heather was "on call" to answer the crisis hotline and attend to any client emergencies. At two in the morning, her SAFE cell phone buzzed loudly on her bedside table. It was from the Sheriff's Department. She was to meet her client at the hospital. Still groggy, Heather reported in her interview that as she prepared to leave, she felt eager, but also weary: "It's early in the morning, and I feel like I just laid down. And I not only have to go to the hospital, but I have to work all day, too [after that]." She was anxious; she had never done this before.

Upon arrival at the hospital, Heather got into "advocate mode." "I'm thinking, 'Just breathe' . . . and then I think how tough it's going to be for the victim and how awful it is. . . . It's so important for me to project, 'You're not alone. You're not alone. You're not by yourself.'" Heather described that the hardest part about the whole episode was watching the forensic evidence literally *taken* from her client. Holding the woman's hand, Heather watched as the sexual assault nurse examiner took three vials of blood from her client, swabbed her vagina multiple times, and collected a total of fifty hair follicles from her head and pubic regions. Plucking the hairs one by one was the most painful for Heather to watch. But perhaps even worse than that was observing the indignity of her client having to remove and leave all her clothes behind. First the nurse passed an ultraviolet light over them to check for semen, then she carefully placed them in plastic bags. Spare clothes were available, but there were no shoes that fit the victim. She had to leave barefoot. The whole time, Heather felt powerless over the process; especially as her client kept whispering to her, "This is so embarrassing. This is so embarrassing." But Heather tried to stay strong. "I sat there and wrote notes, lots of notes, to make myself remember the facts of the case"; as an advocate, she believed that the best way to help her client was to sit by her side as a diligent observer every step of the way.

To see how Heather's efforts constituted moral dirty work, consider how many people would be willing to answer such a call at 2:00 a.m.? What are the rewards for Heather's sacrifices? It is hard, virtuous work that needs to be done, yet few are willing to do it—or even talk about it. When I asked Heather if she had talked about this case (which clearly troubled her) with others, she said that besides her client, coworkers, and a few close friends, no one would ever know what she did that night.

During staff meetings, lunch breaks, and courtroom recesses, staff members at SAFE recalled countless examples of times when interactions with outsiders made it clear that stories like Heather's made others uncomfortable. At any moment, the tone of a conversation that started as light and lively could quickly turn dark once the other person found out exactly where the staff members worked and whom they served. Although some outsiders were encouraging, others became quiet; dinner conversations sometimes stalled, and nervous smiles cued a change of topic.

There are sociological reasons for why people do not like to talk or hear about what it is like to work at places like SAFE. After all, not *all* discussions of violence are taboo. Wars are violent, as are many sports, but cable news and sports channels endlessly discuss the physical and emotional injuries people suffer in these contexts. Similarly, many people have no trouble talking about most types of violent crimes, but the topic of gender violence often provokes a different reaction. The work of advocates and counselors calls attention to gender inequality in general and men's violence against women in particular. To work in places like SAFE is to adopt a completely different kind of explanation for the ultimate culprit of these abuses: a culture that treats men's domination over women as natural and normal, unfortunate but inevitable. To listen to the stories of victim advocates and counselors is to learn that the blame lies not only with sociopaths, but also with society; in other words, all of us.

SAFE staff members often talked about how outsiders avoided the topic of abuse as a way to "keep their heads in the sand." As Jen, a counselor, explained, staying silent was a way for others to ignore the problem. Ironically, she was less frustrated by (mostly) men who blamed victims and referred to advocates and counselors as "feminazis" and "man haters" than she was by seemingly sympathetic women who shied away from the subject when given the chance: "[They assume that] because there is this agency and there are good people working here that these [victims] are going to be okay. They can mark it off their worried list because there is this big nice resource for women." From Jen's perspective, these women want unpleasant things like abuse to be handled by someone else; they know about DV and SA, they just want others to fix the problem for them.

Yet, for all their concerns about the difficulty of the job and the unwillingness of others to talk about it, the advocates and counselors still believed the emotional strain of their jobs was worth it. From their perspective, yes, it was hard, but if it was easy, then anyone could do it. These challenges made victories at work—big and small—all the more sweet. Even if outsiders did not fully understand (or want to know) what they did or how hard it was, they themselves still valued the services they delivered. By working at SAFE, they reaped the satisfaction of knowing that they were doing work that was important and meaningful. In other words, they earned moral wages. And they are not the only ones. In the next section, I show how working with victims is not the only path to earning this kind of symbolic compensation. As shown with the previous example of abortion clinic staff, there are many ways to show that one is a caring and compassionate person. However, the conditions and expectations of some work (like moral dirty work) make this easier than others.

Following, I identify two structural conditions in particular that affect the rate at which workers can earn moral wages across occupations: whether their job requires professional credentials and whether it asks them to take a sympathetic stance toward clients. By using these two dimensions of comparison, I compare the differences between positions inside SAFE—advocates versus counselors—as well as the differences between their workplace and others. Because the opportunities for comparison are endless, I have chosen a selection of other jobs featured in past scholarship on the topics of identity and emotions (paralegals, lawyers, bill collectors, industrial production managers, volunteers, and clergy). The purpose of this exercise is twofold: (1) to show how particular workplace conditions enable or impede the opportunity to earn moral wages, and (2) to highlight the ways that workers can make sense of their sacrifices for others in jobs that offer few extrinsic rewards.

MORAL WAGES IN CONTEXT

Comparing and contrasting jobs according to the moral wages they offer is challenging. Intrinsic rewards are rarely mentioned in classified ads or measured in tax returns. Yet, it is important to analyze how and to what extent workers in different jobs earn moral wages. In many ways, moral wages sustain workplaces like SAFE for the simple reason that they often lack the resources to offer much else.[3] Yet, relying on symbolic compensation to make up for the demands of dirty work has consequences, too— which I expand upon at the end of this chapter.

The Difference Credentials Make

SAFE staff members reported that outsiders were generally unaware of the distinctions between victim advocacy and counseling. Even clients were confused from time to time.[4] This distinction is important, however, because the advocates were more likely to earn (and need) moral wages.

At SAFE, the advocates worked downstairs. They did not have professional credentials or graduate degrees. Most had college degrees, but not all. Despite their lack of professional training, the advocates operated on the front lines of DV and SA victim services. They answered the hotline, processed walk-ins, and helped clients navigate the court system. They were more likely, in their terms, to help those "in crisis" (that is, clients still seeking to meet their basic needs like safety, shelter, economic security). Once these needs were met, clients were then eligible to be referred upstairs to the counselors. Of all the paid staff, the advocates worked the longest hours and earned the least; in addition, a client in need of help could disrupt their workplace routine at any time.

The counselors worked upstairs. They had master's degrees in either social work (MSW) or counseling and clinical licenses to practice (or were well on their way to earning these). These professional credentials were not easy to obtain. In addition to taking classes, licensure required an additional three thousand supervised hours of work and passing a state exam. SAFE also hosted a few nonpaid counseling interns who were enrolled in nearby graduate programs and worked at SAFE as part of their degree requirements. Because of their credentials, the full-time counselors were better paid: $33,000–$37,000 per year compared to the advocates' $25,000–$28,000. To put their salary in context, all staff members made less than the codirectors (who also had MSW degrees and made roughly $45,000 a year).[5] But money was not the only thing that separated the counselors from the advocates. Their interactions with clients were very different. Whereas the advocates helped clients solve immediate problems, the counselors' goal, as they described it, was to help clients develop the emotional and cognitive strategies necessary to develop long-term solutions. The counselors also met with clients only by appointment—either individually, in a group, or in their homes (as part of the "family counseling program"); this allowed them some control over their work schedule. If clients inquired about legal options or expressed renewed concern about their immediate safety, the counselors referred them back downstairs to the advocates.

There was general agreement in the office that the advocates had the tougher job. This is because they worked with the clients with the freshest wounds and who were at the greatest risk of revictimization. I argue that this also made it easier for the advocates to earn moral wages. They may have lacked master's degrees, but—counterintuitively—their lack of formal training garnered them admiration in the office. In theory, almost all their training was based on materials contained within a weighty three-ring binder that sat on an office shelf. This hefty bank of information contained handouts, SAFE policies, and instructions for various legal forms. In practice, however, the advocates relied mainly on experience and one another for guidance. These factors made for less certainty and more stress on the job.

When talking about the advocates, the counselors in the office offered nothing but respect. When I asked Jen about the difference between her counseling job and that of the advocates, she immediately responded, "Oh, I couldn't do what they do." For example, even when the advocates referred clients upstairs, if the counselors decided they were still in crisis, they would send them back down. Until the counselors deemed them ready, the advocates had no one else to whom they could send their clients. At SAFE, the advocates were both the first contact and the option of last resort—no matter how desperate or dangerous their clients' situations.

The pressure of serving vulnerable clients weighed heavily on the advocates. Earlier, Jesse is quoted describing how this job "takes a toll," but she was not the only one. Every advocate confided in me at some point that their clients' well-being weighed on her. They knew that any of their clients could be revictimized at any time after receiving services. Client safety was never a guarantee.

I felt attuned to the advocates' anxieties after having experienced them myself. Volunteering for a few months before beginning my fieldwork at SAFE, I had spent time at the hotline desk at a different agency in the area. I had received about the same amount of training as the advocates at SAFE (thirty-five hours over a period of nights and weekends, plus a two-week probationary period of "shadow" training—that is, following more experienced staff around the office). Also, having studied and researched topics like gender and violence against women, I thought I had a bit of a head start. Yet, when I waited at the desk for my first crisis hotline call to ring, I was nervous. I had doubts. What if I did more harm than good? Callers would often ask if they should file for a protective order or press charges. I would respond with the standard list of strengths and weaknesses of legal remedies that I learned during training (which I outline in more detail in chapter 5), but this just seemed to frustrate callers. At first I thought this was because they were suspicious of me—a man—and would have responded differently if I were a woman. But, after talking to the other volunteers (all women), I learned that they too were experiencing the same types of reactions. Callers were tired and exhausted and just wanted simple answers to simple questions. If we (as volunteers) did not know an answer, we could go ask a more experienced staff member, but they would typically repeat the same list of nondirective options that seemed to upset some clients in the first place.

The other volunteers and myself were taught that when clients asked specific questions, we should offer them support and sympathy, but also respond nonjudgmentally. We were trained to "empower" clients to "take ownership" of their recovery. As a result, we were taught active listening strategies and to respond to questions with questions, like "What do *you* think is best?" or "Trust your instincts, what do you believe would keep you the safest?" These methods helped keep the conversation going, and sometimes callers appreciated this because they just needed to talk; but these tactics also made me question the effectiveness of my service. Could such active listening techniques really work? How would I know?

We were also taught to sometimes stay silent in order to keep clients talking. This was helpful, because on occasion I simply did not know how to respond. When one caller made an offhand remark that she was going to have one of her relatives kill her abuser, I remember sitting there, not saying anything, asking myself, "Should I ignore this? Is she joking? Should I report this? What should I do?" Another hotline caller wanted to know if the agency had money to help her pay rent. I knew that there was some money available, but not always; and even when there was, not all clients ended up receiving financial support. I thought, "Should I tell her that? Should I say, 'I'll ask my supervisor'? Will that get her hopes up? Will turning her down make her hang up, putting her out of contact and in more danger?" We had a few specific remedies at our disposal—cell phones that could only dial 911, a checklist for essential items to pack in case of emergency—but sometimes clients wanted more.

Over the next six weeks, these experiences were the first clue that the worries and concerns I encountered as a volunteer were built into the structure of this work. Yet, despite my concerns, I kept coming back; I still wanted to help. I wanted to dispel myths that men cannot do this kind of work. Not knowing all the answers made my volunteer job hard, but what made it hard also made it more meaningful. At the end of each shift, even though it was sometimes stressful and exhausting, I still felt good about what I had done.

After each call, I was able to hang up the phone and believe that I had done at least *some* good. My answers may not have been perfect, but I was able to derive satisfaction from knowing that I had picked up the phone when someone needed help. I provided something that all callers needed—another voice on the end of the line. The moral wages I earned were modest, but I did not need them very much, either. I was only on hotline duty for a few months. I was only volunteering. This was not my full-time job.

When I talked with the newer advocates at SAFE, Jesse and Cathleen, about their worries and doubts, their experiences sounded similar to mine. Looking back on their first few months on the job, they regularly used metaphors like "trial by fire" and "sink or swim." Yet, by listening carefully to the tone of their comments, I could hear a note of pride in their voices. Their accounts of past confusion and uncertainty were not entirely complaints. Their struggles were also sources of fulfillment. Their work was tough, but getting past the hard parts was satisfying.

The counselors upstairs at SAFE worked under different conditions and expectations. They also had concerns about giving bad advice, but their professional credentials offered them powerful cultural equipment to show themselves and others that they were experts in their domain. Academic degrees and clinical licenses may not guarantee quality or skill among workers, but they do operate as widely recognized symbolic markers of expertise and status (Becker 1970). At SAFE, the counselors' credentials not only enabled them to earn more money, but also allowed them to set the terms of their interactions with clients; this meant having final say over when they met and what they talked about.[6] They defined goals for their clients in therapeutic terms, often using jargon such as "behavioral modification," whereas the advocates described their relationship with clients in much more informal terms. Cathleen, for her part, labeled any type of advocacy a success as long as the client "feels good about it."[7] As a result, the division between professionals and nonprofessionals at SAFE was subtle, but noticeable.

For the credential divide to have an impact on moral wages, however, it had to be seen as "real" among both sets of staff members. As shown earlier, the counselors did not want—nor believe they could do—the advocates' work. The same sentiment applied in reverse. The advocates did not believe they could adequately "counsel" clients, either—at least not in a professional way. The advocates did not secretly resent the counselors for their higher salaries or their less stressful work conditions; they consented to this arrangement. More accurately, they liked it. They took pride in their tougher assignment (clients in crisis), their unpredictable schedules (new walk-ins at any moment), and their relative lack of training (sink or swim). To them, successfully navigating these challenges was exciting and—when things went well—rewarding.

The credential divide was real at SAFE because the advocates saw the act of professional counseling as requiring skills that they did not possess. Lisa believed strongly in this, and she offered a helpful example because she was the only one on staff during my research who worked in both positions. She began her career at SAFE as an advocate and then moved upstairs into the counselors' office even though she did not have a professional degree. Uncomfortable in that position, she later transferred back downstairs to a new "legal advocate" position that served as a liaison with the Sheriff's Department.[8] Throughout her time in the counselors' office, though, she always claimed to be an advocate at heart. Part of the reason for her move back to the advocates' office was because she did not believe she was qualified to counsel: "I was going only on intuition and some of the books that I had read, but that is not the same thing as having a master's degree in counseling. . . . I just didn't feel like it was appropriate for me to be doing therapy. . . . That didn't feel ethical to me." To Lisa, "intuition" was okay for an advocate, but not enough to be a professional.

Pretending to be a counselor was a faux pas among the advocates at SAFE. This had important implications for their capacity to earn moral wages. Had they envied the counselors, they would be devaluing what—to them—made advocacy special. Advocacy at SAFE was less about professional interactions and more about establishing a human connection with clients as peers or equals. And if the advocates believed counseling skills were clearly superior, then they would have a harder time seeing their advocacy skills as an effective means to help victims. Instead, the advocates believed in their abilities, and they showed this by taking pride in their position relative to the credentialed counselors. For example, Rebecca's job in the shelter was formally titled "family counselor," but she identified with the advocates. Her title was more of a bureaucratic formality than an accurate representation of her work—or how she perceived her work. She offered effectively the same services as the advocates in the main SAFE office. When chatting with coworkers, she jokingly avoided the label of "counselor": "I don't know how to do play therapy with two-year-olds. . . . [People] ask where I got my MA, and I would say [laughing] I don't have a master's, I have a bachelor's in English." Her self-deprecating humor, rather than diminishing her moral wages, served to enhance them. A lack of professional credentials was yet another challenge for her and the other advocates to overcome, but when they did—and they believed they had really helped their clients—they could find solace in the fact that they had done it entirely on their own without any professional training or advanced techniques.

Meg, an advocate, was even more outspoken when identifying the boundaries between advocacy and counseling. She enjoyed her informal relationships with clients and was quick to remind others that she was not a professional. When talking about Rebecca's job title in the shelter as a "counselor" without credentials, she worried that a licensed practitioner might suspect Rebecca was claiming more status than she was due: "I'm worried that some MSW [Masters of Social Work] will say, 'She's a what?'" Soon afterward, Meg joked that she was proud of not being a professional: "I've got three letters after my last name, KMA: kiss my ass." Upon hearing this, the rest of the advocates erupted in laughter. Meg's defiance was a way to establish solidarity with other noncredentialed staff, yet the group's laughter also signaled their awareness that the counselors were different. As advocates, they may not have had the professional authority that outsiders usually respect, but they were okay with this arrangement. They may not have had special training, but they believed that they were able to help clients nonetheless.

What can we learn from credential divides within other occupations to better understand the relationship between the advocates and counselors at SAFE? First, we learn that the harmony at SAFE was somewhat special. Past studies have shown that nonprofessionals are not always content with—to the point of being proud of—their lack of credentials within the workplace. Other sociological studies have examined how credentials can foster divisions and distrust. Take law firms, for example. In studies conducted by sociologists Kathryn Lively (2001) and Jennifer Pierce (1995), we learn that the social borders between paralegals and lawyers can be clear and stark. These two studies found that many of the paralegals were conflicted about the ways they were treated by their higher-paid professional counterparts. As a result, it is not a given that workers will trust and respect one another across the credential divide. But the advocates and counselors at SAFE got along better than studies of paralegals and lawyers suggest they would. Why?

There are two primary reasons why the advocates and counselors got along so well at SAFE. First, envy or condescension at SAFE would have made it more difficult for either the advocates or the counselors to earn moral wages. If the advocates had resented the counselors, or if the counselors had dismissed the advocates, it would contradict either of their claims to being caring and compassionate people. Second, they were able to downplay any differences in status because the relative inequality—in terms of salary— was not that stark, at least not as much as the gap between paralegals and lawyers.

The structure of salary allotment within a workplace can have important implications for how both sides of the credential divide can earn moral wages. In Lively's and Pierce's studies, much of the subtext of paralegals' comments about their work was that they were doing similar tasks for much, much less money. Hypothetically, the differences in credentials could have created a similarly cold work dynamic at SAFE. After all, advocates and paralegals share a lot in common. Like advocates, paralegal work often requires only a bachelor's degree (sometimes even a high school diploma or associate's degree will suffice). Both advocates and paralegals work in close proximity to people who enjoy more status and wages while doing different but similar work: lawyers and counselors can do things that paralegals and advocates cannot, but their jobs are not mutually exclusive. Paralegals know law, interact with clients, and sometimes are mistaken for lawyers themselves. At SAFE, the advocates engaged in many of the nondirective, active listening strategies that the counselors did—albeit without the jargon or therapeutic training. But the advocates did *not* resent the counselors for their higher wages. Advocates at SAFE made about 75 percent of what the counselors made. According to the Bureau of Labor Statistics at the U.S. Department of Labor (2012), paralegals, on average, make about 40 percent of what lawyers do. Consequently, the advocates did not covet the counselors' position at SAFE—and this made it easier for both to adhere to their shared selfless, caring, and compassionate identity code.

When the advocates complained about money, they directed their frustration not upstairs (at the counselors) but outside (at local lawyers). They believed they could do many of the things lawyers did. Like paralegals, advocates at SAFE spent a lot of time helping clients navigate the criminal justice system. Sometimes, the advocates had more detailed knowledge about precise DV- and SA-related laws than the lawyers sitting near them in court. This was especially evident when they helped clients file for protective orders. Consider Cathleen's complaint to Heather in the advocates' office regarding the hours they put into helping clients file these legal documents: "Isn't it messed up that we aren't lawyers, and we [know how to file for protective orders], and [lawyers] can charge $1,500 for it?" They never begrudged the counselors' earnings in this way. During my fieldwork, I never heard comments from advocates like, "We can do what counselors do. We should be paid just as much!" Instead, the advocates saw the counselors' professional credentials as a legitimate reason for their (slightly) higher salaries. Of course, the advocates would have liked higher salaries, but if it were all about the money, given their legal savvy, the advocates could have tried their hand as paralegals, doing similar work and making nearly $20,000 a year more. But they did not. And if they had ambitions beyond SAFE, it was not to enter the legal or some other lucrative profession. Instead, they aspired to obtain master's degrees in social work or counseling and continue to work in the nonprofit sector. Thus, by comparing relations inside SAFE with that of law firms, we learn that how extrinsic rewards are distributed within the workplace has consequences for whether—and to what extent—workers can earn moral wages. While it might be easier to see virtue in one's relatively lower salary (for similar work), it can also foster feelings of animosity inconsistent with a moral identity.

Although the counselors were the highest paid at SAFE (although less than the codirectors), they also directed their salary-related frustrations outside—toward their professional colleagues in private practice. Although the counselors may have made more at SAFE than the advocates, they also believed that they *could have made* much more helping wealthier clients with less pressing problems. Although the advocates earn moral wages by pointing to their more difficult and stressful work conditions, the counselors accomplished the same effect by reminding themselves and others that they were passing on greener pastures. When referring to the challenging parts of their job, the counselors used private practice as a foil to frame their services at SAFE as moral dirty work. They sarcastically referred to their private practice colleagues as helping the "worried well." Jen characterized private practice clients as "upset housewives" whose troubles ranged from angst over home renovations or arguments with their hired help. Compared to some of her current clients at SAFE—"I hear some really grizzly stories where there are bruises, and in some cases outright torture"—she thought her peers in private practice dealt with much milder issues. And the confusion Jen caused her friends and peers by staying at SAFE only made her more confident she was doing the right thing. She complained that outsiders, like her former friends in the "country club set," could not understand why she would willingly choose this type of work, "and now when I talk with friends from that time in my life, they are like, 'Why in the world would you do this?'" She and the other counselors believed they could have made more money with less stress in private practice, but again, they chose not to.

As we see in the experiences of those at SAFE, the concept of moral wages can explain why and how credentialed and noncredentialed workers make sacrifices that we might not expect. Those with less pay, power, and prestige earn (and need) more moral wages to make sense of their lesser positions. And those who earn more extrinsic rewards can still point to the opportunities they forego as a way to earn moral wages themselves. However, the moral wages earned by the advocates and the counselors were also enabled by the overall mission of their organization. Their job was to help victims, to listen to them, to not judge them. The mission of law firms is not always as noble. Thus, in addition to the impact of credentials, we should also consider the moral stance different occupations take toward the well-being of their clientele. Whether or not workers are expected to sympathize with their clients has an even greater impact on the rate at which employees are able to earn moral wages on the job. In the next section, I analyze the findings from past studies on bill collectors, corporate industrial managers, volunteers, and the clergy. By examining the sympathetic stance (or lack thereof) that these jobs entail, we can better learn what made moral wages possible at SAFE—and how some jobs depend on intrinsic rewards in order to function.

Sympathy in the Workplace

If we want to learn whether moral wages are offered and earned in any given workplace, we should also look to that occupation's stance toward clients' and others' suffering and misfortune. To return briefly to the example of law firms, Pierce (1995) found that although paralegals conveyed more concern about clients than lawyers, they still saw mollifying clients as a practical matter, not a moral one. Tending to clients' emotional needs was a way to preempt complaints (and fewer complaints meant less work). As a result, paralegals in her study saw their work as largely ambivalent to the personal needs of their clients. Their job was to deliver results; nurturing those they were assigned to help was seen a means to an end. SAFE staff, however, took a fundamentally different approach. The advocates and counselors interpreted their clients' suffering as wrong and unjust, and they saw it as their job to care for them.

Earlier, I argued that because of the difficult conditions of their job, the advocates earned (and needed) more moral wages than the counselors or codirectors. However, by analyzing the sympathetic stance of workplaces, we also learn that long hours and tough tasks do not guarantee more moral wages. After all, many workplaces ask employees to work hard under considerable stress, but not all of them offer symbolic rewards for exhibiting care and compassion on the job. Some workplaces may even discourage workers from sympathizing or worrying about the feelings of others.

Debt collection could be classified as a type of dirty work. It is a job that business owners want done but often ask others to do for them. It does not pay very much and requires interacting with stigmatized clients (debtors). But, even though being a bill collector is hard, it is not *moral* dirty work; thus it offers few moral wages. As outlined in detail by sociologist Arlie Hochschild's (1983) groundbreaking work on emotional labor, *The Managed Heart*, spending all day hassling people with overdue bills is not an activity that workers can easily point to as an indicator of their capacity to be caring and compassionate. This does not mean that bill collectors can never accomplish a moral identity—identities can always be "worked on"—but the conditions of their jobs make things harder.

Bill collecting offers a worthwhile comparison to victim advocacy because their jobs require many of the same skills. Neither job requires professional credentials, and both involve a great deal of personal interaction in order to "read" others' emotions.[9] At this point, however, the comparison ends. Victim advocates anticipate their clients' emotional needs so that they can soothe them or avoid potentially troubling memories; bill collectors look to debtors' feeling for clues on how to exploit them.

Organizational psychologist Robert Sutton (1991) interviewed bill collectors and asked them how they interpreted the feelings of debtors. Although the bill collectors stated that they sometimes felt sorry for contrite debtors, they were trained to respond with irritation and anger. Consider the response from one bill collector on how to treat a debtor: "I just get real tough with them. [I tell them] I want the payment today, express mail. I don't care how or where they are going to get it, short of telling them to go stand down on the street corner. If I can hear television in the background, I tell them, 'Why don't you go sell your television?'" (1991:258). As a result, even if bill collectors privately believe that they are kind and caring people, their work offers few workplace opportunities to act on these beliefs. The conditions of their job make it hard to accomplish a moral identity *as bill collectors*. I do not argue that it is impossible for them to earn moral wages, just that it is an incredibly steep path.

Making a lot of money (extrinsic rewards) can also impede one's access to moral wages. As described in sociologist Robert Jackall's book *Moral Mazes* (2010), being a "nice" corporate manager can hinder one's chances for raises and promotions. As a result, the middle managers in Jackall's study worried that helping workers below them would displease those who ranked above them. In one case, an audiologist tried to advocate for better hearing protection for the loom operators on the floor of a textile manufacturing plant. When he discussed this with his team of industrial production managers, he quickly found that his recommendations were met with displeasure from his superiors. They dismissed his worries, telling him, "[Safety meetings] do not produce cloth" (Jackall 2010:109). His warnings were dismissed, he was passed over for a transfer, and he eventually left the corporation. Like victim advocates and counselors, he privately sympathized with others at work.

Figure 1. Jobs relative to SAFE advocates and counselors

Note: Victim advocates at SAFE earned roughly $26,500 a year, while victim counselors earned roughly $35,000. According to the Bureau of Labor Statistics, U.S. Department of Labor (2012), the median annual pay for bill collectors is $31,310; for family therapists $39,710; for clergy $43,970; for paralegals $46,680; and for industrial production managers $87,160.

However, unlike staff members at SAFE, his compassion was not an asset at work. Conversely, it may have cost him his job. Thus, compared to places like SAFE, there are fewer workplace incentives built into corporate industrial management positions to seek out and earn moral wages (see figure 1).

Learning from the case of corporate industrial managers, it is tempting to believe that extrinsic and intrinsic rewards are inversely related. That is, workers can choose one ("doing good") or the other (pay, power, or prestige) but not both. Following this logic, not making any money—volunteering— would seem to offer an even easier pathway to earn a moral wage. After all, volunteers help others without any benefit to themselves. However, when analyzing the conditions that facilitate or impede moral wages, the same lesson learned from the case of bill collectors (who work long and hard hours) still applies: there are no guarantees.

Making less (or no) money does not *always* make one's work seem more moral. Sociologist Daphne Holden's (1997) study of homeless shelter volunteers offers a good example of how some circumstances make it hard to earn moral wages. For example, the volunteers in her study wanted to establish meaningful connections with homeless people and help them get through their toughest times. Instead, as volunteers, their assigned task was to "help" homeless people by enforcing the rules of the shelter. Instead of being asked to engage in heartwarming conversations, they were trained to police curfew rules and confiscate any unauthorized food brought into the shelter. These policies made it hard for volunteers to see their efforts as an indicator of their virtuosity.[10] Thus, even when offering help for free, some assignments can make it harder for them to see themselves as caring and compassionate. In regard to moral wages, we learn that forgoing extrinsic rewards does not necessarily ensure one will be able to feel good about "doing good."

Conversely, making money does not preclude moral wages, either. One profession that offers relatively high wages and ample moral wages is the clergy. Although no longer the sole purveyor of principled and ethical behavior in contemporary culture, this field still enjoys considerable respect. Religious institutions still claim to represent "the highest values and moral standards in their society" (Lehman 1993:68) and roughly one-third of the American population sees the church as the sole author of morals and ethics (Hackett and Lindsay 2008). Even those who have adopted more relativistic and humanistic assumptions of right and wrong still respect priests, preachers, pastors, rabbis, and imams for the conviction of their beliefs.[11] On average, clergy earn middle-class wages and considerably more extrinsic rewards than advocates or counselors; yet their moral identity is typically not tainted by their pay, power, or prestige. One reason for this is that the clergy have access to persuasive discursive strategies to signify their morality. They describe their work as fostering "community" (Kleinman 1984) and as something that they did not choose so much as they were "called" to do (Simon and Nadell 1995). These rhetorics of morality are so effective that they can be wielded by groups who historically have had a more difficult time claiming the moral high ground in American culture. Sociologist Krista McQueeney (2009) found, for example, that the pastor of a lesbian- and gay-affirming church was able to wield a discourse of Christianity to recast monogamous homosexuality as indicative of congregants' moral worth.

The experiences of clergy also shed light on another way that staff members at SAFE earn moral wages: on the grounds that their job never really ends. Even at the grocery store, both groups may be called on to describe their beliefs or advise others. SAFE staff members all could recount stories about strangers who, upon learning where they worked, would ask questions like "Why don't abused women just call the cops?" Although not "on the clock," they still felt obligated to answer in a quick and confident manner. At any moment, they could be called on to teach what they called "Abuse 101": a brief primer on violence against women, its root causes, and the consequences for victims and others. Clergy share a similar burden. Not only are they expected to "accept, articulate, and act" (Mellow 2006:8) on moral precepts while interacting with their congregations, they know that everyone—not just members of their church—expect them to follow a higher moral code at all times. Thus, while many occupations call upon their members to be moral while on "front stage" and in front of their usual audience, few require members to display their moral identity at all times, with no time to relax "backstage."[12] Consequently, these emotional demands can be hard for clergy (as well as for advocates and counselors) to meet. Yet, if they can, there is a different kind of satisfaction waiting for all of them— one that can explain their perseverance in ways that their paychecks cannot.

CONCLUSION

The primary goal of this chapter is to show how the advocates and counselors at SAFE managed one of the many emotional dilemmas they faced at work: even when the pressure of helping victims of DV and SA was too much to bear, they saw the easiest opportunity to make their work less difficult (by reducing their services) as unacceptable. They believed their work sometimes asked too much of them, but they also wanted to help any woman who asked for assistance. How could they reconcile these competing desires? I argue that they did so by pointing to the positive feelings and sense of satisfaction that come with seeing oneself as caring and compassionate people. These symbolic rewards—which I call "moral wages"—explain how the advocates and counselors at SAFE were able to survive (and sometimes even thrive) during the most challenging times at work.

The second goal of this chapter is to adequately explain how the emotional risks and rewards of moral dirty work are inextricably linked at SAFE—and elsewhere. By comparing work inside and outside of SAFE, I show how moral wages are not just individual experiences, but rather patterned forms of symbolic compensation that are structurally embedded into occupations like victim advocacy and counseling. To understand the extent to which this occurs, I also show how hard work and low pay are not the only determinate of whether—and to what extent—a job offers moral wages. Other factors matter, too. In this chapter, I examine two: whether a job requires professional credentials and whether workers are expected to take a sympathetic stance toward clients' misfortune. By situating work at SAFE alongside these dimensions relative to a selection of other kinds of workers (paralegals, bill collectors, corporate industrial managers, family therapists, volunteers, and clergy), I use the concept of moral wages to offer a different perspective on what factors can impede and enable workers' ability to "feel good" about doing good.

In general, jobs that require professional credentials and take an unsympathetic stance toward their clients make it harder to earn moral wages on the job, but I am also careful to point out that when it comes to intrinsic rewards, nothing is guaranteed. Earning little to no money may make it easier, but depending on the assigned task, volunteers can have a hard time, too. Higher salaries can make the moral wage bargain more complicated— counseling the "worried well" in private practice was seen as a cop-out at SAFE—but not impossible: clergy earn both. Just because it is hard to conceive of jobs that offer considerable pay, power, prestige, *and* are singled out for their sacrifices and compassion does not mean that there are none. CEOs of charitable organizations like the United Way could be one example; professionals working full time for organizations in arduous locations like Doctors Without Borders could be another. These positions may be rare, but they still exist.

As an analytic device, the concept of moral wages also helps explain how workers with higher and lower incomes make sense of their decisions to put up with less. Professionals get applauded for being content with what they have and not asking for more. Thus, their good deeds—even if minor—can receive disproportionate attention relative to the sacrifices of their noncredentialed counterparts. Being better off also means having more things to sacrifice, and sacrifice is an important part of earning moral wages. Nonprofessionals are not afforded this type of admiration; they are not praised for taking a pass on greener pastures. More lucrative opportunities are not available to them in the same way. Thus, with less to give, the only thing left to derive satisfaction from is the relatively more difficult conditions they face.

Although the advocates and counselors at SAFE clearly enjoyed feeling for their clients, it is also clear that there is a downside to moral wages. Organizations like SAFE rely on nontangible forms of compensation like moral wages to keep their employees content. Not because the directors and managers of these places are manipulative or exploitative, but rather because there is not much else to give them. Municipal, state, and federal governments do not offer the financial resources necessary to places like SAFE to increase the salaries of their staff let alone hire more staff to reduce the overall caseload. In the meantime, DV and SA agencies will continue to rely heavily on noncredentialed, less expensive staff. This arrangement "works," in part, because of the prospect of moral wages. Yet, relying on workers to extract intrinsic rewards from difficult work while trying to solve persistent social problems is problematic.

The advocates' and counselors' ability to "make do" under difficult circumstances can be cited as justification that their workplace does not need any more resources. Not having enough money to offer extrinsic rewards, the codirectors at SAFE were left with little more to offer its staff members than opportunities to earn intrinsic ones. Once staff members accept this arrangement, their ability to find meaning in tough, underpaid work can serve to bolster claims by outsiders to deny additional funding. This dynamic creates a perverse incentive for places like SAFE to *not* complain about money so as to not taint their ideological purity or commitment to the cause. Thus, they are applauded for having less (as long as they do not ask for more).

This is the double bind that comes with accepting moral wages. The codirectors of SAFE continually complained that there simply was not enough money to offer all the services women in the region needed. Yet, because their workers relied so heavily on symbolic compensation, the codirectors' complaints could potentially be disregarded on the grounds that their staff members "knew what they were getting in to," and "asked for it," to the point of even "liking it." Sound familiar? These are the same victim-blaming scripts that advocates and counselors fight to debunk on a daily basis. That their capacity to reap intrinsic rewards despite emotionally challenging conditions could be used as evidence *against* their requests for help is as depressing as it is plausible.

As we'll see in the next chapter, moral wages are not the only way that SAFE advocates and counselors have adapted to a perpetual lack of sufficient funding. They have also made the most of their limited resources by adapting policies that sidestep the need for expertise (which can be costly). Instead, they train staff members (especially the advocates) to make clients the experts of their own situation by "empowering" them with options and information so that they may make their own choices. Yet this strategy also sets them up for the next emotional dilemma I address: they want to "empower" their clients by encouraging them to make their own decisions, but they were given little guidance on what they should do if their clients used their newfound power to make dangerous decisions that might put them in harm's way. Should staff members stand back and let their clients make (potentially lethal) mistakes? Or should they risk "disempowering" their clients by stepping in and telling them what to do? Much like the analysis in this chapter, they found a way to manage this dilemma, but their solution also created problems of its own.

Empowerment in Practice

It's not often that we hear a speech or read a pamphlet about helping others that does not mention the word *empowerment*. According to the dictionary, to "empower" is to give someone power and authority to do something—presumably something good.[1] In the legal realm, this typically involves allowing others to make decisions on your behalf—like permitting a lawyer to sign a contract for you. Among social service agencies, empowering others carries a similar, but different meaning. Most often, it entails helping others by offering them the time, resources, and encouragement they need to make their own decisions.

Empowerment was the subtext of nearly everything that happened at SAFE (Stopping Abuse in Family Environments). Although the advocates and counselors rarely used the word with clients—they reserved such policy talk for themselves—the idea was featured prominently in their mission statement and embedded in their policies. Most important, it served as the interpretive filter through which they evaluated whether or not their services "worked." As long as staff members could claim that their clients had been "empowered," they could believe that they had done their job. As a result, empowerment was both ubiquitous and hidden at SAFE: even when staff members were not explicitly using the term, it was clear that the concept guided nearly all their workplace interactions.[2]

As an organization, SAFE defined the concept indirectly: "Empowerment through education, information and support is inherently respectful of each individual's unique experience and abilities and is the most effective tool for creating hope and change." This language was commonly featured on their brochures, newsletters, and handouts and is typical of agencies that assist victims of domestic violence (DV) and sexual assault (SA). For example, the battered women's shelter studied recently by sociologist Amanda Gengler defined empowerment as "regaining strength, courage, confidence, and personal power. In other words, empowerment is taking back your life" (2012:507). Given the expansiveness of the concept, it should come as little surprise that staff members at SAFE found their own ways to interpret and apply the concept.

In the most basic terms, the advocates and counselors believed that empowering clients meant helping them in such a way that one day they could eventually help themselves—even if it meant watching their clients make some mistakes. Staff members understood recovery as a slow process, of which allowing clients to learn from their missteps was an important part. At first glance, this policy would appear to be simple to apply. However, in practice, it was not as easy as it would seem.

Living up to the ideals of their empowerment philosophy was a high-stakes affair at SAFE. Staff members' moral identity was wrapped up in the idea that they did not tell abused women what to do. This made for a lofty standard to live up to. In our everyday interactions, we expect to give and receive explicit advice when interacting with friends, coworkers, and family members. But this was not the case at SAFE. They saw the services they offered victims of DV and SA as clearly different from those offered by cops, doctors, and caseworkers at the Department of Social Services (DSS). At SAFE, they did not sit clients down and tell them they should press charges, follow prescribed remedies, or change their behavior. Instead, they believed it was better to listen than to lecture, to sympathize than to criticize, to support than to compel.

In many cases, living up to this aspect of their moral identity code was relatively easy. When staff members were confident that their clients were making modest and safe decisions, they were happy to stand back and watch them glide toward recovery. Yet, when staff members feared that their clients were about to make poor decisions, this "hands-off" guideline became harder to follow. This did not mean that they never gave explicit advice; if danger was imminent, they gave themselves permission to intervene. It was the cases when danger was possible, but not imminent, that posed the biggest challenge to their empowering approach.

Chapter Three

This is the context of the emotional dilemma I focus on in this chapter. Staff members were asked to help women and keep them from being harmed, but to do so by not "rescuing" them. They feared that being too directive with clients was "disempowering." At SAFE, helping clients "too much" was bad, but so was not helping them enough. When they saw their clients slowly veering toward *potential* pitfalls, they were unsure of how to respond. They wanted to keep their clients free from harm, but they also did not want to tell them what to do. As is the case with the other dilemmas described in this book, SAFE staff members were able to find a way to manage this one, too.

In the end, they capitalized on the ambiguity of their service philosophy to frame nearly any of their services as empowering, even when they nudged clients away from likely hazards—a process I call *steering*. In the conclusion, I argue that their steering strategy was more than just a game of semantics. Framing their services as empowering enabled them to continue to earn moral wages, to forgive themselves when their clients were revictimized, and to maximize the potential of a largely nonprofessional workforce.

To be clear, the purpose of this chapter is not to show how or why empowerment is "good" or "bad." Instead, I explain why this concept has come to be the central organizing principle of places like SAFE and show how its vague and ambiguous meanings serve different purposes (and not always the intended ones). I hope that this analysis will shed light on how the concept of empowerment is used inside agencies like SAFE—and how staff members often put it to work for themselves, too.

WHY EMPOWERMENT?

As a sociologist, I approach the idea of empowerment somewhat differently than do social workers or those who work at places like SAFE. Instead of calculating which services are more empowering than others, my job in this chapter is to outline the social conditions that foster empowerment policies and explain how this concept shapes the experiences of victim-service providers. Nationwide, agencies like SAFE have based their organizational philosophy on a concept whose definition is often difficult to pin down to the extent that inconsistencies in its application often go unrecognized. And analyzing the ways that the idea of empowerment is used—in practice—can tell us a lot about the social positioning of places like SAFE relative to other institutions.

Empowerment emerged as a guiding philosophy in the beginnings of the battered women's movement as an antidote to the powerlessness and helplessness felt by victims of DV and SA. The term became increasingly popular in the 1960s and '70s, and by the early 1980s, second-wave feminists were beginning to talk about empowerment specifically in relation to community-driven responses to violence against women. Today, at trainings and workshops across the country, victim advocates and counselors across the country are taught that "empowerment is a process, a mechanism by which people, organizations and communities gain mastery over their affairs" (Rappaport 1987:122) that can be achieved by helping victims with "goal setting, assessment, inquiry, analysis, and action that may lead to self-determination and distributive justice" (Kasturirangan 2008:1472). These efforts seek to empower those at risk through "an increase in the actual power of the client or community so that action can be taken to prevent or change the problems they are facing" (Gutiérrez, DeLois, and GlenMaye 1995:535).[3]

There are two (related) reasons why the idea of empowerment is so appealing to victim advocates and counselors. The first is that it fits seamlessly into their reframing of abuse as a social—not an individual—problem. According to their line of reasoning, perpetrators of violence against women are not isolated maniacs acting out their own pathologies, but everyday men whose unacknowledged privilege and sense of entitlement cause them to lash out and control those who challenge their dominant position—as men.

Convincing the wider public that DV and SA are the individual manifestations of a wider social phenomenon—patriarchy—was (and still is) a colossal educational task. This message competes against popular assumptions that continue to frame abuse as the product of "lovers' quarrels," misunderstandings, or jealous tempers. Victim advocates and counselors see it as part of their duty to debunk these claims, and the stakes are high. Individualistic explanations of DV and SA render broad structural solutions unnecessary.

This is the political battle that agencies like SAFE have been waging for more than forty years: defining abuse as the systemic denial of power and

Figure 2. The Power and Control Wheel

Source: Domestic Abuse Intervention Project, www.theduluthmodel.org

control over another person's life and well-being that only sometimes takes the form of physical violence (Barner and Carney 2011). This specific language originated from the Duluth Domestic Abuse Intervention Project in 1981 (Pence and Paymar 1993). And to this day, the Power and Control Wheel (figure 2) is a staple handout of DV and SA agencies nationwide.

The second reason why the idea of empowerment is so appealing to the people who work at places like SAFE is that adhering to this philosophy helps them draw a clear distinction between themselves and agents of other institutions (legal, medical, and social service) whose shortcomings were the reason why the battered women's and anti-rape movements were founded in the first place.

Historically, as noted in chapter 1, DV and SA agencies have been very leery of these institutions, especially the criminal justice system. Even the most victim-friendly legal reforms are still viewed with suspicion by advocates and counselors. For example, staff members warned clients that "mandatory" arrest policies—designed to prevent police officers from letting dangerous abusers off with only a warning (Morgan and Coombes 2013)—could sometimes create more problems than they solve. For example, what if a victim only wants the abuser removed from the premises without formally charging him with an offense? They also expressed concern with "no drop" prosecution policies designed to protect victims from being intimidated into rescinding their accusations by their abusers (Ford 2003). They warned clients that the moment an assistant district attorney decides to bring a case to trial, victims no longer have full power and control over whether or how their cases will proceed.[4]

Hospitals were also viewed with caution. Although the SAFE staff members generally had a good working relationship with the sexual assault nurse examiners (SANE) at the nearest hospital, they were well aware that some doctors were incapable (or unwilling) to "sit and listen" with clients enough to meet their emotional needs. This is a common complaint among rape victim advocates: "Insensitive and impatient health care providers can discourage rape reporting by forcing victims to endure poor and sometimes incompetent treatment" (Corrigan 2013:65). Even when done well, the prescriptive advice delivered by doctors is still framed as fundamentally at odds with the "empowering" approach at SAFE. Whereas doctors see diagnosing maladies and prescribing specific remedies as their professional duty, advocates and counselors see telling their clients what to do as problematic. Thus, SAFE staff members operate from a fundamentally different assumption about who is best suited to determine what is best for the people they serve.

Empowerment was also seen as preferable in comparison to the treatment that victims have historically experienced in bureaucratic institutions like the DSS—especially its sub-office: Child Protective Services (CPS). Although SAFE staff members were sympathetic toward the individual social workers who staffed these agencies (many of the counselors at SAFE were themselves licensed clinical social workers or were working to obtain these credentials), they also believed that social service agencies too often stripped caseworkers of the discretion necessary to deal with victims' nuanced, complex, and situational problems. Worries about the possibility that CPS caseworkers would strip custody rights from their clients were frequent at SAFE. This could occur in many ways. For example, evidence that a child has witnessed a mother suffer violence in the home, or that a fleeing mother has temporarily left a child with her abuser (who has abused that child in the past), is often treated as legal grounds for the mother to lose custody (Davidson 1995; Bemiller 2008). Thus, victim advocates and counselors often see the "street level bureaucrats" (Lipsky 1980) who staff these offices in a mixed light (Steen 2009). On the one hand, people who work at places like SAFE identify with the challenges inherent in trying to help vulnerable populations with limited resources; but on the other hand, they perceive the policies underlying public social service institutions to be too directive, rigid, and inflexible (Danis 2003)—antithetical to the empowering approach at SAFE.

DEFINING EMPOWERMENT

During my volunteer training, when we were taught about empowerment, I immediately thought of the ancient proverb: Give someone a fish, feed them for a day; teach someone to fish, feed them for a lifetime. That is, to make sense of the concept, I relied mostly on analogy and metaphor. Those at SAFE did the same. Christina, manager of the shelter, equated empowerment with the ability and desire to do things for oneself. She defined her role as offering clients "the tools they need to meet their own needs. That to me is empowering." This explanation was typical of SAFE staff members. They defined empowerment with broad strokes, leaving the minor details to be worked out on a case-by-case basis.

One reason for this ambiguity was that staff members most often talked about empowerment by explaining what it was *not*. For example, according to Christina, empowerment was not about getting clients hired or placing them in apartments; those actions would be "enabling [them] to continue to be in need." This type of definition by contrast is common, even among scholars of "empowerment." For example, psychologists Mandy Morgan and Leigh Coombes (2013), in their review of the literature on the topic, quoted ample studies that focused primarily on what service providers should *avoid*.

For example, they should not "intrude on her life, reshape her experiences against her wishes or presume that she cannot make decisions in her own interest" (2013:527). At SAFE, talk of disempowering practices (bad) was just as common as discussion of empowering ones (good).

Although there was a consistent definition found in SAFE's written materials (quoted previously), everyone in the office offered me slightly different interpretations during my conversations and interviews with them as part of my research (for more on my methods, see the appendix of this book). This was not surprising; as mentioned in chapter 2, most training at SAFE took place through "shadowing": new staff members observed their more experienced colleagues as they interacted with clients and then asked questions afterward. SAFE had no rigidly organized orientation sessions for new recruits (especially not for advocates).[5] This training method was partly by design—it was consistent with the informal ethos of the organization—but also partly out of necessity: there was no human resources office to process new hires, and diverting experienced staff away from their work in order to teach newcomers would mean asking them to spend less time with their own clients.

One consequence of this method of training was that staff members' definitions of empowerment varied, sometimes even from those of the people who had taught them about the idea. For example, Cathleen, an advocate, first told me that "no one sat me down and said, 'This is the empowerment model,'" but later offered this definition: "I try to connect them to resources that will help them if they are leaving their abuser [and] that will help them get on their feet in terms of basic necessities like food and shelter all the way up to referring them for job training." When I asked who taught her this, she said she was unsure, but that she had probably learned it from Lisa. During Lisa's private interview, she said that she was not entirely sure where she learned about empowerment either: "I have this mental construct of the empowerment model that was kind of verbally handed down to me. But later on I found out that some of the people I was getting the empowerment model from . . . had a different take on that from me." When I asked Lisa for a working definition, she described empowerment as "seeing the person as a total being. . . . It is getting to know them and finding out what will give them personal power on a very individual basis."

To add another wrinkle, Kelly (a SAFE codirector), who remembered training Lisa years before, offered yet another definition: "Empowerment is definitely about respecting their decisions and trying to understand why they're making those decisions. Respecting the fact that they have what they think are good reasons for making the choices that they're making." As the concept was passed down from Kelly to Lisa to Cathleen, we can see slight changes emerge. However, while not identical, their definitions were still similar. They used different phrasing, but all valued the client's perspective when offering services.

Another reason for staff members' slightly different descriptions of empowerment is that their understanding of the concept did not come solely from the SAFE policy manual. This is not uncommon among agencies that assist victims of DV and SA. Other studies of similar organizations have shown that service providers often interpret the concept through the lens of other social issues that are also important to them, such as combatting racism (Matthews 1994:131) or fostering spirituality (Whittier 1995). However, at SAFE, the most pervasive outside influence came from "self-help" folk theories that appear ubiquitously in contemporary discourse. When defining empowerment, staff members seamlessly integrated phrases like helping clients "take charge" of their lives and enabling victims to "own their recovery." Jen, a counselor, frequently invoked these ideas when she described empowerment as finding "cracks where growth is taking place" so that she can help her clients "get in touch with what they want." Lisa wove these rhetorical threads into her description of empowerment, too; she would occasionally switch back and forth between the term *empowerment* and Paulo Freire's conceptualization of *learning* (an egalitarian pedagogical theory of education whereby oppressed people learn from one another) (Freire 2009). Over the course of her interview with me, when I asked her to define the term as she understood it, she used "empowerment model" and what she called Freire's "equal learning model" interchangeably.

In summary, after pressing staff members for precise definitions, it became clear that their interpretations of empowerment varied—not drastically, but noticeably. This is primarily because they most often defined the term through vague analogies or (more often) in opposition to the actions outlined in the "power and control" wheel. The advocates and counselors may have used different words to describe what empowerment was, but there was clear agreement about what it was not (coercion, intimidation, isolation, blaming, and so on). In addition, subtle variations are to be expected considering that SAFE did not own the term. Empowerment talk pervades contemporary discourse; meaning that even if SAFE had posted clear definitions in each office, staff members would likely still be influenced by prior or outside knowledge of the term. As I show in the conclusion to this book, however, the absence of perfect consensus was not entirely a bad thing. The ambiguity of the word *empowerment* caused problems, to be sure—but it also helped solve a few.

APPLYING EMPOWERMENT

Although popular stereotypes depict advocates and counselors as dogmatic and single-minded in their efforts to pressure clients to leave their abusers or to press charges, the atmosphere I observed was quite different. Staff members approached their clients' cases with a wide degree of open-mindedness. They sincerely believed that letting clients make their own decisions was the best solution.

One reason that staff members were so enthusiastic about SAFE's approach—irrespective of its theoretical underpinnings and historical roots—was that they saw it as a good way to keep clients coming back. From their perspective, adopting a friendly, nondirective style of interaction made clients feel welcome; and the more comfortable they felt, the more the advocates and counselors could help them. For example, Lisa believed that taking a hard-line approach with clients would be counterproductive: "I think that whatever decision a woman makes really does have to be her decision and I also am sensitive to not turning her off towards coming here. So I feel like she needs to see me as an ally who is going to boost her up in whatever she needs to do." From her point of view, ordering victims around would make them less likely to seek additional services at SAFE—putting them at greater risk.

When I asked others to explain this logic to me, they typically described a hypothetical scenario whereby an advocate or counselor explicitly tells a client to flee from her abuser (in their terms, a disempowering demand). The client agrees, leaves him, and then changes her mind—deciding to go back.

Weeks later, if the abuse continues, she might not come back to SAFE out of fear that she will return to a chorus of "I told you so" accusations. Thus, staff members believed that telling clients what to do could backfire; if clients eventually changed their minds, they might not return out of embarrassment or shame. As a result, empowerment at SAFE was both a philosophical and practical matter: not issuing orders to clients meant there were no orders for clients to disobey. They believed that this method kept clients close and safe and helped everyone save face when plans went awry.

In many cases, taking this stance did not require much action. Simply listening to clients and encouraging them to continue on their current path could be interpreted as empowering. For example, one client began speaking as soon as she walked into the advocates' office. Cathleen listened uninterruptedly for nearly five minutes before the client suddenly blurted out, "I don't have to wait for him to divorce me, I can divorce him!" Cathleen seemed surprised by the outburst; she paused for a second and then responded enthusiastically, "Yes, you can." Both were elated. Afterward, Cathleen relayed the good news to her colleagues, explaining that her client "felt much more empowered." Cathleen had said only five to ten words during the entire interaction.

Other times, soliciting clients' thoughts while they read through a handout was enough. One common way to help clients in the SAFE office was to help them develop "safety plans."[6] These were practical exercises that involved offering clients a checklist of tasks they could perform to protect themselves. Strategies included stashing an old cell phone—only capable of dialing 911—in a safe place, or having a packed bag ready at all times. Staff members and clients could read over the list and talk about ways to prepare for future contingencies. Clients were usually impressed by the breadth of ideas in the handout. One remarked to Jesse that she knew she would need her personal documents (birth certificate and Social Security card), but had not thought to hide a copy of her children's immunization records in case she needed to flee in a hurry. Moving to a different state would mean enrolling her children in different schools; she had never had the time to think through the logistics of running away. During the exercise, Jesse mostly sat and listened while the client checked off items and talked out loud to herself. Afterward, Jesse explained that the most rewarding part of the session was watching her client slowly realize new possibilities for her future (how to leave, what leaving would be like, how to survive on her own). Jesse then admitted there were times when she wanted to interrupt her client to congratulate her on her progress, but she forced herself to stay quiet until her client was completely finished working her way through the list. From Jesse's perspective, she empowered her client by exerting less control over the session.

Empowering clients became more difficult when clients wanted more explicit advice. Whereas letting clients talk through their problems was an easy decision for staff members, responding to specific legal questions required a more nuanced interpretation of how much or how little they should help. This happened most often when clients needed help filling out legal paperwork to obtain a protective order (a document similar to a restraining order). These forms were confusing—often filled with legal jargon—and they baffled many clients. Because the advocates were not lawyers, they were not supposed to complete the forms for clients. Yet, they could give clients advice on how to phrase certain answers. Sometimes, this was enough; but other times, clients wanted specific answers, and the advocates had to balance their clients' wishes against SAFE's nondirective policy.

To apply their empowerment philosophy during the protective order process, the advocates would first retrieve a copy of the form. After giving a general overview of the costs and benefits of legal remedies, they would then explain the basic requirements of each section as well as the general procedure for getting a judge's approval. If the client wanted to proceed, her advocate would attach the form to a clipboard and sit beside her while she entered responses in her own hand. When one of Cathleen's clients asked how to answer a specific question on the form, for example, Cathleen read it aloud to her and then asked, "Well, if you were a judge, and you were having to think about whether or not to grant this order to you, what do you think are the strongest things that you would want to see in there?" This was typical of the guided—but nondirective—approach advocates took with clients regarding protective orders. If the client filled in the wrong section, the advocate would point out the error. If the client did not write enough, the advocate would suggest she write more. When the client was done, the advocate would read it over one more time, hand it back to her, and tell her when and where to meet outside the courthouse. At court, the advocate would introduce her to the judge (typically during a brief recess), point to the paperwork, and (if the judge agreed) accompany her with the signed document down to the clerk's office to be photocopied and filed. As a result, the advocates' application of empowerment in practice was measured: handing a client the form and writing down the address of the courtroom was not enough; filling out an entire form for her was too much (and potentially illegal).[7] They labeled almost any form of help with protective orders that fell between these lines as empowering.

The biggest challenge to their empowering approach, however, arose when the advocates and counselors believed clients were headed toward danger. They wanted to keep them safe, and they did not want to tell them what to do; but sometimes they feared that these two goals were incompatible. They were careful not to let clients see them as conflicted, so the debates about whether or not to step in often took place behind closed doors.[8]

During one backstage discussion about a recent client, Jesse told the other advocates: "We aren't supposed to tell clients what to do, but [this woman] needs to get out because he's psycho." In another conversation, Melissa, a counselor, described visiting a client's home where she could immediately sense the potential for danger. She sat next to the client on a couch while her abuser was sleeping in a separate room (they were still living together). She described the woman as paralyzed by fear. Melissa later told her colleagues how she spent the entire meeting battling her inner desire to intervene: "My rescuer came out, big time, [but later] I was like, 'Oh God! That is not my job! I am not being paid to rescue her!' But I really wanted to rescue her. I really wanted to take her and her child and put them in my car and say, 'We're out.'" In the end, Melissa left the house without "rescuing" the client. But the other advocates and counselors nodded in agreement during her story; they also had experienced similar desires to rescue clients. Heather, an advocate, described how she was usually able to fight off this impulse by reminding herself of the rationale behind empowerment: "So yes, I do want to say, 'You've got to get out. You've got to get out.' But that is not allowing them to own their own power." Most—but not all—of the time, staff members decided not intervene.

As the level of danger ratcheted up, the battle against their "rescuer" impulse became even more pronounced. In one case, Lisa, an advocate at the time, worked with a client who had recently won a hard-fought legal battle to secure ownership of the home she once shared with her ex-husband. After the case, even though he kept threatening her, she did not want to give up the home. Sticking to an empowering approach, Lisa did not explicitly tell her to seek safety elsewhere. Instead, she pointed out some of the warning signs that she and other SAFE staff members saw regarding her abuser's behavior. He had been suspected of arson before (although never convicted) and hinted to her that he might burn down the home. She was scared, but she did not want to give in to his threats. He still owned an adjacent plot of land and half the title to their car, and he was finding excuses to use the vehicle and mow the lot next door as a means to linger around and intimidate her. Privately, Lisa wanted her to flee: "I had a flash feeling: 'I'm not going to see you alive again.'" Yet, Lisa kept her premonition to herself and continued to gently nudge the client to reconsider.

Eventually, as the warning signs began to mount, SAFE staff members decided to intervene. Kelly, a codirector, talked over the case with Lisa, and they concluded the risk was too great: they visited her home together and urged her to leave. The benefits of empowerment notwithstanding, they believed this case warranted an exception. To Kelly, this was rare: "We pressured her to get out, which we don't normally do." Eventually, the client relented, agreeing to leave in a few days. However, it was too late. The next day, the house burned down with her and her child inside. Police suspected arson, but did not have enough evidence to file charges.

In most cases, when clients were not in immediate danger, empowerment was easy to apply—but this was not one of those cases. It took a long time for Lisa to come to terms with the tragedy. She said it did not really "hit her" until a year and a half later. She avoided reflecting on the client and her child's death until the memory began to overwhelm her: "It's like condensation on the walls, or a critical mass—eventually it just seeps in, and I realize 'I can't handle this.'" However, as time passed, she eventually felt more comfortable with her decision to delay intervention for as long as possible. She admitted that during the case she had been tempted to intervene earlier: "As an advocate, I had to censor that emotion: 'Oh my God, you've got to get out!'" But in the end, instead of blaming SAFE's empowerment philosophy, she used the concept to manage her grief by repeatedly pointing to the client's bravery and strength. Lisa was proud of her client; the woman knew the risks and chose not to give in to her abuser's threats. In the language of SAFE, her client had exerted power and control over her life. This was soothing to Lisa, but it did not wipe away all of her grief. More than a year later, she still believed empowerment was the right approach to helping victims, but cases like this tested her confidence.

DEFENDING EMPOWERMENT

Although the advocates and counselors were quick to cite the benefits of empowerment, some cases (such as Lisa's arson case) created doubts. And if staff members could question the strategy at times, one could imagine that clients might, too. Thus, somewhat surprisingly, I observed staff members spend a good deal of time trying to convince their clients that this was the best way to be helped.

Most of clients' doubts about empowerment stemmed from a different understanding of what constitutes abuse. It may sound strange to outsiders, but many clients who came to SAFE were not sure whether or not they had been victimized. If they did not have bruises, scratches, or scars, they did not know if their suffering constituted abuse. To show their clients that not all abuse leaves visible marks, staff members would show them the Power and Control Wheel and ask them to mark off all things their husbands, boyfriends, or exes had done. They would ask clients whether their intimate partners had ever manipulated, intimidated, or humiliated them. They would ask their clients for examples of times when that same person had isolated them from their friends and family, minimized their complaints, threatened to take their children away, prohibited them from making decisions, or denied them access to household income. The logic of their questioning goes like this: if a woman has been denied power and control over her life, then she has been disempowered; and if she has been disempowered, she has been abused.

The advocates and counselors knew that some clients were confused by their theory of abuse. For those who arrived at SAFE unsure of whether or not they were victims, and not knowing where else to go, this explanation of

DV and SA could take a while to understand. And until they came around to accept SAFE staff members' way of thinking, the empowerment philosophy the advocates and counselors talked about was little more than a handout on a shelf. Convincing others to believe in this approach took time.

Clients who came seeking specific kinds of help (legal assistance, shelter, a job) were sometimes puzzled that the advocates and counselors would not tell them exactly where to go and what they should do. Staff members were ready for this. They were trained that some clients would expect direct commands (call the cops, move out, take the kids and leave town); and if clients asked for clear directions, then staff members would tell them that SAFE was not that kind of place. If clients were still confused, the advocates and counselors were also trained to explain why *not* telling them what to do was better for them in the long run.

Despite staff members' best efforts, some clients still balked at this approach. When I asked Lisa why, if a client wanted to be told what to do, not just tell them, Lisa explained to me, "They need to practice making decisions." Yet, some clients still resisted. Many tried to get the advocates and counselors to tell them what they were "really" thinking—treating empowerment as a kind of guessing game. Lisa referred to this as the "testing stage" of victim services, whereby clients looked for any hints of "fakeness" on part of the advocate. She believed that her clients—as victims—were especially attuned to subtle forms of manipulation and control. She described how one client in particular was persistent in her attempt to tease out any hidden agenda from Lisa. It took a number of sessions before Lisa could overcome her client's skepticism and develop some level of trust: "She would stare right at me, like she was testing me, and I looked right back at her as if to say, 'I'm still here with you, I'm still here with you, I'm still here with you.' And after that, we made a real connection."

Clients' suspicions were not entirely without merit. Away from clients, staff members often shared with me their private opinions about what their clients should do. They believed in their nondirective approach but still debated the ethics of withholding their views. For example, in the hallway out of earshot from her client, Cathleen was conflicted: "I really have the urge to say what I think. . . . If I were a victim, sometimes I would want direct advice." But she also recognized the downside of this approach (discouraging clients from developing their own opinions, denying them power and control, and so on). In the end, Cathleen kept her thoughts to herself: "I guess I could just ask [my client] what she thought she should do." From there, she hoped her client would come to a good solution—as effective as the one she was reluctant to share.

Justifying their hands-off approach to clients became even more difficult when there was not consensus among the staff themselves about how much help was too much. For example, some clients asked the advocates and counselors to contact their past or present abusers on their behalf. Sometimes these clients needed help negotiating sensitive issues (like custody arrangements); other times they just needed someone to tell their abuser when to be out of the house so they could retrieve their belongings from a formerly shared apartment. There was disagreement in the advocates' office over how staff members should respond to these requests. Meg, for example, was willing to contact former abusers on her clients' behalf because she believed this kind of communication could be too traumatic for them; if a simple phone call was all that was blocking a client from getting on with her life, Meg would eliminate that hurdle for her. Jesse, however, disagreed with this approach: "I don't think it is empowering to have clients depend on us to intervene. . . . Relying on us to call for [them] is like holding [them] back . . . . It might give [them] a false sense of security . . . that they can't do it on their own . . . that they need someone to intervene on their behalf." But even though Jesse was firm in her conviction not to call abusers, she made other kinds of calls for clients (setting up appointments with lawyers and DSS caseworkers). Other times she gave clients rides to their appointments.

Although the advocates and counselors enjoyed the flexibility afforded to them to decide when it was appropriate to do things for clients (like make calls or give rides), this also caused problems. If they made one call, should they make a second? What was the appropriate limit? It was hard to tell clients that they would not run an errand for them, or tell them they would do it once but not twice. Consequently, the ambiguity of empowerment could be both a blessing and a burden. Inconsistencies among staff members could have a ripple effect throughout the office. If one client heard that another was treated differently, complaints followed. When Jesse's client became upset when she learned that Meg's clients were receiving different services, it caused tension.

Shelter staff members had an even more difficult time. Unlike in the main office, residents in the shelter were required to adhere to a set of very explicit rules.[9] Whether these rules were mundane (clean up after meals) or more serious (keep the location of the shelter a secret), they posed a problem for staff members: How could they empower shelter residents while simultaneously telling them how they should live and interact with others in a confined space?[10] For example, residents were expected to meet with local social workers. Staff members would help schedule their first meeting, even to the point of arranging transportation; but they expected residents to be responsible for developing a relationship with their social workers and following through with any commitments they made during their sessions. This was the basic principle behind SAFE's empowerment philosophy: staff members believed it was their job to put clients in touch with the tools and resources they needed to solve their problems, but it was the clients' responsibility to use them. Yet, when residents resisted, what could staff members do? They could urge and cajole, but their empowerment philosophy limited how much.

In the case of behavioral rules (no smoking) in the shelter, staff members could make specific demands. Disobeying these cut-and-dried rules resulted in warnings, and continued warnings could lead to expulsion from the shelter. But refusals to engage in tasks labeled empowering (like meeting with a social worker) were harder to penalize. Skipping a meeting with a social worker usually resulted in a meeting with a shelter advocate, developing a new plan, and trying again.[11] In most cases, residents would eventually comply, but not all did. And these kinds of cases were the hardest on staff members. Rebecca wanted her shelter residents to "take ownership" of their healing process, but what if a client did not want to "own" her recovery? What if she wanted to leave the shelter even though she had no place else to go—other than reunite with her former abuser? SAFE's policies offered little guidance on how to respond: *demanding* a client adhere to their empowerment philosophy was—by their definition—disempowering.

Although the wording of staff members' definitions of empowerment varied, they still found the concept relatively easy to apply in the majority of cases. When clients just needed someone to listen to them, staff members had little trouble adopting a nondirective approach. When staff members recognized a possible threat to clients' safety, they had more trouble keeping their inner "rescuers" in check, but they were usually able to do so. And in cases involving extreme danger, they believed it was within their mandate to step in and intervene. Yet there was one remaining type of case that made SAFE's philosophy particularly hard to apply: clients who were not in immediate danger, but were starting to make decisions that were putting themselves at greater risk. These particular cases provoked the emotional dilemma that is the subject of this chapter. When clients appeared unwilling to take steps to improve their safety, or began to make dangerous or seemingly unwise decisions, there was less guidance in either the main office or the shelter on how to proceed. Staff members wanted to enable their clients to help themselves, but what if their clients did not want to cooperate? Or what if they feared their clients' ideas about how best to help themselves were ill conceived? Should staff members sit back and watch their clients eventually suffer in the name of empowerment? They wanted to keep their clients free from future harm, but they did not want to tell them what to do. To manage this dilemma, they developed a strategy I call *steering*.

STEERING STRATEGIES

I define *steering* as influencing clients just enough to nudge them off a potentially hazardous path, but not so much as to be seen—or to see themselves—as telling their clients what to do. All staff members conceded that they influenced their clients' decisions at some point in their careers. Yet, even though they acknowledged doing it some of the time, I observed it happening more often than they admitted and in cases involving less danger than their policies would encourage.[12] Whenever I mentioned that it appeared to me that they sometimes influenced clients more than their (albeit varying) definitions of empowerment would seemingly allow, they felt compelled to reframe their actions as ultimately empowering. These responses were telling. They showed two things: (1) seeing themselves as empowering their clients was incredibly important to them, and (2) they were aware that steering was not entirely consistent with their empowerment philosophy.

In this section, I outline the most common strategies staff members employed to steer clients (planting seeds of doubt, speculating about a brighter future, relying on the authority of others). My purpose here is not to blame those at SAFE for steering—I did not want to see clients revictimized, either. Rather, I argue that their efforts to hide their steering, or frame their subtle forms of influence as empowering, only make sense given the high standards to which they held themselves accountable.

Giving explicit advice or direction is not necessarily a bad thing. Doctors, law enforcement officers, and DSS caseworkers do this all the time. Yet, the advocates and counselors at SAFE saw their approach to victim services as fundamentally different, and this difference circumscribed the contours of their moral identity. Inside the office, controlling others was seen as the problem, not the solution. Staff members were even skeptical of kinder versions of influence, like the "strategic friendliness" or "emotional manipulation of another person for a strategic end" (Pierce 1995:72) that trial lawyers often use to persuade clients and juries. Although such forms of persuasion may be suitable in other occupations, they were seen as potentially disempowering inside the SAFE office. For advocates and counselors, influencing clients' decisions, even if slightly, was something to approach with considerable caution and careful concern.

Let me also be clear that I observed no secret agenda or hidden pattern of whom (demographically) they most often steered other than to claim that it occurred most frequently when staff members believed their clients' could or would not see the danger in their path. Thus, my purpose here is not to argue whether steering is "good" or "bad"; instead, I use the phenomenon of steering to show how idealistic goals can pose problems for the service providers asked to adhere to them.

Planting Seeds of Doubt

If the advocates and counselors believed that a client was making a bad decision, they could steer her in another direction by pointing out hidden snares in her path—but stop short of saying that she would definitely succumb to them. Heather, for example, put it this way with one client who was considering giving her current boyfriend (who had recently abused her) a second chance: "Wow, I hear where you're coming from. I'm just really concerned about what happened the last time and I wonder if it is not going to happen again." Heather did not say, "This will happen again," but rather posed it as a possibility by suggesting that "what happened the last time" might repeat itself. The client was clearly moved by Heather's cautious warning and ultimately decided against her initial decision. I observed this as a case of steering, but Heather told me afterward that she thought it was still empowering to encourage a client to reflect or think over her original plans. If the client thought over their idea for a second time, and still was adamant about moving in that direction, Heather said she would let her go on.

The advocates and counselors had a number of rhetorical tools to plant seeds of doubt in clients' minds. For example, if they wanted to get clients to pause and reconsider their current plans, they would frame their suggestions as merely "opinions" or "concerns." Melissa, for example, would preface suggestions like this: "This is very much my opinion, this is very much from me, but I'm very worried about you." This approach allowed Melissa to express her fear for her client—who was considering going back to her abuser—without claiming this was SAFE's official position. And it worked; afterward, the client decided not to move back in with him.

Staff members learned this strategy from a SAFE codirector, Kelly, who prefaced nearly all of her warnings to clients by characterizing them as based on her experience—not because she was the final authority: "I really take pains to let them understand that this is my opinion, coming from where I'm coming from. And I understand that they might not see it that way at all, but I feel like I have an obligation to share with them what I've learned and seen over the years, working with lots of different people." This was an effective steering strategy because in these examples Melissa and Kelly never told clients they should do X, Y, or Z. Rather, they outlined what has happened to past clients who did X, Y, or Z. This way, SAFE staff members could frame this strategy as empowering because clients were still given the freedom to decide what to do with this information. In the end, clients could feel like they were making their own decisions, and staff members could see their actions as consistent with their moral identity code.

A similar indirect approach to steering was to walk clients through a list of "concerns" about what might happen. For example, when a resident in the shelter wanted Rebecca to drive her back to her abuser's house, Rebecca confided in me that she thought this was a bad idea. However, she did not admonish the resident who she believed was in a fragile state. Instead, she refused as gently as possible: "I never said [to her], 'I don't think you should go.' Or, 'You can't go.' I said, 'If you want to go, these are my concerns for you going. I'm not going to stop you from going and that's your choice.'" Later in her interview, Rebecca said that she tried to balance her client's safety with her commitment to an empowering approach: "I do believe in honoring choices, and, in that sense, that's her choice." Eventually, the resident chose to stay in the shelter. In Rebecca's mind, this was the best of both worlds; her client was both safe and empowered.

Reminding clients of how they used to feel was another way to encourage them to rethink going back to their abusers. Although the advocates and counselors repeatedly asked clients to "trust their feelings" when the clients suspected danger, they also believed that clients could be misled by their own emotions after leaving their abusers. Staff members believed that it was common for clients be overcome by wishful thinking and to believe they could go back as if nothing had happened. They described how it was natural for clients—once the immediate trauma had passed—to be optimistic, hopeful, or even happy about reconciling with their abusers. When Melissa suspected one of her clients was experiencing this type of premature euphoria, she encouraged her to remember what she felt during a specific time when he had abused her: "Okay, when that happened, where was that in your body? How did that feel in your body?" Melissa explained to me that this kind of memory exercise was important for clients because it would allow "their body to be their best friend." For this client, Melissa believed that tapping into forgotten feeling states would help her to recapture that "sense of danger in [her] body." After a few moments of remembering—and re-experiencing— what she felt like when she made her original decision, Melissa's client decided to hold off on a quick return to him. Afterward she reminded her client that she could change her mind in the future: "And I said, 'Okay, that doesn't mean that you have to do anything, now you just know that you're scared, and a good way to deal with fear is to go really slow.'" Ending the session by reminding her client that she was the one who would make the final decision—while still nudging her to "go really slow"—helped Melissa frame the interaction as an empowering one. From Melissa's perspective, she never told her client not to return to her abuser, she just empowered her to change her mind by re-equipping her with forgotten memories.

Speculating about a Brighter Future

When seeds of doubt did not change clients' minds, advocates and counselors could steer them by encouraging them to imagine how making a few
small changes could result in an alternative—better—future. For example,
one of Lisa's clients did not want to leave the trailer she rented with her
abuser. She wanted him to leave, not her. She was adamant, telling Lisa, "I
shouldn't have to leave because of him doing this." This put Lisa in a difficult
position. Like Lisa's other client who had died in the fire, this client wanted
to stand her ground—a sign of nascent empowerment at SAFE. Lisa wanted
to applaud her courage, but she also worried that letting her client take a
stand might put her in danger.

To steer her client away from harm, Lisa first applauded her willingness
to stand up for herself: "You're right, you really shouldn't have to be going
through this, you really shouldn't have to leave. It's terrible that you're being
put in this position and I understand where you are coming from." Then, she
began to offer a series of "What if?" questions to encourage the client to
rethink her decision. "What would happen if you went away for a couple of
days, what would that be like?" Lisa explained to me the rationale behind
her approach: "If I could get [her] to have a visual picture of [leaving] . . . if I
can help [her] say, 'Well, it wouldn't be that bad, just three days.' And I
would say, 'Well, you know, it's one thought; because if this went on, this
could be worse. Hopefully it won't, but this could be worse.'"

In the end, the client left the trailer. She believed she had made her own
decision and Lisa was proud of her for initially wanting to stand her ground.
Lisa admitted to me that she knew she leaned on the client a bit to move out,
but she qualified her remarks by reminding me that this was okay because
she only asked her client questions about her decision—she never explicitly
told her to leave.

In the shelter, Rebecca had seen a number of clients move out before they
were ready, only to return weeks later. So when one resident proposed moving in with another former resident in town (who had a long history of drug
dependency), Rebecca immediately saw red flags. She worried that this was
an unhealthy environment—especially for a resident's first post-shelter living arrangement. In private, Rebecca was clear to me that she thought this
was a bad idea. She had seen other residents make similar decisions, and

nearly all came back to the shelter soon after, looking to be re-admitted. When talking with the client, however, Rebecca took a more subtle approach. First, Rebecca asked the resident to brainstorm the possible risks of such a move. From Rebecca's point of view, encouraging a client to imagine what might go wrong was still empowering: "That wasn't a stable situation to be going into. And personally I was like, 'I don't know about that.' But I wasn't going to present it like that . . . [so I asked her] 'Do you have any concerns about this? What would they be? What would happen if they came true?'" She then asked the client to consider the benefits of waiting a bit longer before moving out. Ultimately, the client decided not to leave the shelter.

SAFE staff members saw it as their responsibility to provide clients with a number of options from which to choose. As long as they did not tell them which option to pick, they were not being directive. Heather said it was a routine practice to "put certain scenarios out there" for clients. She believed that asking clients, "If you took this avenue, what do you think would happen?" was empowering, because "they're still, ultimately, choosing the avenue. But sometimes, if it's put out there in a different way, they realize that there's a choice of different avenues to take." They believed that asking clients to imagine alternate futures encouraged them to rethink past decisions and open their minds to what their lives *could* be like. From their perspective, this gave clients an extra chance to pause and reflect on their decision, and reverse course if need be.

Relying on the Authority of Others

When SAFE advocates and counselors believed that their clients were no longer listening to them about the potential dangers that awaited them, they could invoke the advice of others to speak for them. When one client (who was recovering from strangulation injuries in a hospital room) was considering returning to her abuser, Cathleen saw multiple warning signs. The client (a teenager) was much younger than her abuser, who had an extensive criminal record. She also had a newborn baby, who made her more financially dependent on him (which he could exploit). In Cathleen's mind, this was a recipe for disaster—possibly meriting a direct intervention.

In the recovery room, Cathleen was particularly frank with her client about how dangerous he was: "He's as crazy as a loon. . . . He's a bad dude."

Privately, Cathleen told me that she believed that her client's child had already suffered from being exposed to violence in the household, describing an instance where the infant screamed in panic when left alone for only a few moments. Cathleen considered explicitly telling the client to leave, but decided to stick to the empowerment approach a bit more. Instead of telling her client to leave him, Cathleen showed her his criminal record and read it aloud, offense by violent offense. When the client was not moved, Cathleen was unsure how to proceed. But her internal debate about whether to intervene was rendered moot as soon as the sheriff's deputy (Paul) assigned to SAFE's clients showed up. During her interview, Cathleen recounted to me: "I'm thinking, 'You need to take out a [protective order] and press charges . . . because eventually [CPS] will find out and they might take the baby.' . . . But Paul was there, and he told her she needs to cooperate with the DA. . . . I wouldn't say it directly. . . . I'd explain the [protective order process] more." Rather than tell her client to press charges, Cathleen described her strategy as "seconding" what Paul the deputy said. Because Paul did not claim to be bound by SAFE's empowerment philosophy, she believed he could speak more freely and directly with clients than the advocates or counselors could. When the nurses in the room also agreed with Paul in front of the victim, Cathleen decided to stay silent. Later telling me, "I'm thinking [the same thing], but I didn't need to say it because the nurses were saying it." This case was one of the clearest examples of steering that occurred during my research. Cathleen secretly wished her client would change her mind and was able to accomplish that goal without saying a word.

Outside experts did not even have to be present for SAFE staff members to wield their influence. Having clients imagine how a judge *might* rule was an effective way to get clients to reconsider legal plans. There were practical reasons for this. Allowing weak cases to go to court could do more harm than good. Abusers could become enraged when served a warrant and emboldened if later victorious in court. Consequently, the advocates were trained to not rush clients into court, especially if clients' claims would be hard to prove. However, if a client persisted, the advocates were also trained to "honor" her wishes. This put them in a tough position. To untangle themselves, instead of explicitly asking clients to drop their requests, they achieved the same result by asking clients to evaluate their cases from the perspective of a judge.

Most clients had never been to court before, so they trusted the advocates' characterizations of how judges handle cases involving DV and SA. For example, when a client pressed Jesse on whether to file for a protective order, she listed the reasons why a judge might strike down her application in court. Yet, Jesse was also careful to qualify her remarks by saying, "I'm not a judge . . . I'm not a lawyer . . . I can't tell you exactly what will happen." From this information, clients believed they could predict how a judge would likely decide given the details of their case—meaning Jesse could keep her thoughts to herself.

Heather put this logic to work when she steered a client away from a protective order by pointing out the ways a judge would be skeptical of her application. Her client, for more than an hour, detailed example after example of her abuser's past tactics of manipulation and intimidation. Yet, when Heather pressed her for evidence that she was in "imminent danger" (language specific to the legal form), the client had a hard time answering. Heather believed the client was currently being emotionally abused; however, Heather also knew that SAFE's definition of abuse was more expansive than the legal definition in court. Yet, even after the client came to realize that a judge might turn down her request, she still persisted. Eventually, the client admitted that she only wanted the protective order as a means to obtain sole custody of their child. This was understandable, and Heather began to explain the legal process for a custody hearing, but the client interrupted. She had contacted a lawyer about obtaining custody and he had quoted her legal fees of around $2,000. Heather responded by explaining that judges would only grant custody via a protective order in cases of specific and recent abuse: "I'm not telling you not to fill out the paper work . . . [but] it takes a lot, a lot, a lot to keep a parent away from their child [with a protective order]. . . . It takes something drastic." Eventually, the client opted not to file for a protective order.

After the client left the SAFE office, I chatted with Heather for a moment outside while she smoked a cigarette. She admitted to me that she had tried to change her client's mind. She defended her actions by pointing out that a court battle over a protective order would not accomplish her ultimate goal (custody). Additionally, a protective order battle would incur substantial costs in terms of time and energy, and might even inflame an already unstable abuser. In the end, Heather knew that she did not tell the client what she wanted to hear: "It was like she wanted to get a [protective order] as cheap custody . . . and I still would have assisted her [with a protective order], but when she learned it wouldn't give her custody she didn't want to do it. I'm not worried that he's going to assault her. . . . I'm worried about her health. . . . She needs social services and an attorney. It's sad when kids are in the middle of this bullshit." The client left SAFE looking frustrated and exhausted; as Heather ground her cigarette butt into an ashtray on the porch, she looked the same. It was a draining session, but ultimately a successful one. Heather had prevented her client from a future defeat in court.

When clients proposed ill-fated plans, it put SAFE staff members in a bind. But why? Why did Heather wait until she was alone with me to share her private thoughts? Why not tell her client early and explicitly, "This is a bad idea." The answer: from Heather's perspective, taking such a directive approach would have been disempowering. So what could she do? Heather wanted her client to make her own decisions (like fight for custody), but she did not want her client to make bad decisions (like enter into a doomed protective order battle). In this case, Heather could not have both. This was the dilemma she faced, and it only makes sense in relation to the high standards of the moral identity code to which she held herself accountable: directly telling clients what to do was unacceptable. To manage this dilemma, Heather invoked the likely skepticism of higher authorities (in this case, judges) and arrived at the desired destination via an indirect route.

CONCLUSION

I am not arguing that steering is wrong. Sitting next to the advocates and counselors as they gently persuaded clients to follow different paths, I agreed with the tactics previously outlined (planting seeds of doubt, speculating about a brighter future, relying on the authority of others). If these strategies kept clients safer, why not embrace them? Few people would blame the advocates or counselors for using whatever means possible to keep their clients free from harm. In very few cases involving imminent danger (like Lisa's case involving arson), they gave themselves permission to suspend their empowerment philosophy and directly tell clients what they thought they should do. But in most other cases, they saw directing or "rescuing" clients as something to resist and avoid. Why? Why was it so important for them to label their services as empowering? Following, I outline three explanations.

Enabled Moral Wages

The concept of empowerment signified the core elements of the advocates' and counselors' moral identity. Claiming allegiance to this approach served to show themselves and others that they were caring and compassionate peers and allies of victims. As I argued in chapter 2, the positive feelings and sense of satisfaction they experienced when they believed they were empowering clients were incredibly important to them. These were the rewards that helped make their work seem worthwhile and meaningful—even during the most trying times. But earning these moral wages was not always easy. This was because in order to adhere to their moral identity code, they had to believe they were empowering clients. And to believe they were empowering clients, they had to be able to see their interactions with clients as qualitatively different from doctors, lawyers, cops, judges, and DSS case-workers. To embrace steering enthusiastically would be to break the code—potentially sealing off access to the moral wages that sustained them.

If they interpreted their services as steering, they would have to admit that they were engaging in similar—albeit much milder—tactics that victims could expect from other institutions that have traditionally served the needs of victims. For example, in Cathleen's case involving the particularly dangerous abuser described above ("He's a bad dude"), she privately hoped that her client would seek legal remedies. However, she resisted saying this out loud. Instead, in the emergency room that evening, she stayed silent while a sheriff's deputy told her client that she should cooperate with the district attorney. By letting him do the talking, she was drawing a clear line between her kind of work and his. In the end, she could still lay claim to offering nondirective—and thus empowering—services.[13]

Holding on to the idea of empowerment also helped staff members maintain their egalitarian stance as peers or allies to victims. Clients who resisted SAFE's philosophy by asking for "too much" help made it hard for staff members to envision their relationships with clients as an equal one. Ironically, to keep from being seen as "in charge," staff members sometimes had to say "no" to clients' explicit requests of help. This could cause conflict, but framing their refusals as empowering helped soften the blow. For example, when a resident became mad at Rebecca for refusing to call a DSS caseworker for her, this made Rebecca upset: "I felt guilty, but the resident needs to be independent. If we follow an empowerment model, some residents need to do these things for themselves. But at the same time I'm being made out to be the bad guy if I didn't do it." Rebecca wanted to like and be liked by her shelter residents. Clients' resistance to SAFE's approach stripped some of the shine off staff members' claims to being equal partners. Recasting the tension as ultimately empowering helped restore it.

As long as staff members could see their services this way, they could also manage their frustrations when clients resisted their steering by citing their clients' stubbornness as evidence of their nascent empowerment. For example, when Rebecca feared a resident was leaving the shelter too soon, she tried to steer her back. When the client refused, Rebecca was frustrated, but not angry: "It's her choice. . . . I can say I have safety concerns, but it's her own choice." Had she disavowed SAFE's philosophy and insisted strongly that her client stay, it would have been impossible to frame her relationship with the resident as an equal one. Instead, by calling upon the rhetoric of empowerment, Rebecca was able to wipe away any residue of conflict. The resident did not disobey by leaving, because she had never been ordered to stay. Thus, keeping to the empowerment frame helped both save face when disagreements arose, and enabled Rebecca to experience the positive feelings and sense of satisfaction that came with seeing herself as a caring and compassionate person.

Mitigated Feelings of Fear and Guilt

Frustration was not the only emotion that the idea of empowerment could help staff members mitigate. Helping victims carries a lot of responsibility. What if a client leaves and is revictimized? What if a piece of advice unintentionally puts her in harm's way? As Heather put it, "To tell someone what to do is the most dangerous thing to do, because if they do it, and it is a flop, then it's your responsibility." These concerns linger in the background of places like SAFE—especially considering that past tragedies were discussed in the office for months and years later. However, if staff members can claim that their clients made their own decisions, they could mitigate some of their fear when their clients returned to dangerous situations and the guilt that arose if they were revictimized.

In the months after Lisa's client died in a fire—the case where staff members suspected arson—her coworkers offered her a set of cognitive strategies to ease the pain. They told her, "Don't accept blame for something that he did." "If he really wants to kill her, he'll find a way." "Leaving is no guarantee he won't find her." There were more variations, all tailored to the specific details of the case, but they all attempted to convey the same message: "It's not your fault." Yet, no matter how many times staff members heard these phrases in the aftermath of clients' suffering, they still had doubts. Self-blame was an occupational hazard at SAFE.

One way the advocates and counselors were able to keep feelings of guilt and grief in check was by calling on the concept of empowerment to remind themselves of their role vis-à-vis their clients. According to this logic, it was not their job to rescue clients or tell them what to do; it was their job only to offer them options and encourage them to make their own decisions—because clients who made their own decisions had power and control over their lives. As long as they did not take a clear stance on what clients should do, staff members could never be wrong; not giving directions meant never giving bad directions.

Not having to have all the answers means one less burden to bear. Looking back on my time as a volunteer before coming to do research at SAFE, I remember how comforting this was to me. During my training, we were taught that if a client called the hotline and asked, "What should I do?" we were trained to answer by turning the question back on them, "Well, what do you think you should do? What do you think might be the solution? What would keep you safe?" I did not have to offer expert advice; I did not have to "fix" my clients' problems. I thought back to those lessons each time my anxiety rose waiting for the hotline phone to ring.

The advocates and counselors at SAFE did not cling to the idea of empowerment for selfish reasons or as a cynical ploy to deny emotional liability. Mitigating guilt may have been a consequence of empowerment, but it was not the intended purpose. Rather, staff members embraced the idea of empowerment for a number of practical and philosophical reasons. Their reluctance to "take ownership" of clients' cases was partly because they thought it was counterproductive to the healing process, and the dynamics of abusive relationships were simply too complex to be able to know precisely what clients should do. When they were reasonably certain that they knew what was best, they shared those thoughts with clients in immediate danger. But in other cases, uncertainty reigned; sometimes, there are no good choices to offer clients—all come at a cost. In those cases, as long as staff members were able to identify empowerment as the limit of their responsibility toward clients, they could sidestep the pressure of having to come up with perfect solutions and avoid the guilt that could come should they offer bad advice.

Remedied Structural Deficiencies

The idea of empowerment helps agencies like SAFE stay afloat—financially. When it comes to offering services to victims, expert advice is costly; situating clients as the experts of their situations is less so. To understand the ubiquity of empowerment in places like SAFE nationwide, we must also look to ways that this ideology enables them to rely heavily on staff and volunteers without professional credentials.

Empowerment philosophies are well suited to difficult conditions—that is where they were created and where they most often operate today (Gutiérrez et al. 1995). They were developed in opposition to the "expert" services offered elsewhere. Although SAFE did have expert professionals on staff (the counselors), they still relied heavily on the nonprofessional staff (the advocates) to do some of the hardest work of the organization. By training the advocates that it was okay (even preferred) to not have all the answers, they can be quickly deployed to help vulnerable clients in crisis situations.

Would the codirectors of SAFE have hired professionals if their budget could afford it? I do not know. Hiring more counselors, let alone keeping attorneys on retainer or housing an onsite physician, was not feasible, thus never debated. Yet, it is important to note that the codirectors framed the advocates' lack of professional credentials as a strength, not a weakness. This was not a veiled ploy; they believed in this. The advocates did, too.[14]

Helping victims costs time, money, and energy. Where local, state, and federal resources end, places like SAFE are expected to make up the difference. As long as neoliberal reforms continue to ask more and more of nongovernmental agencies to solve persistent social problems, these financial constraints are not likely to go away any time soon. Viewed in this light, empowerment offers nonprofit organizations a flexible and cost-effective way to help those they serve. This philosophy legitimizes the work of nonprofessional "peers" who help clients to help themselves. Adhering to this approach not only helps staff members define their identity as caring, compassionate, and egalitarian people, but it also helps the organization survive in a challenging fiscal environment.

In this chapter, I showed how steering helped staff members keep their clients safe while still laying claim to an empowering approach. Yet, sometimes steering failed and clients still did not cooperate. There were some clients who, no matter how much nudging and prodding, resisted SAFE's philosophy of victim services. For them, appeals to an empowerment approach did little to keep them from breaking SAFE's written and unwritten rules like skipping appointments, lying to staff members, and returning to dangerous abusers. In the next chapter, I show how staff members dealt with these clients that they labeled "difficult."

Difficult Clients

"There is no such thing as a 'perfect' client." I heard this the first day of my volunteer training. As it turned out, this lesson has weighty implications: whether or not a client lives up to the "ideal victim" stereotype can mean the difference between getting a protective order signed by a judge or having the police not believe her recollection of events. The victim advocates and counselors at Stopping Abuse in Family Environments (SAFE) saw this as unfair and were highly critical of what they called "perfect victim" myths.[1] They argued that real-life victims of domestic violence (DV) and sexual assault (SA) were not always the sad and stoic figures portrayed in the media. They believed that victims' bouts of "difficult" behavior (lying, expressing anger, skipping appointments, breaking rules, and even returning to abusers) were part of the healing process. As a result, staff members were willing—even eager—to forgive their clients when they acted in these ways. Instead of scolding them or questioning their claims to victimhood, staff members tried to be as patient as possible with their clients—couching any disapproval of their behavior in the softest language possible.

Yet, as I came to learn, forgiving clients was not always so easy. A single lie, for example, was a relatively simple thing for staff members to absolve; but if a client lied to them twice, rationalizing her behavior became more of a challenge. If the behavior escalated—lying three times? Ten?—it became increasingly harder to explain it away. This caused problems at SAFE, not only for those seeking help, but also for those offering it. For clients, difficult behavior could get them in trouble, put them in danger, or both. For staff members, clients' difficult behavior created a daunting emotional dilemma to overcome.

In this chapter, I analyze the ways that staff members at SAFE forgave their clients for their difficult behavior despite their grave concerns about the consequences should it never stop (or at least diminish). With few enforcement tools to change their clients' ways, staff members believed there was little they could do to change their behavior. Cutting off the flow of sympathy was one way, but they worried this tactic might push clients away from SAFE to fend for themselves. Continuing to offer sympathy unconditionally was another way, but they worried that solution might inadvertently encourage clients to keep up their ill-advised ways.

Sympathy was important at SAFE. Victim advocates and counselors see themselves as caring and compassionate people, and sympathizing with victims is an important component of their identity code. As long as they can believe that they are the sympathizers of last resort—willing and able to care for victims more than anyone else—they can experience the positive feelings and sense of satisfaction that comes with accomplishing a moral identity. In short, offering sympathy to clients was the surest path to earning moral wages at SAFE, and the frustration caused by difficult clients disrupted this process. The victim advocates and counselors I observed and interviewed wanted to offer their clients ample amounts of sympathy, but they also did not want their sentiment to enable bad behavior. There was no perfect solution to this problem; and, as in the rest of this book, I show how their attempts to reconcile these competing aims created new problems all their own.

To understand how they managed the emotional dilemma posed by difficult clients, I first analyze how and why staff members set limits on what they would tolerate from their clients. I then offer an extended case study in which their patience with a client completely ran out.[2] In general, staff members worried that continuing to serve clients "no matter what" could have negative repercussions on their clients' safety, their reputation as advocates and counselors, and their ability to help other clients in need. Thus, they framed their decisions to cut off the flow of sympathy—in the most extreme cases—as in the best interests of their clients, the agency, and the larger movement against DV and SA. In their minds, refusing sympathy in some cases made sense both practically and politically.

From a sociological perspective, however, I offer two alternative explanations for why they stopped sympathizing with some clients. First, their decision showed that they were not immune—despite their training—to idealized assumptions about victimhood. In theory, they knew that there were no "perfect" victims; however, in practice, their responses to clients' difficult behavior revealed that they still expected them to be *somewhat* honest, cooperative, and grateful. That the advocates and counselors occasionally fell back on dominant frames of compliant victimhood speaks less to their flaws as individuals and more to the pervasiveness of these cultural tropes. Second, their discernment over how much they were willing to forgive clients was part of a wider pattern of sympathy as a subtle mechanism of control in our culture. Staff members had few means to keep clients from heading in dangerous directions. If their efforts to steer clients to safety did not work (see chapter 3), granting and refusing sympathy was their last-ditch mechanism of influence. By setting limits on how much sympathy they were willing to express, they preserved the value of this sentiment—and its usefulness at keeping other clients in line and out of danger. In the end, by investigating how staff members dealt with difficult clients, I show how sympathizing with victims does not always come easy. However, for those who can care when others cannot, or know when to stop caring for the right reasons, moral wages are theirs to claim.

ANTICIPATING "DIFFICULT" BEHAVIOR

Although outsiders might think that difficult behavior could drive a wedge between victims and those who help them, this was not always the case. At SAFE, "bad" decisions could bring service provider and recipient closer together. Once forgiven, clients were grateful that someone else understood their problems, and staff members could feel good knowing that they understood the lingering effects of abuse in ways that others did not.

But, just how far were they willing to go to explain their clients' behavior? The short answer was that it varied by how much a client had suffered. Those who had endured the worst were afforded ample and lasting sympathy, those who had gone through less were offered less (although much more than they could expect anywhere else). The long answer involves what sociologist of emotion Candace Clark (1997) calls the "micropolitics" of sympathy, which I explain in more detail later in the chapter. Briefly, although sympathy can create an emotional bond between two people, it also sets the terms of the relationship; offering sympathy to others signals one's relatively greater status at that particular time and place. But first, I describe the ready-made explanations for difficult behavior that staff had on hand before clients even walked through the door or called the hotline.

Clients Who Lie

Staff members did not expect full honesty from their clients—especially at first. They explained that clients arriving at SAFE's doorstep might lie for a whole host of reasons. They might hide information as a way to test staff members to see if they were worthy of trust. They might shade the truth to keep embarrassing details under wraps. They might be deceptive because honesty had never worked for them in the past. Whether new clients were being untruthful through omission or commission, staff members were ready to forgive them. As Meg—an advocate—put it, "Victims who lie are still victims."

The more the advocates and counselors got to know individual clients, the more likely they were to frame their lying as a strategy of last resort. When clients needed protective orders, for example, they had to convince judges that abuse was either recent or imminent. Some clients had no such evidence: either they had successfully kept themselves out of harm's way for the past few months, or their abusers' rage lay dormant for long periods of time before erupting at any moment. As a result, some shaded the truth on their applications; and when they did, staff members were quick to remind others that it was not because they were bad people, but rather because of the unrealistic requirements of the legal system.

They applied this same logic to explain why clients might lie for the opposite reason: to protect their abusers from cops and judges. Because of mandatory arrest policies, staff members told me that some clients lied to sheriff's deputies to keep their abusers out of jail. If a client was dependent upon her abuser's income to pay the rent and feed their children, having him locked up could make things worse, not better. Although the advocates and counselors at SAFE wanted their clients to be truthful, they also reasoned that under some circumstances clients might have no other choice but to lie.

Implicit in these explanations so far was that staff members saw lying as a savvy and intentional move by their clients to make the best of a bad situation: a calculated act of desperation. In this framing, they cited cases in which clients lied only because they had no other way to combat the lies of their abusers. The advocates had an endless number of stories of how abusers had convinced police officers that they were not at fault. Citing the "Power and Control Wheel" handout (see figure 2, chapter 3), they rattled off the ways that abusers evade responsibility: "She not really hurt, it's only a scratch" (minimizing), "I didn't do anything, she's making it up" (denying), "I was just protecting myself, she started it" (blaming). Consequently, if a client thought her abuser could deceive others, staff members defended her efforts to deceive on the grounds that fighting fire with fire might be the only option she had left.

However, not all explanations assumed clients' dishonesty was tactical or strategic. In some cases, lying was interpreted as an uncontrollable response to deeper root causes. When Cathleen suspected a client was lying to her and could not understand why, Kelly, her supervisor, offered her this advice: "I don't have doubts that victims are lying sometimes. They may lie for any number of reasons. I also try to keep in mind that [lying] may also be the effects of substance abuse. Also, some lie to get revenge." Both of these explanations forgive the client—but from different angles. The first blames lying on the power of addiction. The second blames lying on the emotional desire to enact revenge. When combined with all of the other explanations outlined earlier, we learn that clients' dishonesty could be a sign of their rationality, irrationality, or both.

Clients Who Stay with Their Abusers

The most common questions that the victim advocates or counselors at SAFE get from outsiders are "Why doesn't she just leave?" and "Why would she go back?" At any given moment, staff members could fluently justify almost any client's decision to stay. The common denominator in their responses was that abusers—by denying victims power and control over their lives—manipulate circumstances so that leaving and staying away become nearly impossible. In the advocates' office, I overheard Heather cycle through four variations on this theme in less than a minute when talking over the phone with someone from the Department of Social Services (DSS): "[Abusers] threaten them with violence if they leave," "keep all the cash and control access to the bank account," "threaten to take kids or hurt the kids or turn the kids against them," and "convince them that everyone hates them and no one else will take them in."

Staff members never underestimated the ability of abusers to manipulate victims into staying or coming back. After one day in court, Cathleen came back to the office shaking her head. A few days earlier, she had spent hours helping her client apply for a protective order. But in court, her client changed her mind at the last minute. Cathleen described her client as if she were under a spell: "She was talking and she had her head in her hands, it seemed like she was trying to remember what he coached her to say." For all her efforts to explain her client's decision, cases like this still made her mad. This is not entirely uncommon: past research has shown that "despite training specifically designed to recognize battered women's agency and to honor *all* the choices they make (including 'staying'), victim advocates have considerable difficulty doing this" (Dunn and Powell-Williams 2007:977–78; see also Powell-Williams, White, and Powell-Williams 2013). Cathleen tried to hide her feelings, but she admitted to me in private that she thought this client was making a mistake; however, to the client, she tried to put on a calm face. When I asked Cathleen how she was able to keep her negative feelings in check, she put the blame back on the abuser: "And I just get frustrated. Not so much at her, but really it is with him. . . . He has that level of control." In this case, blaming the abuser was enough for Cathleen to manage her feelings toward her client; however, blaming abusers was such a common tactic at SAFE that its effectiveness could be diluted with excessive use. As a result, sometimes staff members had to be more creative.

One way they did this was by speculating that "going back" was caused by the emotional roller coaster that was victimhood. Because the lows were so low, staff members believed that any high could produce a cathartic effect so powerful that it often fooled clients into believing things were permanently better. After winning in court, for example, clients might be so emboldened by their fresh "win" that they might be overcome by feelings of nostalgia—causing them to make poor decisions. When one of Lisa's clients returned to her abuser soon after facing him in court, she cited this rationale

Chapter Four

in her explanation of her behavior: "Sometimes, once they finish the [protective order process], they get all their bad feelings out and they start having positive feelings about them [the abuser]." Thus, Lisa believed that short-term victories caused clients to see things through rose-colored glasses and make decisions they might later regret.

Clients Who Break the Rules

Staff members were conflicted about imposing rules on clients and tried to enforce as few as possible. According to their empowerment philosophy, the last thing victims needed was another person telling them what they could or could not do; staff members saw their job at SAFE as providing clients with options and resources but leaving the final decision on what to do up to them. But, for all their policies that promoted such a hands-off, indirect approach, staff members still believed that some rules were important—especially those designed to keep clients safer. They knew some clients would likely break these rules, and they were ready to forgive them when they did.

The most likely place for clients to break rules was in the shelter. The shelter's staff members and residents spent a considerable amount of time together, often in cramped quarters. Whereas a client might visit the main office for an hour or two, residents lived in the shelter for days—sometimes weeks. This meant more opportunities for conflict. On more than one occasion, staff members likened the shelter to a house packed with relatives over the holidays. When tempers flared, residents could retreat to different rooms, but they were never far away from each other. Arguments over who ate more than their fair share of a particular cereal could simmer for days. Thus, staff members spent a great deal of energy managing emotions (theirs and clients'). This was especially important in the shelter because the stakes for difficult behavior were higher: continued violations could mean expulsion. As a result, the communication and enforcement of rules in the shelter were much more regimented than in the main office.

Upon entry, potential shelter residents were given a list of rules and asked to sign a "contract" that outlined the consequences for breaking them. Some of these rules were routine—dishes must be washed before leaving the kitchen, while others were safety oriented—never let a stranger in the house.

If a resident broke a rule (for example, letting a candle burn unattended in her room), she would be warned. After a number of warnings, a resident could be given final notice that she must leave within twenty-four hours.[3]

Although expulsion was rare, the possibility of it was very hard on the staff members. Christina (the shelter director) explained that kicking people out was the last thing she wanted to do: "I hate to ask people to leave." Standing next to a cement urn filled with cigarette butts on the patio behind the shelter, she explained that playing the authoritarian was the worst part of her job. She wanted to make the shelter a caring, warm environment. As we talked, she moved a plant out of the shade caused by the high-walled privacy fence. Watching Christina talk, it was clear that conflict wore on her. However, she made sense of this tension by pointing to the consequences of *not* enforcing the rules. She was careful to point out that the rules were designed with the residents' interests in mind. If someone "broke the contract" by bringing illegal drugs into the house, the whole shelter could be shut down. If one resident played music too loud in her room, another caring for an infant might not be able to rest. As a result, even though no one at SAFE liked enforcing them, they believed that rules kept everyone safe and happy. And when residents did not follow them, staff members relied on a stock of interpretive strategies to make sense of their dual roles as both peers and enforcers.[4]

The most common strategy for explaining bad behavior in the shelter was to cast it as an inevitable by-product of the tension found in any crowded living environment. This meant that they believed that difficult residents *could* follow the rules, just not under such cramped circumstances. As Rebecca described it, residents could resent staff members for simply being the person in charge: "Some don't like us." This explanation helped her make sense of why some residents not only refused to follow the contract (for example, no smoking in the house), but were also unremorseful when caught. Before Heather became an advocate in the main office, she worked the night shift at the shelter. She also framed friction in the shelter as unavoidable: "It's hard with different personalities." From her point of view, difficult residents were just having a hard time coexisting with too many other people with too many painful memories living too close together for too long. Given the stressful conditions they were living under, rule breaking would occur no matter what the rules or how they were applied.

When pressed to explain the root cause of residents' personality "issues" with each other and staff members, the standard explanation typically fell back on the idea of empowerment. Breaking rules could either be a symptom of clients' disempowerment, a sign of burgeoning empowerment, or both. One resident, whom Christina characterized as "really pushing the rules," continually asked for more money to buy clothes and more time to stay out past the shelter curfew.[5] She also used the communal phone longer than her allotted time. When gently asked to stop these behaviors, she refused. Although Christina was not happy with this, she explained to me that this resident was "testing boundaries" to see how far she could go. She then went on to describe how victims of DV and SA have little experience at pushing the limits of others' patience without risking harm. As a result, this resident's continued disobedience was a source of frustration, but also a sign of growth to Christina. From her perspective, allowing the client to test her authority was a way to help her. Christina saw this challenge in a positive light: "This is a person who I am going to have to really use my skills to empower, for her to figure out another way." Even if she feared her client was making the wrong decisions, Christina still gave her credit for trying to find new ways to exercise power and control over her life.

Clients Who Lash Out at Staff

The advocates and counselors at SAFE expected clients to be on edge. They believed that people who suffer abuse experience a mix of unsettling emotions; sometimes these feelings bubble to the surface through tears, and other times they erupt through anger and rage. Although staff members found these outbursts unsettling, they were also seen "part of the job." Kelly, as a SAFE codirector, could recount hundreds of stories of being on the receiving end of clients' displaced frustration during her career, described it this way: "[It's] okay, that's what we are here for." As long as clients were able to keep their outbursts to a minimum, the advocates and counselors were able to see clients' anger as a beneficial and therapeutic way for them to "get it all out" and regain their "voice." Although everyone at SAFE had a story of an upset client, the advocates had the most. They dealt with clients in the most precarious "crisis" situations, and everyone in the office agreed that they were more likely to bear the brunt of clients' anger than others on staff.

Some clients' anger was explained as a negative reaction to SAFE's non-directive approach. They described some clients as confused and frustrated by the advocates' explanations of why it was better for them to help themselves rather than have someone on staff do it for them. As explained in chapter 3, SAFE advocates and counselors held themselves to a very high standard of victim services. Although staff members reported being tempted on occasion to "rescue" clients or solve their problems, they feared that such a directive approach was counterproductive—or, in their terms, "disempowering." Yet, for clients who expected more to be done for them, this hands-off style caught them off guard. Some clients understood—or at least accepted—the rationale behind it, but not all clients were as obliging. When clients resisted SAFE's empowerment philosophy, the subsequent tension could create a "ripple" effect throughout the office—especially if clients learned that others were receiving different kinds of services.

This frustration led to an ancillary kind of difficult behavior staff members called "advocate shopping." Some clients, upset that their advocate would not make calls on their behalf or give them rides, would switch from one advocate to another until they found one who was willing to do what they wanted. When asked, the advocates would explain that these clients were just looking for the best deal (that is, treating them like rational consumers). However, even though they could appreciate why clients would do this, it still hurt. Having one of "their" clients ask for another advocate by name was tough to fathom. When Jesse complained about a client calling at different hours "to see if Cathleen or Meg might help her more than I would," she was both confused and frustrated: "I don't understand because I have worked with her in the past. I had driven her to the court and advocated for her there before." Jesse wanted her clients to like her. This was one of the ways she earned moral wages: she offered sympathy and her clients accepted it; completing this kind of emotional transaction felt good. Given the sacrifices she made for her job, it was troubling that a client would refuse her emotional offering and shop elsewhere.[6]

Clients Who Stop Coming Back
In all the explanations previously mentioned, staff members knew each of the clients whose behavior they were defending. They had a history with them.

They could tell a story about their past, present, and future that explained why they lied, went back, broke rules, or got mad. But some clients skipped appointments or stopped showing up before the advocates and counselors could gather enough information to make sense of their absences. When Lisa sat waiting in court for a potential client who never came, she was at a loss to explain why. Instead, she walked me through the scarce details of what she knew about her client's relationship: it had begun with care and love, but had suddenly turned violent. "She's trying to make a huge adjustment in her mind," she explained to me. But when I pressed Lisa for more details relating to the client, her history, or her abuser, it quickly became clear that Lisa knew very little about the woman. As an advocate, she wanted to forgive her, but in place of facts, all she could do was insert a generic story line of a woman caught off guard by her abuser's actions that could have been applied to almost any SAFE client. Without easy clues or hints as to why a client failed to reappear, the advocates and counselors were left with bits and pieces of information that they wove together until they could patch together a reason why their client was not there. Thus, ironically, the less in their case files, the wider the range of possible scenarios explaining clients' departure and eventual return.

It took a considerable amount of time before SAFE clients were categorized as "never coming back." Staff members always held out hope that they might return. When one of her clients skipped her day in court, Meg took this wait-and-see approach: "I don't know if I would say [I'm] disappointed, but I know I'll eventually see her again." This rhetorical strategy was especially effective because no matter how unlikely her client's return, the possibility was always there. No evidence—other than tragic news of her client's death—could refute Meg's claim.

Staff members found it trickier to explain why some clients stopped showing up in person but were still willing to talk over the phone. When a client missed a counseling session, Jen called her. The client offered a tepid excuse about meeting a friend. After hanging up, Jen dismissed the client's explanation and offered me her own: victims have been made to feel worthless by their abusers, thus they have a hard time realizing that their absence will be noted. "Because they feel invisible, powerless, and have no self-esteem, they don't see how they affect others because they don't think they are important." This account shifted the blame away from the client (that is, "She doesn't know how her actions make me feel") back onto the abuser (that is, "He told her no one cares about what she does").

A variation on this forgiveness script was to frame appointments as something that some clients only agreed to because they were too disempowered to refuse in the first place. Andrea, a counseling intern, offered this explanation as I sat with her for more than an hour while she waited for a client who never came. The client had indicated over the phone that she wanted to talk with Andrea about the lingering effects of a long-past sexual assault. During the first fifteen minutes of waiting, Andrea talked rapidly about how she had prepared for the session. Yet, as we both watched the clock, her attitude changed from enthusiasm to boredom to frustration. Her social work graduate program required that she spend at least forty "contact hours" with clients during her internship at SAFE. As a result, she needed clients—not just to earn moral wages, but for practical reasons as well. When I asked her why she thought her client was a "no-show," she answered, "I called her to set up a time, and she was probably too embarrassed to turn down the offer [of free counseling]." According to this logic, her client's lack of self-esteem led her to make a commitment she could not honor. Andrea believed that if her client had been more empowered, she would have had the confidence to turn down the initial offer to meet at the SAFE office. As Andrea kept on defending her client, I could see the frustration drain from her face. Talking through the possible reasons why her client would have made—and then skipped—an appointment had a calming effect on her. Explaining them to me was a way for her to stand up for her client in absentia. By the end of her shift, Andrea packed up her papers and left; she seemed at ease.

Clients who stopped coming back (or engaged in any of the other behaviors labeled difficult) were a source of frustration at SAFE, but they also served a potentially useful end: they offered staff members ample opportunities to affirm their sense of themselves as caring and compassionate people. In other words, although clients' difficult behavior rubbed their patience raw, forgiving them proved to be the best salve. After all, their identity was staked around the idea that when assisting victims of abuse, they were the sympathizers of last resort.

In the next section, I describe how—despite their extraordinary capacity to forgive—they still had limits. In a few extreme cases, when clients went too far, staff members believed the only remedy was to sever the relationship.

REACHING THEIR LIMIT ②

Previously, I outlined staff members' most common ready-made explanations for clients' difficult behavior. In most cases, these strategies to forgive and rationalize were enough. However, sometimes clients' behavior persisted, and these efforts failed. Even though the advocates and counselors saw themselves as the most compassionate and forgiving audience their clients would likely encounter, they did not claim that their patience was infinite. Nor did they believe that it should be. Consequently, from time to time, their well of sympathy ran dry.

The advocates and counselors believed that setting limits on clients and refusing services to the most difficult ones was best for everyone (the client, the agency, and the DV and SA movement in general).[7] For the client, they believed that continuing to offer services without any signs of improved behavior was unethical on the grounds that it enabled bad behavior. For the agency, continuing to defend exceedingly difficult clients could potentially tarnish SAFE's reputation. When they stood next to clients in court, they implicitly vouched for them; if those clients went on to lie or break laws, the advocates and counselors knew judges, cops, and lawyers might later accuse them of being "too biased" to determine who was a real victim and who was not. Staff believed that clients' current behavior should not be used to disprove their prior claims to victimhood, but they feared this argument would prove ineffective against deeply entrenched stereotypes that cast victims as innocent, pure, and compliant. If the honesty of staff members was called into question, they feared the DV and SA movement as a whole could suffer.

Without the public trust, SAFE and agencies like it would have a hard time garnering the resources necessary to help fund their cause; as I discuss in the conclusion to this chapter, public sentiment effectively pays the bills for nonprofits that "do good." Consequently, the advocates and counselors believed that ending their relationship with the most difficult clients could sometimes serve the greater good.

Although these practical concerns were likely correct—hostile skeptics *are* looking to frame places like SAFE as run by overly biased "feminazis"—

there are also larger sociological reasons why staff members ultimately severed their relationships with some clients they labeled difficult. By stepping back and looking at DV and SA victim services from a broader perspective, we can see how other social forces shaped staff members' reactions. In the following section, I offer an extended vignette of one of the most difficult clients ever to seek services from SAFE. After this lengthy case study, I offer two arguments as to why SAFE advocates and counselors eventually drew the line for this client and others like her (besides the practical explanations espoused by staff members themselves).

Tammy's Story

By the time I began conducting research at SAFE, Tammy had already been in jail once, for resisting arrest. That time, she had kicked out the window of a police cruiser from the inside. This had happened months earlier, and the SAFE advocates responded by scrambling to get her a lawyer and visiting her in jail. The next time around, during my research, she was caught selling drugs to an undercover sheriff's deputy. However, this second time, SAFE advocates did not rush to get her a lawyer or see her in jail. Initially, it was hard for me to understand how they could treat a client this way. To see Tammy's case from their point of view, I had to learn the whole story.

Tammy's case began with one of the most brutal cases of abuse anyone at SAFE had ever seen. Her first abuser—a man the advocates labeled "psycho" without a hint of exaggeration—had strangled her to the point of unconsciousness and left her for dead. The photos of her injuries were so shocking that a regional group representing DV and SA agencies statewide used them to lobby lawmakers to make attempted strangulation a felony (it was previously only a misdemeanor). These photos were stored in a binder on an office shelf. The advocates would flip through them when discussing the most vicious cases; the close-ups of petechiae in and around her eyes were office lore.

Despite their admiration for her bravery, any discussion of Tammy inevitably led to the number of times she had frustrated SAFE staff members. They had tried to help her so many times, only to be disappointed after each attempt. The first story they told was about the scholarship they had secured for her to attend a local community college. At first, they were elated by her progress. Tammy was transforming from victim to survivor. She had over-come obstacles. She had become empowered. However, to their surprise, within weeks she stopped attending classes and eventually dropped out.

Although quitting school was something the advocates usually would have no trouble forgiving, this situation was complicated. SAFE had a his-tory of successful applications with the charity that had funded the scholar-ship. In the past, it had paid for Christina (the shelter director) to attend a regional conference. Having Tammy's award go unused could put future applications in jeopardy. Despite these worries, SAFE advocates welcomed Tammy back in the office and worked with her on creating new plans, tempering their goals to fit what they believed she could accomplish. They told each other that clients sometimes "stumble out of the gate." They reminded each other that small tasks that seem simple to outsiders, like attending classes, can be more challenging for victims of DV and SA. They generated plausible scenarios about classmates who might not understand what she was going through or teachers who were insensitive to her needs. But this was just the first time Tammy made a decision that frustrated SAFE staff members.

When the advocates tried to find Tammy a new apartment so that she could sever all ties with her former abuser (he had moved out, but hinted he might return), Tammy became uncooperative. She refused any option that did not accommodate her pet. They told Tammy that they understood her connection with her dog, but staying in her current apartment exposed her to a lot of risks. Her abuser was out of jail, back in town, and the apartment they shared would be the first place where he would look for her. Eventually, Tammy found a new place to live, but did so by moving in with a man who also had a record of violence against women. Working within the confines of their empowerment philosophy, the advocates did not tell Tammy in clear terms that she should leave him—issuing clients orders like that was seen as too directive at SAFE. Instead, they spelled out all the possible ways that this arrangement could have a bad ending. Yet, despite their steering, these appeals had no effect. She was insistent on moving in with this new man.

As they spent more and more time with Tammy, they became increas-ingly bewildered by her temper. She had a habit of lashing out at people trying to help her. SAFE staff members tried to explain these outbursts as evidence of her recovery and newfound sense of power and control. However, they began to reach their limit as Tammy continued to get in heated verbal arguments with the pro bono lawyer SAFE advocates had arranged for her. She also yelled at sheriff's deputies that served as liaisons between SAFE and the sheriff's department. These outsiders were crucially important in order to help other clients. Staff members started to question how much attention any one client deserved—especially if she took time away from their ability to serve other clients.

Eventually, Tammy's difficult behavior proved to be too much. The advocates had given her some money from a small SAFE fund to spend on rent and utilities for her new apartment. They viewed these payments as a temporary measure to help her "get back on her feet." Soon after, Meg began to hear rumors from sheriff's deputies that Tammy was buying and selling illicit drugs around town. Putting two and two together ("How is she using the money we give her?"), the advocates did some investigating to find out what really happened before ultimately confronting her. Tammy denied it, but Meg did not believe her: "I know for a fact that she has sold drugs to officers, yet she has said straight to my face that she hasn't." After detailing all the ways that Tammy had fallen from grace, Meg finished by saying, "There has to come a time with any victim where I say to myself, 'I've done everything I could have done for her.' . . . Is it possible to empower someone too much?" The other advocates within earshot nodded in agreement. SAFE staff members had provided her with nearly every tool and resource available, yet they could not control what Tammy did with them. Now they began to worry that their help was having the opposite effect—enabling bad behavior.

At this point, all patience for Tammy had come to an end. Cathleen and Jesse were openly critical of Tammy, referring to her around the office as manipulative and dishonest. After Tammy called one more time to ask for more money, Jesse finished the conversation with a simple "no," and quietly hung up the phone. I watched her closely as she looked at the phone for a moment with an exasperated look. As if seeking affirmation for telling a client, "no," Jesse asked anyone within earshot, "Is she still in crisis?" to which Cathleen replied in a sarcastic tone, "Not really, but she pretends like she is for money." I had never heard anyone in the SAFE office talk about a client like this before. The laundry list of Tammy's behavior had stretched the advocates' reserves of sympathy to the limit.

The advocates started to treat this case like no other. When news of Tammy's most recent arrest on drug charges reached the SAFE office, they made no effort to reach out to her, arrange a lawyer to help her, or speak to law enforcement officials on her behalf. In a court hallway a few weeks later, Meg and Lisa were talking to Paul, the sheriff's deputy with the closest ties to SAFE. Paul referred to Tammy as a lost cause: "She's in jail, and she deserves to be in jail." Meg and Lisa looked a little surprised at Paul's blunt characterization, but they nodded in agreement. When I asked them later about his statement, both offered only half-hearted defenses of Tammy. Meg referred to Tammy's difficult childhood and how she might be acting out of frustration that her initial abuser (who had strangled her) never served any significant jail time. Lisa speculated that Tammy was suffering from post-traumatic stress disorder, although she admitted she was not qualified to make such a diagnosis. When court was called back into session, they re-entered the courtroom to find their seats. I did not observe another conversation about Tammy for months. I later learned that she was eventually released from jail, but did not seek services from SAFE again.

ANALYZING THE LIMITS OF SYMPATHY

Why were the victim advocates and counselors at SAFE willing to tolerate so much difficult behavior from Tammy at the beginning? Why did they eventually cut off their flow of sympathy at the end? Those at SAFE had practical reasons for being patient and nondirective with clients. From their perspective, sympathizing with clients and hiding any frustration kept clients close and safe. If clients thought staff members were angry or disappointed in them, they might not return out of shame—putting themselves at risk. However, if they believed a client's difficult behavior (like Tammy's) was getting to be too much, they reserved the right to cut her off in order to preserve the reputation of the staff, the organization, and the wider movement. Yet, while these matter-of-fact justifications are persuasive, they do not tell the whole story. There are other sociological reasons for why their sympathy ran out. Next, I outline two explanations: the lasting power of ideal victim stereotypes and the limited effectiveness of sympathy as a mechanism of social control.

The Myth of the "Ideal" Victim

Socialization into the world of victim advocacy and counseling means relearning how "real" victims behave. During my volunteer training, we heard again and again how victims often say the wrong things, at the wrong time, to the wrong people. We heard testimonials from past and current victims to learn how they were not like the quiet figures featured in made-for-television movies who proudly take off their sunglasses before the judge to reveal their blackened eye or boldly pack their car to leave town to start a new life. Relearning how victims behave was important, we were told, because no matter how much they would test our patience, they all deserved sympathy for their abuse and forgiveness for their missteps on the path to recovery.

For the advocates and counselors at SAFE, debunking popular perceptions of victims was part of their job. They thought that the false images of victims as pure, innocent, and weak were inaccurate and put their clients in an impossible situation.[8] For example, victims are generally cast as helpless, passive figures. Yet, passivity can also be cited as evidence that a victim does not want to get better—implying that she relishes her victimhood. Instead, ideal victims are supposed to be proactive and show that they want to move on and get better. Yet, being too proactive works against them as well. For example, as Dunn (2002) found, stalking victims who aggressively and repeatedly lobby law enforcement for help can be labeled a "pain in the ass" (Dunn 2002:99), inviting suspicion that their demeanor provoked their stalkers in the first place. As a result, being a perfect victim is an impossible task. They must demonstrate weakness, but not too much; they must show strength, but only in moderation. Put simply, the trope of the ideal victim puts abused women in an inescapable double bind.[9]

Legal scholars have gone to great lengths to catalogue the ways these assumptions influence legal proceedings. Wendy Larcombe, for example, found that in order to prove their cases in court, victims have to present essentially perfect selves; they have to simultaneously prove that they are "chaste, sensible, responsible, cautious, dependent" (2002:133) while also being "polite but not compliant, co-operative but not submissive" (2002:144). Melanie Randall (2010), in her study of sexual assault law, argues that some social circumstances can make it effectively impossible for a person to be considered a rape victim at all. For example, in sexual assault cases, victims' claims are often (unfairly) dismissed on the grounds that they had engaged in risky behavior (like being intoxicated, or staying out "too late"). However, as Randall argues, some "risky" behaviors are actually long-term states of being. For example, to be homeless (out of doors, late at night) is to engage in risky behavior. To be addicted to illegal drugs (and intermittently intoxicated by them) is to engage in risky behavior. By virtue of merely inhabiting these sets of social circumstances, claims to victimhood can be discredited by cops, lawyers, and judges—indefinitely.

As if these behavioral expectations were not demanding enough, cultural assumptions about ideal victims dictate how victims should *feel*, as well. In one study of rape victims preparing for trial, sociologist Amanda Konradi (1996) found that women have to walk an impossibly thin line in regard to displaying their emotions in court. On the stand, they have to be emotional, but not overly so. When recollecting the events surrounding their rape, for example, tears are obligatory; without them, proof of injury can come into question. Too many tears, though, signals irrationality and lack of control, which jury and judge might use to question their past and present judgment. When there are no bruises or physical markers, facial expressions and posture become skeptics' testing ground for whether victims are feeling the "right" way. The flash of a smile or a brief sneer can shatter a woman's case in the eyes of jurors. This is partly because ideal victims of DV and SA are presumed to be eternally wounded to the extent that they can never get "over it" (Lamb 1999:115). Logically, this reverse causation (that is, later emotional expressions disprove the occurrence of prior abuse) rests on shaky grounds; but in relation to other victim stereotypes, it is par for the course.

Having watched the advocates and counselors interact with clients for fourteen months, I can confidently state that their claims to offering their clients ample compassion were well warranted. Their patience with most clients was impressive. Even in Tammy's case, they never questioned the events around her original injuries, and she likely received more "last chances" at SAFE than she would have anywhere else. However, despite their exhaustive efforts, they still set limits—even if they were lenient by outsider's standards.

In the end, for all of the criticism of victim stereotypes inside SAFE, the actions of staff members showed that they were not entirely immune to them either. At their wits' end, talking behind closed doors, they complained that Tammy was too defiant—unwilling to follow the advice given to her; that Tammy was dishonest—lying to the only people who would forgive her for telling the truth; that Tammy was manipulative—cashing in on her past suffering. Unrecognized during these "vent" sessions was that these complaints mirrored the jabs that they were trained to debunk. They had been taught that it was unreasonable to expect victims to be uniformly tranquil, sincere, and cooperative. They told themselves that they were the ones who denounced the unfair standards to which our culture holds victims accountable. However, when exhausted and pressed to the limit, they fell back on popular assumptions about how victims should behave to make sense of Tammy's actions, too.

Tammy's case showed that the SAFE policy regarding how victims respond to DV and SA was just that: a policy. It was something to be learned through training and practice, but acquiring a belief system that goes against the grain of popular logic is no small task. As a result, the advocates and counselors at SAFE, while more receptive to new ideas about victimhood than outsiders, still had to work to put prevailing stereotypes behind them. No matter how hard they tried to put them out of their imaginations, the ideal victim frame proved to be lingering in the background, ready to be applied when the advocates and counselors had used up all of their other explanations to excuse and absolve.

Another reason the advocates and counselors had such a hard time with Tammy was the lack of guidance offered by SAFE's empowerment philosophy on precisely how much difficult behavior was "too much." For most clients, this was not an issue. However, it was during the extreme cases—the most emotionally draining ones—when the staff members needed specific criteria the most. At what point does giving clients the freedom to make their own decisions shift from "empowerment" to "enabling bad behavior"? At what point does telling clients to change their behavior shift from "preventing self-harm" to "disempowerment"? In both cases, the former interpretation earns staff members moral wages while the latter provokes doubts about their purpose and mission. In some ways, the ambiguity of empowerment helped (it allowed them to see a silver lining in almost any outcome), but this flexibility also came at a cost (upon reflection, any service could be reinterpreted as potentially harmful).

Although staff members began each case by trying to explain away all difficult behavior, in some instances they found this strategy unsustainable. Because there were no hard and fast rules on where to draw the line in relation to the frequency or intensity of difficult behaviors, staff members had to develop those boundaries on their own. They did so through a practical assessment of how their choices might affect their personal reputations as well as that of the agency and others like it. Consequently, the pristine explanations regarding how to respond to victims' difficult behavior outlined in their handouts and training manuals became fuzzy when viewed through a cultural lens smudged with the residue of victim stereotypes. And when forced to come up with new reasons of why some clients were so difficult, it was easy to fall back on the ones in which they had been culturally immersed all their lives.

Sociological Perspectives on Sympathy

For an agency that had a surprisingly sociological view of abuse, staff members still interpreted their own emotional responses to clients in very individualistic and psychological ways. Yet, sociological perspectives on sympathy can explain a lot about how and why SAFE staff members would try so hard to "feel for" their clients.[10]

In Tammy's case, her original suffering afforded her a substantial reserve of sympathy—like a bank account. As Tammy kept receiving sympathy from staff members over time, she slowly drew down on her account.[11] At the beginning, if she neared her limit, it was easy for staff members to restock her sympathy reserves by reflecting on her past suffering. Thus, the amount of sympathy a client is entitled to is not only related to her most recent wounds but also can grow upon consideration of her entire history of suffering. From this perspective, the advocates offered Tammy sympathy on the basis of her fresh injuries *and* for her years of past abuse. In other words, even without being revictimized, staff members could look back to her past suffering to summon up additional sympathy sentiment from within. This is an important point because it shows how anyone can generate sympathy for others through introspective reflection (Clark 1987; 1997). In Tammy's case, simply reopening the binder that contained the photos of her blood-stained irises could evoke another wave of sympathy and replenish her account.

SAFE staff members had an incentive to cultivate and maintain a consistent flow of sympathy toward their clients. It was one of the most effective ways for the advocates and counselors to earn moral wages. In exchange for the stressful work, long hours, and low pay, SAFE staff members garnered substantial satisfaction from their ability to understand and believe their clients when few outsiders would. Feeling sympathetic toward victims felt good to them. Running out of sympathy for a client—like Tammy—would not only signify a failure to adhere to SAFE policy but also make it harder to accrue the symbolic rewards that made their work worthwhile. However, this was not the only reason they worked so hard to excuse and forgive their clients for their missteps.

Offering sympathy to clients (or threatening to withhold it) was also one of the few ways the advocates and counselors could influence their clients without explicitly telling them what to do. Yes, they wanted to feel like caring and compassionate people, but they also wanted to keep their clients away from danger. But how could they keep clients from making decisions which they feared might put them in harm's way?

As shown in the previous chapters, making explicit demands on clients was deemed disempowering at SAFE. Sure, they could gently steer their clients toward particular directions, but the effectiveness of these strategies was limited, especially with strong-willed clients like Tammy. Consequently, holding out the possibility for more or less sympathy was one of the only ways left that they could subtly communicate their disapproval while still laying claim to their empowering approach.

Sympathy is rarely talked about as a mechanism of control. Instead, the emotion is generally thought of as something that nice, polite people do as a gesture of concern. Yet, as sociologist Candace Clark's (1997) work has shown, sympathy can also be used to achieve "micropolitical" ends. In this sense, sympathy serves to bind people together—and not always as equals. This can be seen in the subtle ways that expressing sympathy toward another person is a quiet way of communicating who has more status during an interaction.

In everyday life, we witness countless examples of those with status offering sympathy to those with less. These interactions garner praise and admiration. Yet, the reverse—those with less status offering sympathy to those with more—happens much less often; and when it does, it can provoke confusion. For example, a teacher who pats a child on the head is seen as considerate; a child who pats a teacher on the head is viewed as impish. Or, consider how a boss can sympathize with an employee who is about to make a big presentation, but for the employee to do the same would be awkward. From boss to employee, the gesture is typically seen as kind and caring; from employee to boss, it is likely to be seen as intrusive, or out of place. Of course there are exceptions, but the same pattern can be found during sympathy exchanges between doctors and patients, cops and criminals, veterans and rookies, and so on.

In regard to status, sympathy usually flows down, not up. The reason: to sympathize with other people is to delve into their personal lives, imagine the hardship they might be experiencing, and feel entitled to offer an opinion on the matter. To accept sympathy is to allow another into one's private realm and admit vulnerabilities—something that people with status are rarely keen to do with people who have less. Advocates and counselors at SAFE never spoke of sympathy as an indicator of their relative power vis-à-vis clients, but this kind of analysis can help explain why they tried so hard to forgive their difficult clients.

When a client like Tammy sought services from SAFE advocates and counselors, she was accepting a subordinate position relative to them. Although the egalitarian rhetoric at SAFE obscures what Candace Clark (1997) calls the "microhierarchy" between sympathizer and sympathizee, the disparity became clear when staff members refused clients' requests (for rent money, in Tammy's case).[12] To maintain some influence over Tammy, they needed to keep the sympathy flowing. There were practical reasons for this. Sympathy bound them together; it kept clients close as a means to keep them free from harm.

Refusing to sympathize with particular clients signaled the end of the relationship. Once disconnected, staff members had no way of guiding them away from future danger. This is why forgiving clients was so important. For example, when Lisa was upset about one of her clients moving back in with her ex-abuser, she knew if she let herself get upset it could drive her client away. She then quickly came up with a list of potential explanations for why her client was doing this. Whatever negative feelings were left, Lisa hid for strategic reasons. She equated disagreeing with a client as taking a side against her, which could harm the relationship: "If you take a side, she won't come back." Leaving open the possibility of future sympathy maintained the relationship—and microhierarchy—between service provider and recipient. By ratcheting the flow up and down, Lisa could use it to encourage and discourage different behaviors. This was a weak mechanism of influence, but one of the few she had. The only way to measure its strength is to observe the effect were Lisa to stop using it. If she cut off the flow of sympathy entirely, she would lose her last lever of influence—with nothing left to nudge her client to safety.

In some cases, like Tammy's, this was a sacrifice that staff members were willing to make. Continuing to offer sympathy in the face of unrepentant behavior could potentially harm the reputation of staff members, SAFE, and the movement as a whole. If staff members allowed one client to use SAFE money to sell drugs, what else would they tolerate? As a result, cutting some clients off showed others that their sympathy was still special, not something that they just gave away to anyone at any time. For example, when the advocates stood silent in the court hallway when Paul, the sheriff's deputy, said Tammy "deserves to be in jail," they saved their micropolitical capital for another client on another day.

CONCLUSION

SAFE staff members believed that most outsiders generally did not understand the dynamics of DV and SA. Expressing frustration over victim myths was a common lunchtime activity at SAFE. At least once a week, an advocate or counselor would report an insensitive comment they overheard at the gas station or the grocery store; someone, somewhere, had opined on an issue related to DV and SA and demonstrated their lack of awareness of why victims behave the way they do. What they did not realize is that they have not even heard the worst of it. As a man, I have overheard even more outrageous stereotypes by other men who felt free to say what they "really thought" once confident that "the feminazis" had left the room. Yet, for all the frustration that victim-blaming scripts and myths have caused advocates and counselors, they serve an important purpose: by distancing themselves from popular beliefs, staff members signal that they understand the dynamics of DV and SA in ways that others do not. Thus, by telling each other stories of how unsympathetic or ignorant other people are about the topic of violence against women, they paint themselves in a more favorable and virtuous light.

These myths did more than just help individual staff members accomplish their moral identities, though. In many ways, agencies like SAFE are heavily dependent upon these myths because they are drivers of public sentiment from outsiders. They need them to harness financial and political support for their cause.

To show how DV and SA agencies "need" these myths, let's consider one with which they often took issue: the popular assumption that victims must act like victims forever because they can never "get over" their abuse in any way. The underlying premise of the "perpetual victimhood" myth is that "even a single, brief incident can have consequences that extend throughout the victim's life" (Best 1997:11).[13] This myth caused SAFE staff members all sorts of problems in the courtroom. For example, if a victim in court was unable to summon and display pain and anguish months (sometimes years) after being abused, judges and juries might not believe her (see also Konradi 1996). Additionally, any evidence that she has "moved on" could be taken as a sign that her original wounds (physical and emotional) were not as deep as she once claimed. Yet, for all the trouble caused by this myth, it is also an effective conceptual image to show outsiders that victim advocacy and counseling services are always in need.[14] In the public marketplace of ideas, this myth lays the conceptual groundwork for why places like SAFE are so important. After all, if the effects of victimization continue in perpetuity—at least to some degree—any woman who has ever been abused might need a place like SAFE one day.

Ironically, women who defy this eternal victimhood frame put places like SAFE in a difficult position. One of Jesse's clients, for example, initially came to SAFE completely petrified after her abuser threatened to sexually assault her and kill her animals (a few pets and some chickens). But a few months later, Jesse came across the woman in town and hardly recognized her: "She had on make-up, sunglasses, stylish clothes. She was a different person." This client never returned or called SAFE again. By most accounts, this was a success story, and the advocates and counselors had many others just like it. Yet, the image of former clients transforming—in the span of a few months—from terrorized victims to walking around town in stylish clothes does not foster the emotional currents that are necessary to sustain a nonprofit organization like SAFE with public funds. The myth of enduring victimhood "helps" in this regard. This myth casts recovery as something that can be undone at any moment, meaning places like SAFE will always be needed—especially when women who thought they had "moved on" come to realize they still need more help.

Although disproving the myths of DV and SA victimhood was a goal of SAFE's, too much success at swaying conventional wisdom could also cause problems. What if cultural perceptions about victimhood change before rates of abuse subside? If the public became convinced that being a victim is not always a permanent experience, public support for SAFE services might erode while DV and SA continue unabated. Convincing outsiders that *some* victims can recover completely is thus a double-edged sword. It may improve public awareness, but it could also invite a skeptical policymaker to ask hypothetical questions like "If victims are more resilient than popular perception would have us believe, then why does the public need to devote so many resources to help them heal for such extended periods of time?" Of course, administrators of places like SAFE would have quick and ready answers for such questions: "Some clients may be resilient, but not all." "Some clients who think they are 'over it' may later realize they are not." "Each victim responds to abuse in her own way, and we need to be there to answer the phone whenever she decides to call." But shades of the perpetual victim myth can be found in each of these hypothetical responses, too. As a result, even though victim myths might cause headaches for those inside places like SAFE on a day-to-day basis, they also helped staff members frame their relevance to potential donors, volunteers, and politicians.

SAFE depended upon public sentiment to support its cause. The nearby sheriff's department did not have to hold bimonthly fund-raisers at a local restaurant to help make payroll—SAFE did. Staying afloat was not easy. When traditional sources dwindled (as when a state funding program was cut), they marketed their moral position to make up the difference. This meant convincing a skeptical and unaware public that their services were unique: they served those whom other institutions (legal, medical, and social service) had failed. Thus, popular images of victims—even if inaccurate—help rally public opinion. SAFE fundraising newsletters always offered at least some vignettes or images of quiet and stoic women who were slowly rebuilding their lives. These images imply that victims can get better, but will always need a place like SAFE in case they ever fall apart emotionally or are revictimized. The subtext of these appeals is that no one becomes an ex-client of SAFE; they are either "current" or "potentially returning" clients. This is how myths can ironically help places like SAFE. As long as the wider public believes that the healing never ends, there will always be a reason to fund the healers.

Readers should not mistake my analysis of the ways that victim myths "help" places like SAFE as an argument that these myths do not cause incredible harm to victims of DV and SA. The contradicting and interlocking norms of victimhood placed the women who sought services at SAFE in an oppressive bind from which there was little escape. Staff members at SAFE were ready and willing to confront outsiders who believed in these myths; what they were not prepared for, however, were the ways that they were not completely impervious to them. It was this last struggle that they rarely articulated, but one that I was able to observe them manage during their interactions with the most difficult clients who tested their limits.

I admit, the first time I observed staff members criticize and otherwise stop sympathizing with a client, I was surprised. All my volunteer training and experience had taught me that there was always an explanation for why clients behave in difficult ways. But, over time, I saw how some clients simply exhausted all of the patience SAFE staff members had to offer. At some point, the advocates and counselors came to see that continuing to work with clients like Tammy could do more harm than good to everyone involved. But refusing sympathy has consequences, too: it can feed some of the myths of victimhood that SAFE workers spent so much energy trying to debunk. Even by their generous standards, they believed that some victims had to be held to account for their most egregious actions. In this way, cutting off services to clients like Tammy could potentially serve to refute notions of victimhood as a total and eternal identity. However, the advocates' emotional responses after talking with Tammy on the phone that last time were not political calculations aimed at changing theoretical understandings of victimization. They were upset and angry—and their feelings signal that even the people we least expect (victim advocates and counselors) also have baseline assumptions about how victims *should* behave. To be fair, their expectations were milder and more forgiving variants than popular stereotypes. But, by acting on them and refusing sympathy to some clients, they also breathe new life into these myths. True, their voice is but one in a chorus. Yet, as moral entrepreneurs in the domain of violence against women, their message carries weight.

In the next chapter, I show that the moral wages they earned for work with victims sometimes did not make up for the relative lack of respect they received outside the office for their capacity to care. In most cases, this was not a problem. The support and respect they received from their peers and colleagues were enough to keep them going, even when dealing with difficult clients. However, the general lack of appreciation for their emotional and interpersonal skills—partly due to the devaluation of women's care work in general—made some aspects of their work in and around the criminal justice system more appealing and satisfying to them than their training and policies led me to expect.

CHAPTER FIVE

The Allure of Legal Work

When it comes to incidents of abuse, many people assume that calling the police is the best thing a victim can do. The thinking goes, if someone is harmed, they should call on the law to help—immediately. To choose not to do so is a sign of something wrong: only the misguidedly loyal would choose *not* to call 911. However, inside places like SAFE (Stopping Abuse in Family Environments), the criminal justice system is viewed with more suspicion than outsiders would expect.

Even though legal remedies can do a lot of good for victims of domestic violence (DV) and sexual assault (SA), advocates and counselors fear that they can also do a lot of harm. They view arrest warrants and restraining orders with caution, and they worry that legal victories can give a client a false sense of security, or enrage her abuser, or both.[1] Sure, sheriff's deputies and assistant district attorneys might be able to get him locked up, but what good would forty-eight hours in jail do? What would happen when he got out?

I spent a lot of time with SAFE staff members in and around courtrooms and quickly learned that although the criminal justice system could do many powerful things, attending to the particular needs of individuals was not its strongest suit. SAFE clients needed precise and exact measures to solve their problems; legal solutions, however, operate more like a broadsword than a scalpel. A client might rely on her abuser to cover the costs of food or housing. Putting him in jail might get him fired; without his paycheck, how would she make ends meet? Untangling clients from their dependency—often by abusers' design—is a messy and complicated process; one that rigid legal arrangements are rarely able to accomplish in subtle and nuanced ways.

In the language of SAFE, the legal system could potentially take away clients' "power and control" over their lives. Irrespective of what a client wanted, judges had the final say over verdicts, prosecutors decided whether or not to bring charges, and cops picked whom to arrest; this approach—ultimately dictating how victims' cases were handled—was antithetical to SAFE's empowerment philosophy. As a result, staff members warned their clients that the criminal justice system offered victims a fundamentally different set of services from those delivered by advocates and counselors. Inside the SAFE office, clients were in charge; in and around courtrooms, they held no such sway.

These concerns about legal remedies are not new. As explained in chapter 1, second-wave feminists initially created agencies like SAFE in large part to serve as a countermeasure to the criminal justice system. Although relations have improved, many leaders in the DV and SA movement still characterize collaboration with law enforcement as "fraught with danger" (Corrigan 2013:30) and continue to see police stations and courtrooms as potentially hostile territory (Barner and Carney 2011).

The most visible evidence of this lingering distrust could be found in SAFE's training sessions and policy documents. SAFE advocates were taught to "sit, listen, and then talk" to clients before hurrying into legal remedies. Their boss, Kelly, a SAFE codirector, put extra effort into teaching advocates not to presume that pressing charges or—more commonly—obtaining protective orders was the best answer: "I go to great pains, very verbose introduction: 'Don't run get the protective order forms when the woman walks in! Sit down with her and let her tell her story. Listen to her. And be sure you have a range of options to offer her including a protective order.'" Even in cases where clients came to SAFE explicitly asking for legal help, Kelly trained her employees that the empowering solution was to inform victims of *all* possible alternatives. After that, if clients still expressed interest in legal paperwork, the advocate should then detail all of the risks and rewards of bringing in the law to help. Kelly made sure that everyone working for her knew that the legal path should be tread with caution: "I try to train the advocates not to just assume that [a legal solution] is the best option or the first option they think of. Because until they hear the woman's story and her situation and think about what has she tried before. . . . They're not going to know whether a protective order is their best option, or not a good option. . . . So it's just critically important that advocates take the time to spend with that woman and hear her story and understand her situation." From Kelly's perspective, bringing in the criminal justice system "upped the ante" between the client and her abuser. This strategy might help—showing him that she is serious; but it also might hurt—making him angrier.

The effectiveness of protective orders was a particular source of concern inside SAFE. Kelly described them like this: "It is just a piece of paper that depends on enforcement by law enforcement. . . . Sometimes they might make the situation worse." This refrain—protective orders are "only a piece of paper"—was not unique to Kelly or the SAFE advocates. This rhetoric is part of the lore of DV and SA work nationwide. Even the sheriff's deputies who served as liaisons with SAFE used the same phrase.[2]

Courtrooms were also painted in a negative light. SAFE staff members were trained to expect defense attorneys to challenge their clients' assertions and otherwise discredit their accounts. Past research has documented this pattern at length (Campbell 1998; Maier 2008a); going to trial can leave scars: "Even successful verdicts exact a price. [Victims] may be dismayed to learn that the record of their police report is public, they are expected to testify about graphic details of sexual assault in open court, and even rape shield laws fail to guarantee that they will be protected from questions about their social and sexual history when these issues are ruled relevant to determining consent" (Koss, Bachar, Hopkins, and Carlson 2004:1441). Yet, despite these risks, some clients desperately wanted to go the legal route—and if this is what they wanted, the advocates were ready and willing to guide them through the cold and confusing channels of the criminal justice system.[3]

Going to court was not a pleasant experience for clients. The contrast between the quiet and comfortable confines of the SAFE office and the courtroom was stark. In the SAFE office, clients could relax among filtered light, soft chairs, and friendly faces. In the courtroom, they sat on hard wooden pews under humming fluorescent strips. Once court was in session, clients had to pay attention at all times: the bailiff commanded them to sit and stand, and if the judge was behind the bench they were not allowed to talk out of turn. Past studies have documented the ways that courtrooms "are not inherently set up to—or necessarily overly interested in trying to—attend to victims' needs or experiences" (Bell, Perez, Goodman, and Dutton 2011:72), and clients quickly learned this lesson while waiting for their cases to be heard. After the gavel drops, they have no control over how or when their hearing will proceed.

Although the SAFE advocates were usually able to secure a copy of the day's schedule—printed by the clerk—the order and pace of the hearings were largely opaque. An abuser's name might appear to be the next item on the list, but a quick huddle of lawyers and a motion of the hand by the judge to the clerk could mean that the matter had been delayed or settled. During all this, clients typically sat confused and worried. During recess, the advocates could rush off to sleuth in the back hallways to figure out what had happened, but clients rarely understood all that was going on around them.

This lack of control victims of DV and SA have over court proceedings causes more than emotional distress. Court delays can create practical problems for clients who have to negotiate other obligations—like work. Is a protective order worth getting fired over? To get a better sense of the problems that victims face in court, sociologist Jill Adams documented the hurdles that one victim faced in her efforts to obtain a civil restraining order in Canada: "To appear in front of the judge for numerous one to four minute hearings, and one 13-minute hearing, [the victim] has taken half and whole days off work on several occasions. Without knowing how long she will be waiting on Thursday, coupled with sudden notice to appear for subsequent hearings, it has been difficult to give her employer sufficient notice that she will be absent" (2009:206). My observations and interviews of SAFE staff members generally yielded similar findings regarding clients' experience in court. Taking time off from work could put their jobs in jeopardy and there was no guarantee that their cases would even be heard on any given day.

Although victim's experiences are important, the focus of this chapter (and book) is on the experiences of the service providers. After watching them for months helping clients through the criminal justice system, I found something that I did not expect. For victims, court was a confusing and intimidating place; for those helping them—the advocates—the subjective experience of court was surprisingly different: they liked it.

THE LEGAL WORK EMOTIONAL DILEMMA

Despite their worries about the risks of legal remedies for their clients, SAFE staff members found work in and around courtrooms (which I call "legal work") to be challenging and rewarding in ways that their work inside the SAFE office was not. Their training, policies, and rhetoric framed legal work as something to avoid as much as possible, yet they were still drawn to it in ways I found surprising. Although their interactions with police officers, judges, magistrates, bailiffs, and lawyers were tense at times, these exchanges could also be exhilarating. My earlier volunteer training did not prepare me for this, and I did not fully understand it until I engaged in some legal work myself (which I describe later in the chapter).

The skepticism surrounding legal work in places like SAFE is the basis of the emotional dilemma that is the focus of this chapter: victim advocates worry about the consequences of legal work for their clients, but they also find this kind of work energizing. Staff members value their caring and quiet interactions with clients inside the SAFE office, but they also know that outsiders do not always share the same respect and admiration for those specialized skills. As a result, they are torn between two aims: to establish meaningful, caring, and private relationships with their clients, and to be respected for their ability to obtain justice on behalf of victims. Sometimes these goals are compatible, but not always. In the end, SAFE advocates were able to manage this dilemma. By emphasizing the "concrete" and "immediate" benefits of legal remedies for their clients, they justified any divergence from their policies and training. As long as legal work "worked" for their clients, it was worth it.

To analyze the underpinnings of this dilemma, I begin by outlining the ways that legal work was different from other tasks at SAFE. First, the symbolic architecture of courtrooms enabled the advocates to showcase their skills in a respected public venue (something that their private work inside the office did not). Second, legal work offered staff members a chance to win; unlike the uncertainty, ambiguity, and secrecy that shrouded the outcomes of their confidential listening sessions with clients, verdicts in court offered black-and-white measures of their effectiveness. To argue this point, I offer an extended description of the courtroom experiences of one advocate (Meg) to show just how good victories in court felt. However, by themselves, these two immediate causes do not adequately explain why legal work was so alluring at SAFE.

To fill this gap, I then outline two additional sociological reasons for why the advocates were drawn to legal work. One, the organizational stance of places like SAFE toward the criminal justice system has changed dramatically over the years; what was once seen as an institutional foe has now become a source of revenue and validation. Two, outsiders' inability to understand and respect their emotional and interactional skills is part of a wider cultural devaluation of women's care work. To "sit and talk" with victims required incredible patience and sensitivity; yet, in a culture that assumes women are "natural" nurturers, there are few rewards for those who exercise "instinctual" caring skills that presumably require no training or practice for them to learn.

Typically, the scholarship on violence against women addresses legal remedies for victims from a different angle. Most studies (which I briefly outline later in this chapter) focus on whether or not the criminal justice system works for victims—that is, Does it protect them? Does it effectively penalize those who abuse them? My sample is small and my focus is different. Instead, I analyze broader social phenomena to explain why—despite continual reminders that legal remedies should be viewed with caution—legal work can be so attractive to those who help victims.[4]

TANGIBLE WORK

When I asked the advocates about their thoughts about using protective orders and arrest warrants to help their clients, they uniformly opened with the same cautionary tales outlined previously. However, after detailing all the things that could go wrong with legal approaches, they also finished their warnings with a surprising addendum: legal work felt real to them. In a job where it was hard to tell which news was good news, and where successes were often measured in a client's small smile or a brief upturn in self-confidence, winning in court was easy to celebrate. The clearest example of this during my research occurred one day when Jesse returned from a victory in court. Word had gotten back to the office ahead of her that she had good news, and upon arrival she was surrounded by the whole staff in the kitchen. She was peppered with questions: "What did the judge say?" "How did [the abuser] respond?" After walking them through the details of what happened, Jesse finished with the grand finale: "She got custody!" and promptly received a "high five" from Cathleen. As the small crowd dispersed, Kelly invited Jesse to her office upstairs for a congratulatory debriefing.

What I learned from watching Jesse and the rest of the staff that day was that legal work offered them something that their other interactions with clients could not. When sitting, listening, and talking with clients, it was hard to determine exactly how much a lengthy conversation or hours of "safety planning" really helped; but in court, a win was a win—both for the client and for the entire movement against DV and SA. In a term used by the advocates, legal victories felt "tangible." After months of observations, I had suspected as much. But I did not fully understand the way it felt until I engaged in some legal work myself. It was a simple task, but it helped me understand how and why the advocates found this kind of work so satisfying. Afterward, when my job was done, it was done; I could move on to the next thing. When finished, I could say to myself—for the moment—that I had done something good: I had helped a client.

The Protective Order Process

The request for my help came on a quiet morning in the SAFE office. Clients rarely came in before 10:00 a.m., and it was not unusual for only two or three staff members to be in the office that early. This morning, though, Melissa was the only staff member in the office (others had not yet returned from a breakfast meeting with representatives of other community organizations). I found her sitting with a client in the downstairs waiting room. The day before, this client had worked with the advocates and a local lawyer to fill out an application for a protective order. However, by the time they had finished, the clerk of court's office had closed. Now the client was back, and she needed someone to walk her to court, get the document signed by a judge, and file it with the clerk's office.

Technically, because Melissa was a counselor, not an advocate, it was not her job to help clients with protective orders, but she often helped out in a pinch. She wanted to accompany the client to court, but she could not leave the office unattended. Instead, she asked me if I could take the client over and walk her through the process. I agreed. The client looked a little surprised when first meeting me—a man—but I was used to this kind of reaction. I tried to put her at ease by smiling and telling her this should only take about thirty minutes. She looked weary and a little nervous, so I tried to help her by appearing calm myself (even though I was a little nervous, too).

The court was only a few blocks away. As we walked, the client clutched her paperwork tightly under her elbow. Like most SAFE clients, she was white, but she was also a college student, so her likely middle-class status meant she was better off financially than most clients. Because the walk was short, there was not much time for small talk; I began spelling out what to expect—who we would talk to, where we would go—and she mostly just nodded in response.[5]

Although I had accompanied the advocates through the entire protective order process on about ten separate occasions by this point in my research, I had never done it by myself. I admitted this to the client, but I assured her that if needed, I would tell court officials that I was volunteering with SAFE and that I would likely be able to get her pointed in the right direction. This was partially true. Technically, I was not a SAFE volunteer, but I did help out in the office on a number of occasions. I had a pick-up truck, and I could speak Spanish. Consequently, I did some driving, furniture moving, and phone answering from time to time when things got busy. As for my assurance to her that we could get help navigating the offices in the court building, that was mostly correct, too. Court officials would not sit down with applicants and help them fill out the form like the SAFE advocates would, but it was not uncommon for the clerks, the bailiffs, and (to a lesser extent) the judges to show applicants where they needed to go and what they needed to do. Although I still found the courthouse a little intimidating, I knew who and what to ask; I was confident we could get the order signed that day.

Technically, the civil protective order process was designed so that applicants would not need lawyers. In theory, any applicant should be able to read the form, insert the necessary information, and get it signed by a judge on their own. In practice, SAFE advocates or pro bono lawyers visiting the office would sit next to clients and walk them through the questions one by one. Careful attention to detail was important because the meanings underlying the questions on the application were not always intuitive. For example, one item on the form asks applicants if "the defendant has attempted to cause or has intentionally caused me bodily injury; or has placed me or a member of my family or household in fear of imminent serious bodily injury or in fear of continued harassment that rises to such a level as to inflict substantial emotional distress; or has committed a sexual offense against me in that: *(Give specific dates and describe in detail what happened.)*" What first-time applicants do not know, however, is that most of the judges in SAFE's district were primarily interested in the most recent incidents of abuse (that is, in the past days or weeks, not months or years). These judges reasoned that if the applicant had been free of abuse and fear for months, then there was no "imminent" danger. This was confusing to many SAFE clients. Many assumed that they only needed to provide cursory details or describe the most violent episode of abuse they had ever experienced, even if it took place years before. What they did not know was that these were the most common reasons for getting their paperwork rejected.

Ideally, women who had practice filling out detailed forms might not need a lawyer or an advocate to complete the application process, but most SAFE clients had no such experience. And even ones that did—like the college student I accompanied to court—still needed help. Filling out the application, however, is just the first step of many. The next was to make our way to the clerk of court's filing office. I had been there before, but the client had not. We made our way through a maze of hallways and shoulder-high cubicle partitions. There was a small sign on the door that read "Clerk of Court," but it was easy to miss. We made our way to the clerk's desk, I introduced myself as a SAFE volunteer, and the client handed in her form. The clerk looked over the application for the most common mistakes: Is the protective order being filed in the county where the applicant lives (not the county where the abuser lives, or where the abuse took place)? Has the applicant included the full name and address of the defendant (that is, the abuser)? Has the applicant accidentally filled in portions designated for court officials? After a quick review, the clerk produced a palm-sized Bible upon which she asked the client to place her hand and swear that the information on the form was accurate, and then sign her name to this effect. This swearing-in ceremony may sound solemn, but the length of time it took the clerk to retrieve the Bible, have the client swear and sign, sign herself, and squeeze the notary embosser lasted roughly twenty seconds. Once finished, the clerk told us to "get this signed" and come back.

Although I knew what the clerk meant by this, the client had no idea. I had been with advocates as they tracked down judges before, and I knew that the client was likely baffled by the clerk's last request. I could see confusion in her eyes: How does one get a judge to sign a document? I knew the answer, and it felt good to reassure her that everything would be okay.

To get a signature, first you have to find a judge. This means knowing when court is in session (not every day of the week); when the judge is on the bench (only a few hours per session); and where they go when not behind the bench (usually to their chambers). We exited the clerk's office, made our way up some back stairs, and came to the metal detector before entering the courtroom, which was largely empty. Upon entry, I told the bailiff we needed a signature for a protective order, and he agreed to walk with me back to the judge's chambers. I told the client she could sit down in one of the back rows of the court. She waited in one of the long, wooden pews, like in church, while I disappeared in one of the back hallways. I quickly saw that the judge was not in chambers, so I returned to the main courtroom and sat next to the client until some of the district attorney's staff started trickling in. Like the clerk and the bailiff, I recognized them from my past fieldwork visits in court with the SAFE advocates. I waved to the assistant district attorney; he did not know my name, but he recognized my face and gestured for me to come forward. I told him we needed a protective order signed, and he said he would mention this to the judge after the next few cases were wrapped up.

When the judge returned to the bench a few minutes later, I sat next to the client as we both listened to a couple of cases so mundane that it put the details of abuse on her application in stark relief. The two cases involved juveniles who had stolen candy from their school. The client was quiet and even smiled a few times as the judge lectured the boys in a parental tone. After the boys were ushered out, the assistant district attorney pointed over to us and muttered something to the judge we could not hear. The judge then announced, "Is anyone from SAFE here?" I stood up and said that I was volunteering today at SAFE. I held up the paperwork and said that it had been checked over by a lawyer the day before—which was true—in the hopes that the judge would give it less scrutiny, figuring that everything was in order.

The judge waved her hand to signal that we both should approach the bench and flipped through the paperwork as she told the client, "You're in good hands with SAFE. You do whatever they ask you to do; keep in touch with them." This judge was the most sympathetic to SAFE clients of the three on rotation in this district. I had been secretly happy when I saw that she was on duty today, but I did not say anything to the client until she signed the application—which she did.

With the signed application in hand, the client seemed relieved. We made our way back down the stairs, through the maze of cubicles, and into the clerk's office a second time—this time she knew the way. The clerk took the forms without a word and walked over to the copy machine, "How many?" I did not know how many copies were appropriate, so I said nothing. I waited a moment until the clerk broke the silence: "Two copies okay?" she said, and the client nodded in agreement. Later, I asked around, and the advocates said they typically make more copies for clients back at the office. One to keep in SAFE's files, one for the client to keep on her person at all times, and others to stash at her house, place of work, and with nearby relatives and friends. That way, if the abuser violates the order, she will be sure to have one nearby to show the police in case she cannot find her own copy.

As we walked back to the SAFE office, I explained to the client the next couple of steps she should expect. Going over the logistics of her protective order seemed to put her at ease; she had commented earlier that she did not really understand how it would work, even though her SAFE advocate and pro bono lawyer had tried to explain it to her. With all of the uncertainty of the past few days, she said it was nice to have some clear details to grab on to. And, to be honest, it put me at ease as well.

Fairly quickly, I was able to rattle off the standard "Protective Order 101" spiel that I had heard in the advocates' office so many times before. It went like this: Although the client had a signed protective order in her possession, this document was only a temporary measure. Her abuser was not in court to defend or explain himself when the judge looked over the order. As a result, the client had only acquired an "ex parte" protective order— meaning that the judge's decision had been made "by or for one party" in the absence of the other. Likely, the first time her abuser would learn of the protective order would be when sheriff's deputies served him in his county of residence. At this point, the order would only be in effect for about ten days. Then, a hearing would be held where he would have a chance to contest the order in court (the SAFE advocates referred to these follow-up hearings as "ten-day hearings"). If he showed up, he could bring a lawyer to challenge the client's assertions. He might also use a lawyer to extend the process by asking for more time and a new date for the hearing. Or, he might not show up at all. As long as the judge knew that he had been served notice of the order, and he had been given a reasonable chance to appear in court, the judge could let the hearing go on without him. In either case, the judge would ultimately decide whether or not to extend the protective order for a full year. If the client wanted to extend the order after that, she'd have to request a renewal annually—and the process would repeat itself.

Another confusing aspect of protective orders in the state where SAFE was located was that they were civil documents, but they evoked criminal penalties if violated. These distinctions are unclear to many clients because most people conflate civil and criminal court proceedings. To outsiders, if you are in court with a judge behind the bench and a bailiff at the door, it is hard to tell the difference. To make it simple, SAFE advocates explained to clients that the purpose of civil court is to solve disagreements between individuals, whereas criminal court oversees disputes between individuals and the state. As a result, protective orders require that an abuser abide by certain restrictions on his behavior toward another person. For example, he may not be allowed to contact her (directly or through intermediaries). If he owns a gun, he will likely have to surrender it to law enforcement. Depending on the judge's decision, he might also have to leave the house, give up custody of their children, enroll in "batterer intervention" classes, or all three. If he refuses to abide by the protective order, he is subject to criminal penalties (either a misdemeanor or felony, depending on how severe). This is why the SAFE advocates were careful to remind clients to keep copies of the order with them at all times. Typically, sheriff's deputies and police officers do not arrest people for being in a home that they own or for calling their spouse on the phone. But, if they are shown a civil document signed by a judge prohibiting that person from doing those things, they are required to stop them—with force if necessary.

By the time we got back to the SAFE office, the client was nodding in agreement. She was tired—she had not slept well in days—but she seemed relieved to get this chore out of the way before she could embark on the long drive back to her parents' house. The other advocates had returned to the SAFE office by this time and were glad that the paperwork had gone through. They made her additional copies and reminded her that one would always be on file in their office if she ever needed it. The client promised to keep in touch with SAFE and her pro bono lawyer before her ten-day hearing. She looked exhausted. After all that talking, I was tired, too. But I was also proud of my work. I felt good—like I had done something worthwhile.

WHAT MADE LEGAL WORK SO ATTRACTIVE?

Given all of the warnings about the criminal justice system, why did the advocates—and I—find this kind of work so rewarding? All of SAFE's training materials and brochures suggested cautious skepticism. Yet, after my experience helping a client with her protective order, I began to see more clearly the differences between how legal remedies were written about in policies versus how they were experienced by staff members. The doubts and worries on paper gave way to excitement in the moment. In the rest of this chapter, I try to explain why.

The Symbolic Architecture of Legal Work

Court days were special for the advocates. Not just because it was a change of pace, but also because they made it special. The advocates dressed up for court: skirts or dress pants and blouses—no jeans. They carried legal pads on clipboards and spent a lot time rushing around, juggling paperwork, and ushering clients around the maze of hallways and stairwells. They were continually busy; as soon as they arrived they would pore over the docket to look for DV- and SA-related cases that day. Then, acting on tips, they would peek their heads in waiting rooms and around corners to find the women involved in these cases to tell them about SAFE. They recruited a considerable number of clients this way. During the four-hour session of court each week, they initiated roughly 850 "client contacts" a year. This constituted nearly one-third of all new SAFE "contacts" in any given year.

As I followed the advocates around court, I continually struggled to keep up as they dashed through closed doors and back hallways. Taking field notes was a challenge. The sheer number of people they talked to (past clients, prospective clients, friends of clients, family of clients, and sometimes even abusers) was daunting. This list does not even include all of the "official" people they also interacted with around court (lawyers, probation officers, clerks, bailiffs, sheriff's deputies). After each session, my notepad was often a tangled mess. Back in the office, I would have to debrief the advocates to make sure I had gotten my facts straight regarding the specific charges and outcomes of each case (see the appendix for a description of my methods).

By itself, busyness is not enough to make court days special. Folding newsletters and sealing envelopes back in the office made for busy work, too. Instead, the symbolic architecture of the courtroom made it easier for the advocates to show themselves and others that they were uniquely equipped to help clients solve problems. As a venue, the courtroom offered them ample dramaturgical opportunities to display their skills: a stage on which to shine.

Conceptually, the courtroom can be divided into two areas: one public and one restricted. At the bench, the judge and the clerk faced a large open room. Facing them were two long tables, behind which sat the opposing legal teams. Visitors were allowed to watch the proceedings if they sat in the pews behind a three-foot-tall wooden partition in the public area. In front of the petition, in the restricted area, the SAFE advocates were allowed to sit alongside lawyers, witnesses, defendants, bailiffs, and parole officers.

When court was not in session, the advocates were free to escort clients through the back door to the area behind the courtroom. This private entrance, unlocked by passcode, also allowed the advocates to enter conference rooms to conduct private meetings with lawyers and assistant district attorneys. There, they discussed plea bargains or other arrangements. On occasion, these meetings drifted down the hall and concluded in the judge's chambers. These areas were not especially attractive (the carpet and furniture were typical office grade), but that was not the point. Their access was limited, and this made them special.

It might be tempting to assume that the advocates enjoyed court so much because they secretly wanted to be lawyers. After all, being a lawyer would mean more prestige and more money. However, after asking them directly and observing their behavior in court, I came to see that they did not envy lawyers (although they would have liked to earn more money). What they wanted was the *respect* that came to lawyers. Like professionals, the advocates believed that their legal work indicated that they possessed "a monopoly of some esoteric and difficult body of knowledge" (Becker 1970:94). They knew that lawyers had larger salaries and more social status; they were okay with this. What they really wanted was to be recognized as experts in a small niche of law specifically related to DV and SA.

This desire put them in a bind because they did not have the credentials necessary to claim expert status in the courtroom, even though they knew a great deal about the laws affecting their clients. They knew the paperwork, the terminology, and the statutes very well. Sometimes they knew more than the lawyers with whom they interacted; but, like paralegals in a law firm, they understood that knowing the things that lawyers know does not mean they get the same rewards and respect.[6] They understood that professional status was out of reach. However, legal work still offered them a chance to be respected by an audience broader than just other colleagues in victim services.

For one thing, legal work was easy to explain to their friends and families. Protective orders are complex, but they are easier to explain than the relationship between patriarchal values and violence against women. The advocates reported that their friends and family already had a general understanding of "restraining orders" and how courtrooms operated. Explaining their interactions with clients inside the SAFE office was more difficult—made even more challenging by confidentiality rules that forbade them from revealing specifics about their clients' cases.[7] In contrast, tales of their courtroom exploits impressed outsiders. Put another way, mentioning that they spent the day working in court served as an "ideological code" (Smith 1993) that signified that they were people with authority and expertise. For decades, the popularity of legal dramas on print, screen, and stage (*To Kill a Mockingbird, Law and Order, LA Law,* and *Perry Mason* are a few examples) has generated a vast amount of cultural capital around legal work. Nonlegal work inside places like SAFE offers no comparable cachet.

The cultural valuation of legal work was something over which they had little control, but it shaped their everyday experiences at work. They wanted to help their clients by listening and talking to them about a wide range of issues, but their legal skills enjoyed much more widespread respect and admiration than their caring skills. The wider public may not fully understand the importance of sitting quietly and letting a victim tell her story, but they do know what a plea bargain is. Compared to stories about helping clients enroll their children in a new school, staff members reported that tales of whispering into the ear of the assistant district attorney between cases yielded much more immediate respect and admiration.

Another reason staff members found legal work special and exciting was that it offered them a chance to hold abusers accountable. Courtroom victories signified a win not only for individual clients, but also for the entire movement against DV and SA. In the next section, to show how important legal battles were to those at SAFE, I trace the path of one advocate—Meg—toward a newly created "legal advocate" position in the office. Meg was unique among the advocates in that she was the most enthusiastic about legal work; yet, Meg's subjective experiences are also generalizable to other staff members who were not as vocal or demonstrative. What others in the office found exciting and energizing, Meg found more so. As a result, she offers the clearest example to explain how and why advocates for victims of DV and SA can be drawn to legal work even though their training and policies advise them to be skeptical and leery of it. When Meg was not offered the legal advocate position (in her words, she was "passed over"), her eventual disappointment was visible and heartfelt. The other advocates who did not get the job (all of them applied) were also upset, but not as much as Meg. Not getting the position meant a significant reduction in the time she spent in court; this was too much for her, and turned out to be the main reason she ultimately decided to leave SAFE. Legal work was incredibly important to her. Charting her trajectory to and from SAFE helps show how and why it was important to others in the office, too.

A Chance to Win

As a SAFE advocate, Meg had been a weekly fixture in court for years. She knew all the sheriff's deputies, court clerks, and lawyers by name. Every time I had lunch with Meg in town, a lawyer or a sheriff's deputy would inevitably stop by to chat for a moment. She joked with probation officers, knew gossip about all the bailiffs, and could rattle off the pet peeves of the three rotating judges without missing a beat. Of all the advocates, she was drawn to legal work the most. When she described her work to outsiders, she always mentioned her years of experience "in the criminal justice system"; when it came to tallying up her years of working with victims, she always made sure to count her time at a legal services agency before coming to SAFE.

If challenged about her expertise, she did not hesitate to show what she knew. In an anecdote she told me on more than one occasion, she described an argument she had with her brother about whether or not a family member should file for a protective order. He continued to dismiss her arguments, stating that only a lawyer could help the family. Finally, after describing all the minutiae of the paperwork, she convinced him that she knew what she was talking about: "He finally realized that I really did work in the criminal justice system doing this stuff and I really did sit in court and watch all these cases. I really did attend legislative hearings and know a little bit about the law."

Talking to Meg about her work in court, it became clear that legal victories were special. To her, they offered her clients a chance to win. She resented the ways that abusers manipulated arrangements to keep their victims subservient and weak. In court, she could help her clients restore the balance. When I asked her for an example, she recalled a time when an abuser was defiant during a hearing. As she replayed the scene, she mimicked his deep voice and arrogant tone. When asked by the prosecutor if he had assaulted his girlfriend, he said, "I didn't assault her, I just pushed her." Meg paused, smiled, and waited for me to join in on the fun of laughing at his expense; but I did not understand the joke. She saw that I was confused, so she continued the story: "The district attorney, she just looks over at me. And it takes her a second to figure out what he just said. And she says, 'The state rests.' And then the judge said, 'Well, I guess so.'" At this point in the story, Meg could clearly see that I did not understand what was going on. Shaking her head and laughing loudly, she gave away the punch line: "The man didn't realize that pushing someone *was* assault!" At that point I "got" the joke. I smiled, but Meg kept laughing—her schadenfreude in response to the abuser's mistake was palpable.

Although more subtle in court, Meg's joy and excitement was still visible—as was her disappointment during losses. During a criminal hearing, for example, Meg sat near the assistant district attorney as he cross-examined a man accused of felony assault. SAFE advocates had worked with the woman accusing him and taken pictures of her bruised wrists and neck. Besides that, though, there was not much evidence other than her testimony. The assistant district attorney repeatedly asked the man to explain how her wrists could have been bruised so badly. At first, he answered that he had no idea. But later, he stated that he had grabbed her wrists in self-defense. Upon hearing the contradiction, Meg immediately raised a manila folder to hide her smiling face. Behind the folder, she got the attention of someone else on the prosecutor's staff seated off to the side. As I watched their secret interaction, I could see they were both trying to hide their exhilaration and appear as if nothing had happened—lest they tip their hand to the defense attorney.

Unfortunately, their happiness did not last. Without eye witnesses, the judge claimed it was impossible to ascertain exactly what happened. He was acquitted, to the audible relief of his family. Meg shook her head with pursed lips. Afterward, as she consoled her client, she kept repeating her annoyance at his—and his family's—exuberance: "They were a little too happy, if you ask me."

Although losses in court were painful, Meg believed they were outweighed by the joy that wins brought. Put together, she—and the other advocates—drew from the energy and ultimate finality of legal work. When a judge made a decision, clients knew exactly where they stood. A decision could help clients immensely, but it could also make their lives much, much worse. In either case—exciting victories or demoralizing losses—court offered the advocates a heightened experience; there was little ambiguity about whether the outcome was positive or negative. However, this was the same reason that Kelly warned Meg and the other advocates to "go slow." Court was exciting because it increased the stakes. Comparatively, the "sit and listen" approach of care work that occurred inside the office produced victories typically measured in shades of gray. In court, final results were black and white.

Perhaps the most powerful example of the importance of legal work to Meg was her disappointment when it was taken away from her. As part of the increased coordination between SAFE and the local criminal justice system, Kelly and Liz (the other SAFE codirector who worked in a satellite office) submitted a joint application with the Sheriff's Department and the District Attorney's Office for federal funds to pay for two new positions. The first would be a "legal advocate" position at SAFE, and the second would be a new sheriff's deputy position assigned exclusively to cases involving DV and SA. Both would be hired "in house" from their respective agencies. As proposed, the legal advocate position would absorb most of the legal work duties previously done by the advocates.

The new position did not offer extra pay or better hours; it merely offered the opportunity to focus more on legal matters. However, as stated previously, all the advocates applied for the job. They all wanted it, but Meg wanted it the most. Although everyone else in the office agreed that Meg was the most qualified in regard to her legal skills, they also knew that her application had one main weakness—she did not speak Spanish. Other advocates in the office did. This put Meg at a disadvantage. The county that SAFE served was experiencing a tremendous growth in the Latino population.[8] Interacting with this community would be an important part of the new legal advocate's job duties. In the end, Meg believed that this was the reason she did not get the position.[9]

The codirectors hired Lisa, from the counselors' office, instead of Meg. Lisa had previously worked as an advocate before becoming a family counselor. This initial move to the counseling office had been to help fill a vacant position, but she did not have a professional degree or license and worried that despite her on-the-job training she was not fully qualified to counsel clients. For this reason, she said she never felt comfortable in the counselor's office. Also, she wanted to make the switch to the legal advocate job because of its "problem-solving element." This would be a welcome change from counseling, which she characterized as emotionally satisfying, but not "as productive" as helping clients accomplish "immediate" goals. For Lisa, working in court was something that she liked and believed she was good at. Unfortunately, Meg felt the same way.

Meg left SAFE within a few weeks of learning that her hours in court would be diminished. When I interviewed her after she had started working in a different DV and SA agency in a different county, she said that not getting the legal advocate job was the main reason she left SAFE. She had other complaints, too. She believed she never got the support that she had needed in the aftermath of Shelly's murder (see chapter 1). But Meg's lingering grief and doubts about what she could have done differently during Shelly's case also speak to how drawn she was to legal work. Shelly's case was one of the most glaring examples of how legal remedies can fail victims. Meg had helped Shelly make use of almost every tool available in the criminal justice system, from protective orders to arrest warrants; yet Shelly was murdered anyway. When it came to keeping her safe, these instruments really were just "pieces of paper." But Shelly's death did not cause Meg to lose faith in the criminal justice system. Despite the great risks, she explained to me, there were also great rewards. When it worked, victims could get justice. And, to Meg, that felt good.

VICTIM WORK IN BROADER CONTEXT

To offer some broader perspective on why Meg and the other advocates were drawn to legal remedies in ways that seemed out of step with the warnings contained in their training manuals and policies, I analyze their subjective experiences from a wider sociological perspective. In addition to the symbolic architecture of courtrooms and the ability to hold abusers accountable, how might SAFE staff members' individual wants and needs be explained by larger social trends? First, I outline how the relationship between places like SAFE and the criminal justice system have evolved over the past three decades. In particular, political reforms fought for and won by places like SAFE have bound them to legal remedies in ways that few could have imagined at the birth of the DV and SA movement. Second, the private nature of the advocates' care work is rendered relatively invisible in the occupational marketplace because of gendered stereotypes that cast woman as "naturally" suited to listening and sympathizing. These political and cultural patterns were difficult for advocates to see while working "in the trenches" on a day-to-day basis. Yet, analyzing them is important. No matter how well designed, civil and criminal reforms still rely on advocates—primarily women—to do much of the work administering them. As a result, we should understand how and why the "helpers" subjectively experience legal work as exciting and rewarding.

Evolving Stance toward the Criminal Justice System

In isolation, the advocates' eagerness to delve into legal remedies may appear to be a product of idiosyncratic preferences and personalities. However, there is also a pattern to their experiences: their excitement toward legal work was enabled by the gradual integration of DV and SA agencies with local criminal justice entities. Decades earlier, the movement vanguard fought tirelessly for the better treatment of victims by cops, judges, and lawyers. They pushed for comprehensive legal changes to streamline paperwork, treat victims with more respect in court, and ensure that first responders were sensitive to the dynamics of abuse. In many of these political struggles, they have made real progress. Lawmakers who were previously indifferent to the plight of violence against women now see places like SAFE as potential allies in their movement to get "tough on crime."

In recent decades, more and more prosecutors' offices have adopted "no-drop" policies that allow for "evidence-based prosecution" to counteract abusers' tactic of intimidating victims to "drop the charges" against them during criminal and civil proceedings.[10] Mandatory arrest policies have denied law enforcement officers the ability to let dangerous abusers off with a warning (Morgan and Coombes 2013). The Violence Against Women Act of 1994 (and reauthorized in 2013) has made protective orders more accessible, restricted abusers' access to firearms, made stalking a crime, and added interstate provisions to make some forms of DV and SA that carry federal penalties (Moracco et al. 2010). Additionally, a series of state and federal grants have funded "coordinated community response" programs to enable local agencies such as SAFE to work with legal, medical, and social services institutions to fight abuse. These reforms have meant more and better services for victims nationwide. This does not mean the fight is over—political battles continue to this day—but it does complicate SAFE's oppositional stance toward the criminal justice system. Nowadays, victim advocates and counselors coordinate with legal representatives in ways that would have seemed alien in the 1960s and '70s.

One consequence of this investment in the legal process for places like SAFE has been a shift in organizational philosophies. Whereas before, DV and SA agencies operated according to principles like "shared decision making, limited hierarchies, and a mission-driven approach to service linked to feminist principles"; over time, these hard-and-fast rules have become blurred: "The acceptance of private and public funds often bound these agencies to the rules and regulations of their funders, including documentation and evaluation" (Bennett, Riger, Schewe, Howard, and Wasco 2004:816). Winning grant monies may mean helping more clients, but it also means abiding by a new set of rules. Empowering women to regain power and control over their lives may be a worthy goal, but how do you determine precisely whether it has been achieved? Federal and state funding agencies want evidence. How do you show them that this qualitative transformation has occurred?

Legal victories are easier to measure. To show that their victim advocacy and counseling has helped clients, places like SAFE can count the number of abusers in jail, protective orders approved, and custody decisions in clients' favor. In contrast, to demonstrate their effectiveness at empowering clients to take control of their lives, they can only offer anecdotes of clients "becoming whole." This kind of information is less quantifiable and thus less persuasive according to the rubrics outlined in funding protocols. As a result, after DV and SA agencies fought for and won reforms from legal institutions, they were then held accountable by their standards and methods of measuring results.

Although the political successes of the DV and SA movement explain why agencies like SAFE would try newly reformed legal remedies, it is not enough to say that they would continue to use them if they did not work. And there was a general perception at SAFE that they did. Even though staff members commonly derided protective orders as "just a piece of paper," they were still regarded as one of the strongest cards victims had to play. During the time I conducted research, the advocates processed—on average—two hundred protective orders each year. This frequency was not unique to SAFE. More than a million protective orders are issued in the United States each year (Tjaden and Thoennes 2000). Most studies have found that protective orders do help; however, if an abuser already has a criminal record, they have much less of a deterrent effect (Jordan, Pritchard, Duckett, and Charnigo 2010). Thus, like the advocates argued, they have shortcomings. In the United States, 60 percent of protective orders are violated each year, and fewer than half of those violations result in arrests (Tjaden and Thoennes 2000). Despite these limitations, a recent meta-analysis of all research on protective orders found that they generally lead to a slight decrease in physical violence (Fleury-Steiner, Fleury-Steiner, and Miller 2011).

The same positive—yet mixed—support applies to arrest warrants. Under the right circumstances, they can offer victims a significant amount of protection. However, these benefits can also be quickly outweighed by other mediating factors (Buzawa and Buzawa 1996; 2003). If the abuser is already unemployed, for example, an arrest may exacerbate "assaultive behavior" (Iovanni and Miller 2001:303-27).

Yet, focusing exclusively on the effectiveness of protective orders and arrest warrants sidesteps an important but often overlooked aspect of work inside DV and SA agencies. Why did the advocates derive so much satisfaction from the act of legal work itself? They were trained to view this work with skepticism. The evidence of the effectiveness of legal remedies was positive, but by no means overwhelming. Something else was going on. Legal reforms and funding incentives help explain the wider movement toward criminal justice solutions, but there is an additional reason why legal remedies garnered so much respect in the SAFE office and the culture at large.

When reviewing the statements made by Kelly and the advocates during the time I spent with them, it became clear that they found something special about legal work. Again and again, I heard the same stock phrases ("It's concrete," "It's immediate") to describe how satisfying this work was in relation to their other duties. The reason Kelly went to such great lengths to train the advocates not to rush into legal remedies is that she knew—from experience—that they would be drawn to it because of the straightforwardness of the work. She described how filing paperwork and getting signatures from judges can be "comforting to people. It feels like they've really done something." What are the implications of Kelly's statement for the staff members' other forms of help? Why were they unable to derive similar satisfaction from their care work services: listening, sympathizing, and safety planning? These are worthy and noble services, yet they did not garner the same amount of excitement as legal work. Why?

The Devaluation of Women's Care Work

Inside the SAFE office, care work practices earned a lot of respect. Heather would often listen to her clients at length, at times letting fifteen to twenty minutes go by before interrupting them with a question or a comment. Any time a client "opened up" about her past or expressed optimism about her future would be a victory for Heather. She would smile and bask in the after-glow of successful "sit and talk" sessions with clients, describing the emotional reward she got from these sessions. Lisa also took pride in her caring ability, saying that during the years she had acquired an ability to connect with her clients: "With women, I know the words to say to them, to help them see that light again." She described her work with clients as fostering a special bond; she talked about it in mystical terms: "I feel it. I see us as healers . . . and being a conduit for that . . . I feel people are affected by that."

Quiet and private time with clients could be moving and special at SAFE. Shelter staff, for example, described the increased amount of time spent alone with residents as a "bonding experience." Christina described the purpose of her job as shelter director as creating a "nurturing place . . . to help with stability and peace." As we can see, the emotional component of their work was very important to them. This was evident in the ways that they reminded each other to cherish the "little" moments when things went well. Simply getting a phone call from a client updating her progress, for example, could change their whole day. In sum, at SAFE, caring mattered; it helped them feel good about their work. Exchanging emotional sentiment with the clients they helped was part of their moral identity code as victim advocates and counselors. Living up to this code garnered a sustaining and heartfelt sense of satisfaction. In my terms, effectively delivering this kind of care work earned them moral wages. However, this emotional subculture was not the only environment in which the advocates lived. What earned respect inside the office did not necessarily garner the same outside of it.

The SAFE advocates believed that outsiders respected their care work abilities—but not as much as they ought to. For an example, remember Meg's account of how her brother was not impressed by her advice until she pointed out her legal experience. Or consider the generic ways that legal work can be articulated that caring work cannot. To "sit and listen" to a client for hours requires considerable patience and experience. And the stakes are high—without establishing a trusting relationship, a client might leave to return to an abusive and potentially lethal situation. But the advocates reported that many of their friends and family—although sympathetic—had a hard time listening to these care work success stories. The topics were not only emotionally troubling (as was their legal work), but the complexity of their clients' lives could not be explained as easily as courtroom dramas could. Although most people will never step foot in a courtroom, they "know" how it works through popular media depictions in ways that they do not understand care work with victims.

Staff members' disappointment that their work was often misunderstood and underappreciated did not occur in a vacuum: it was caused by the larger devaluation of care work in our culture. On a large scale, the interpersonal skills of the advocates are not highly valued by outsiders. This is primarily due to stereotypical assumptions that any woman can exhibit them. As a result, because care work skills are seen as coming naturally to women, the SAFE advocates had a hard time getting credit for them. As sociologist Ashley Mears explains this perspective, as long as "women are devalued in our society relative to men, jobs associated with women, and especially those coupled with women's essential 'nature' (such as being nurturing and expressive) are devalued by association" (2011:216).[11] Viewed from this angle, the allure of legal work becomes more reasonable. Staff members were not drifting away from SAFE policies out of disregard for their clients' safety or rogue ambition; they wanted to help their clients. But they also wanted some degree of credit and respect for their specialized skills and training. Legal work offered this opportunity in ways that their care work did not.[12]

This is not fair, but gendered arrangements never are. Sociologists of gender and work have long documented the ways that men earn more in the workplace than women. Yet, the reasons for income disparities are not entirely due to women earning less for the same work than men (although there is evidence of that). Instead, the primary cause of gender inequality in regard to earnings is job segregation. That is, jobs most often associated with men pay more than jobs associated with women. This is not because females are biologically incapable of doing "men's jobs." It is because of the subtle mechanisms that funnel women and men into gender "appropriate" occupations. For example, when those who recruit, hire, and promote people consider who might be the best fit for a job that requires empathizing and sympathizing with victims, they think of women. When they consider who might be the best fit for a job that requires aggression, assertiveness, and "inexpressiveness" (Sattel 1976), they think of men. Of course, there are exceptions (Mears 2011), but the trend is clear (Cohen, Huffman, and Knauer 2009).

"Women's work" typically involves attending to the emotional needs of others, based on the popular assumption that women are innately suited to occupations that require "emotion work" (Hochschild 1983). The association of women with emotions is so strong in American culture that caring is the central activity that defines women as women (DeVault 1991). One consequence of this popular belief, however, is that no matter how well women in caring occupations (like the advocates at SAFE) listen, empathize, and sympathize with their clients, there are few symbolic and economic rewards for their abilities.

These stereotypes about women, and the subsequent devaluation of their care work, help explain why the SAFE advocates were drawn toward legal work in ways that their policies and training cannot explain. Whether it was because friends and family were more impressed by some work stories than others, or because grant applications asked for quantitative evidence of success, it was easier to get credit for their legal work. Again, independent of gender, managing clients' emotions is no less difficult than handling legal paperwork and procedures, but the SAFE advocates did not live in a world independent of gender.

In this cultural context, the technocratic and adversarial skills on display in the courtroom were more socially valuable for the SAFE advocates because they were displaying skills typically associated with men. Thus, when they exhibited their expertise in this stereotypically masculine domain, they earned even more respect because they were stepping outside of their "innate" abilities and fighting for clients on hostile—gendered—turf. When they stayed inside the SAFE office, their affectual and interpersonal skills associated with "women's work" earned quieter and more subdued forms of praise—and what recognition it did receive came mostly from others who did the same kind of work. They earned moral wages in exchange for these activities, to be sure, but sometimes the advocates wanted to see themselves as more than just caring and compassionate. They wanted to believe that they had done something specific and tangible for their clients. The courtroom helped them come to that conclusion. And the reason it was such an impressive venue in which to excel was that it represented all of the things that SAFE was not. It was "men's work," even when women were doing it.

The satisfaction they earned from their care work, however, was a largely hidden experience. I witnessed these moments as brief embers of sentiment, but only because I was doing fieldwork. I might have missed them had I not been looking closely. Other advocates saw them, too, but their responses— subdued smiles—were quiet occurrences. When it came to care work "wins," there were no office-wide celebrations. There were no high fives after sit-and-listen sessions. Through both care and legal work, clients benefited as a result of their advocates' help. Yet there were clear differences in the recognition the advocates garnered afterward. Care work wins were private, and produced slow rolling currents of positive feeling; legal work wins were public, and churned steep crests of elation (and despair). These differences were not random; they are part of a larger pattern of how "women's work" is rewarded across occupations today.

CONCLUSION

My objective in this chapter was not to argue that legal remedies are somehow good or bad, or should be used in some instances but not others. Rather, I highlighted the dilemma posed by legal work for victim advocates. On the one hand, they are trained not to rush into legal remedies and prioritize "sitting and listening" as part of their empowering approach to victim services. Yet, to adhere to this approach and focus primarily on caring would be to engage in work that is generally devalued in the American marketplace— especially when women do it. In a perfect world, they could accomplish both—getting credit for their care work while also engaging in legal work with the confidence that cops, lawyers, and judges would treat their clients with consideration and respect. But the world of victim advocacy and counseling is not perfect; people who work inside places like SAFE cannot control how others value their work or how the criminal justice system treats victims. Instead, they make the best of a difficult situation.

In the case of legal work, the dilemma I analyze in this chapter is largely a product of the high standards outlined in SAFE staff members' moral identity code. They are not only expected to help their clients heal and keep them free from harm, they are asked to do it with a weary eye directed toward an imposing criminal justice system that has failed so many victims in the past (Bumiller 2009; Matthews 1994) and continues to fail so many of them today (Corrigan 2013). Had they trusted the legal system, this dilemma would not exist. But they did not trust it—and for good reason. Until the criminal justice system can prevent clients like Shelly from being murdered, it will never earn their full and complete confidence.

Although the risks and rewards of legal work were hard to manage, SAFE staff members found a way. They resolved their competing desires (to care for their clients, to be validated for their ability to help clients get justice) by putting the focus back on clients' outcomes. Even though they were drawn to legal work more than their policies and training would suggest, they still believed that the ends—helping their clients in immediate and concrete ways—justified the means. Legal work may have presented some worrisome risks, but it also offered their clients the chance to experience unambiguous and powerful wins.

I admit that although I was surprised at first by how drawn staff members were to legal work, by the end of my research I came to understand it more clearly. For one, I experienced the pressure and rush of getting a legal task done myself, and that helped me to better see their work through their eyes. But the allure of legal work also made sense for a different reason. In a job that largely offered symbolic compensation—like moral wages—in exchange for hard work under tough conditions for low wages, is it any surprise that they would make the most of every opportunity to earn credit and respect for their special skills? Is it any surprise that when the new legal advocate position opened up, every advocate would apply for the job? At the beginning of the DV and SA movement in the 1960s and '70s, it would have been shocking to see such eagerness to work as a liaison with the Sheriff's Department and the District Attorney's Office. Yet, things have changed. The organizational philosophies of places like SAFE are evolving—a process incentivized by legislation like the Violence Against Women Act. Meanwhile, there are no comparable cultural shifts in the valuation of women's caring labor. As a result, the stigma associated with legal work inside places like SAFE is slowly fading away.

In the next chapter, I analyze one final emotional dilemma. The victim advocates and counselors at SAFE were well aware of popular stereotypes about them. Hostile skeptics often claim that places like SAFE are filled with "man-hater" zealots (Huisman, Martinez, and Wilson 2005). In a small way, there is some truth to this stereotype. The advocates and counselors at SAFE *were* leery of men who abused their clients—and they worried about them coming to the office to seek revenge. However, for the most part, they were very welcoming to men. And they needed men. SAFE was staffed almost entirely by women, but a few men did work within the organization. More important, SAFE staff members depended upon the help of men in other local organizations and the wider community for support. Being seen as dismissive of and hostile toward all men could harm their reputation and influence. Thus, "man-hater" stereotypes could impede their ability to help their clients. As a result, they wanted to dispel rumors that they found all men unacceptable, even though there were some men they would not tolerate. This created a difficult dilemma: they needed some men's help, but did not want to open their doors to all of them indiscriminately.

CHAPTER SIX

Men at Work

When I meet new people and tell them about my experiences at SAFE (Stopping Abuse in Family Environments), I usually get one of two responses. The first is typically a quick acknowledgment that it must be emotionally challenging to spend so much time in a place like that. This reaction is understandable and reveals the moral terrain that victim advocates and counselors travel on a daily basis. Outsiders have a lot of respect for people who help victims. Even skeptics of places like SAFE still indicate some degree of admiration for people who help others in need. It is not an easy job. It is a "dirty job," but not in the ways we typically think of messy work. The residue of hours spent on the hotline or "safety planning" with a client does not come out in the wash. The effects are hard to see, and their invisibility makes rinsing them away all the much harder. That people feel compelled to acknowledge this to me underscores the value-laden nature of their work.

The next most common response I get goes something like this: "So, what is it like, being a man inside a place like SAFE?" My answer usually surprises them: being a man made my research easier. Some find this hard to believe—pressing me to admit that the women I studied were leery of my presence or otherwise eager for me to leave because they did not trust men. I first respond by telling them that these stereotypes are caricatures drawn up by hostile cynics. But, if they seem genuinely curious and concerned about the inner workings of places like SAFE, I reveal that there is a grain of truth to their suspicions. At first, the women at SAFE *were* suspicious of me. Before agreeing to my initial request to meet and discuss my research project, they checked up on me (I later learned) with their friends at the agency where I did my volunteer work. Upon arrival, they asked me a lot of questions. They waited a few weeks before telling me the location of the shelter. Their guarded approach is understandable. Not many men stop by the office; and when unfamiliar ones do, staff members trace their path to the front door with watchful eyes. However, if men can pass a series of tests—which I outline later in the chapter—their presence is welcomed, if not applauded.

In this chapter, I analyze the dilemma that men pose for victim advocates and counselors at work. Some men were seen as unacceptable, and keeping them away from SAFE was seen by staff as the best way to protect themselves and their clients; but turning away too many men away could—indirectly—impede their ability to help their clients. They were torn about how to proceed.

Obviously, abusers were not tolerated at SAFE. Instances of angry men looking for their ex-wives—or someone to yell at—were rare, but they did happen. The location of the shelter was not publicized, but the address of the main office was well known in town. As a result, a consistent trickle of men—including those with good intentions—had a way of making its way to SAFE's door. Theoretically, new men offering assistance would be welcome with open arms. However, as I show, some men brought with them strange ideas about how to help. "Macho" guys looking for chances to teach abusers a lesson, or "creepy" men seeming a bit too eager to spend time with vulnerable women were to be shown the door at the first available opportunity. Yet, despite the potential risks of letting in the wrong men, being too restrictive could also cause a different set of complications.

Places like SAFE need men. This is not because men are somehow better suited to help victims or solve their problems, but because highlighting the presence of men is an effective way for victim advocates and counselors to push back against the "man-hater" stereotype that makes their job more difficult. Places like SAFE have faced a political backlash since their inception. The existence of battered women's shelters and rape crisis centers stirs strong emotions among both supporters and detractors. This is because places like SAFE serve as reminders that violence against women is a persistent social problem. Such a claim can be threatening to some.

To those accustomed to the way intimate relationships work today, rethinking the deeper root causes of abuse means entertaining the notion that domestic violence and sexual assault (DV and SA) are not just the random outbursts of psychologically flawed individuals. If the cause is broader—at the societal level—then almost everyone is implicated in its reproduction. Thus, to accept the perspective of places like SAFE is to think critically about the institution of gender as a whole. The prospect of such an alternative worldview can cause an angry mixture of shame, fear, and resentment in some. These emotions ebb and flow in our culture, but victim advocates and counselors bear the brunt of them; they are constant targets for slurs old ("bitch") and new ("feminazi") (Anderson, Kanner, and Elsayegh 2009; Maier 2008b). The feelings these terms indicate are the viral strains on which the man-hater trope thrives in our culture, and this stereotype—more than any other—made their work difficult on a daily basis.

In most cases, staff members could dismiss insults directed toward them as vapid bluster, but some attacks they could not let go unanswered. In practical terms, they knew that these labels could (unfairly) hamper their ability to do their job. The more lawyers and judges saw them as overly biased, the harder it was to defend their clients' interests in court. If dispatchers believed that staff members would say anything to get back at men, they might be slow to send sheriff's deputies to enforce protective orders. The advocates and counselors at SAFE had thick skins—they could tolerate harsh language—but they did not want stereotypes about them to indirectly harm their clients. As a result, the social and political landscape in which places like SAFE operate have put advocates and counselors in a bind. Opening their office doors to all men could potentially invite danger, yet not letting any men in would breathe life into the stereotypes that hindered their work. Neither option was desirable.

As with the other dilemmas in this book, SAFE staff members found a way out of this predicament. They did this by first subjecting new men to a series of litmus tests. Like abusers, men who were seen as "tough guys" or otherwise harboring questionable intentions were screened out. For those who passed these tests (like me), their relationship with SAFE was underlined as a signifier of the organization's inclusivity. Although I would like to think that my invitation into the SAFE community was based entirely upon my sensitivity and knowledge of DV- and SA-related issues, that assumption would be naïve. My (and other men's) presence served an additional purpose. By showcasing the participation of men in the movement, DV and SA agencies can deflate the man-hater image that makes their job harder. This is what I mean when I say that places like SAFE need men. We—myself included—inoculate places like SAFE against accusations that they are places where *all* men are seen as the enemy.

Becoming a male insider did not happen automatically, though. I first had to prove myself and allay their fears. However, once I was accepted, I was applauded. In exchange for my genuine interest in their work, I earned a *progressive merit badge* of sorts that signified that I "got it" when it came to women's issues.[1] Once affixed (metaphorically), I became eligible for "extra credit" as a guy who understood their point of view and willingly affiliated with their mission. This phenomenon is not unique to the fight against DV and SA; members of privileged social groups who express solidarity with progressive causes or organizations earn their own kinds of merit badges, too. The implications of this process deserve attention: for the men associated with SAFE, their special status paid off in real ways both inside and outside the agency.

To analyze the causes and consequences of privileging men like me, I begin by explaining how the pattern of doling out progressive merit badges is indicative of the structurally weak positions inhabited by places like SAFE and the women who work in them. As an organization, SAFE rewarded "good" men in this way because they needed their help yet had little else to offer in return. Institutions that have traditionally served the needs of victims (legal, medical, and social service) do not have to make similar bargains with men. Additionally, were it not for the man-hater stereotype that made SAFE staff members' work more difficult, men's contribution to the cause would not have seemed so valuable. Women do not receive as much admiration for their commitment and effort; their participation in the struggle is seen as admirable—but expected. In the wider cultural context, the burden of "fixing" DV and SA is still women's to bear.

As I argued in chapter 5, because women are seen as innate nurturers, they are not sufficiently rewarded for accomplishing tasks like empathizing, listening, sympathizing; women are assumed to do these things naturally. In this chapter, I analyze the flip side of this argument. I show how men can parley small amounts of caring at places like SAFE into disproportion-ately large amounts of social esteem. As long as helping victims is seen as women's work, men who lend a hand can earn accolades for simply stick-ing around. Thus, men affiliated with women's organizations can accrue more appreciation while doing less. Later in the chapter, I show how grant-ing symbolic rewards like progressive merit badges (to men) and moral wages (to women) may help places like SAFE recruit and retain the staff members and affiliates they need to help victims, but this strategy also comes at a cost: symbolic compensation schemes often obscure workplace inequalities.

Although I enjoyed my time at SAFE, the extra credit I received during my time there came with a twinge of guilt. The other men and I did less for the movement, but were appreciated (as men) for cleaning up a mess that other men created. These pats on the back may seem trivial, but they are not. Handing out progressive merit badges should not be dismissed as merely a polite gesture; its use within places like SAFE signals a lack of sufficient tools to combat a pervasive social problem. It is because these resources are likely not coming any time soon that all of the emotional dilemmas outlined in this book will likely persist for advocates and counselors in the indefinite future.

PROGRESSIVE MERIT BADGES

By the phrase "earning their progressive merit badges," I mean the ways that members of privileged groups can accrue symbolic credit by virtue of their "special affiliate" status with progressive causes or organizations. These badges signal a person's sensitivity and commitment to aid others in their fight against persistent social problems. Progressive merit badges were selectively doled out to men who helped out at SAFE (I earned one), but they are not exclusive to the fight against DV and SA. For example, the wealthy can earn them by coordinating volunteers to serve food in soup kitchens; whites can earn them by helping to organize events on Martin Luther King day; heterosexuals can earn them by recruiting friends to walk in pride parades. In short, they are earned by helping others solve *their* problems, not one's own.

To be clear, progressive merit badges are not conferred automatically; one must work to earn them.[2] Members of less privileged groups are wary of fair weather friends who wish to use them as props for photo opportunities. However, despite their guarded skepticism, the less powerful still need allies. Consequently, for each hour that members of privileged groups volunteer, organize, or march, the closer they become to being considered "different" by virtue of their commitment to solving the problems faced by those less fortunate.

Ironically, the more privilege one enjoys, the smoother the path to earning a progressive merit badge. We do not look twice when members of beleaguered communities mobilize and work on their own behalf; we assume they do so out of self-interest. We expect the poor to lament the effects of poverty. We expect people of color to fight racism. We expect members of the queer community to call out heterosexist policies. It is the participation of people in these causes who do *not* suffer the same injustices that catch our attention. Their presence is deemed special by virtue of its apparent selflessness. This is why the presence of men inside a place like SAFE was seen as surprising, and thus admirable.

Rather than suffer because of their "rare" status, men benefited from it. This is not always the case for minorities. Research in the sociology of work has found that for women and non-whites, being the token representative of another gender or race means being treated (at best) with indifference or passive aggressiveness (Kanter 1977). However, for men, being a token can be a good thing—at least for those working in female-dominated occupations (nursing, elementary school teaching, social work, and librarianship). They do not suffer because they are few in number. Instead, studies like the one conducted by sociologist Christine Williams (1992) have shown that men ride a "glass escalator" to the top of these "women's" occupations on the basis of their special status. Williams interviewed women in these workplaces and found that they genuinely believed that the presence of men was an asset to the organization. They would fast-track male teachers to get them out of the kindergarten classroom and into the principal's office. These men were treated as rare and valuable commodities—not as obligatory tokens. In these settings, Williams found that the leaders of these organizations saw these men as special *because* of their willingness to work on foreign terrain, not in spite of it.

Men at SAFE rode a glass escalator of sorts, but with one important distinction. Their special treatment was not contingent on full-fledged membership or allegiance. They were granted a symbolic badge of honor from SAFE, but as tangential "associates" only. They worked with SAFE, but not *for* SAFE; and this positioning was to their benefit. It served as a hedge against social penalties that trivialize men who claim to be singularly devoted to "women's" causes.

Although men risk ridicule from other men for spending so much time in a "women's place" like SAFE, they can also refurbish their manhood by pointing to their "real" jobs as evidence of their masculinity. Men engage in these kinds of trade-offs all the time. As long as they can successfully signify their masculinity through "manly" acts (like exhibiting physical strength or earning wages) most of the time, their claims to manhood can withstand critique for engaging in "non-manly" acts some of the time (Ezzell 2012; Schrock and Schwalbe 2009). For example, sheriff's deputies could work with SAFE and be seen as trusted confidants, yet project an image of manhood with their peers back in the department. They could do this in two ways. Either they could be selective about to whom they showed their progressive merit badges—revealing their association with a women's organization to some but not others. Or, if they were mocked for being too sensitive, they could easily point to other skills or experiences that bolstered their "rough" identity as law enforcement officers. Thus working toward— and accepting—a progressive merit badge is a relatively low risk "side bet" (Becker 1960) for men whose toughness (physically and interpersonally) has been previously established.[3] In some career tracks, the payout for being seen as both masculine and sensitive to women's issues can be quite high.

In my experience, earning a progressive merit badge from SAFE was not particularly hard. Sure, I had to pass a series of tests, but to prove one is not an abuser, for example, is a pretty low hurdle to clear. At the end of my volunteer training, I did not have to utter a word during our "graduation" ceremony in order to be pulled aside and told by an elderly woman from the community that she was so glad to see "men getting involved." To be fair, the men who earned their progressive merit badges at SAFE *were* "different" than most men. These men were accepted into SAFE's community because they offered special and valuable services that the advocates and counselors needed. Most (but not all) of these men could clearly and persuasively talk about DV and SA in a way that showed that they understood how the causes of abuse were a product of wider patriarchal currents within our culture. Men who can articulate these kinds of ideas are rare. Yet, because they were men, they (and I) also benefited from simply "being there" in ways that the women with more experience and commitment to SAFE did not.

Litmus Tests

Because SAFE was almost entirely composed of women, the question of how staff members should interact with men was a tricky one. SAFE workers were skeptical of unknown men—and rightly so. Statistically, many more men abuse women than vice versa (National Coalition Against Domestic Violence 2007). In regard to reported crimes (a conservative estimate), 85 percent of victims of intimate partner violence are women (Catalano 2012). However, when taking into account self-reports, the difference becomes much greater. For example, nearly one in five women (living in the United States today) are estimated to have been raped in their lifetime compared to one in seventy-one men (Black et al. 2011). Hence, the advocates and counselors saw their services as geared almost exclusively toward women. Even though they knew that not all men were abusers, they still checked to be sure.

Interactions with men were not the norm in the SAFE office. Men from affiliated organizations came to the SAFE office for meetings with staff members, but not many, and not every day (with the exception of Paul, from the Sheriff's Department, whom I discuss in more detail later in the chapter). There were even fewer male clients. During more than a year of research, of the hundreds of cases I observed, only one involved a man who staff members believed had actually suffered abuse, and this case involved a father who feared physical abuse from his son. In four other cases, men sought services from SAFE, but their stated concerns were to protect their children or a female relative. Also, in six other cases, staff members believed that men had sought out SAFE services as a means to enact revenge on their female partners (such as a man seeking an arrest warrant for his female partner after he had been released from jail).

Although it was rare for abusers to come to the SAFE office, it did happen. For example, when a client's estranged husband came to the SAFE office looking for their children (who were upstairs in the counselors' office), staff members quickly came out of their offices to see what was causing all the commotion. While yelling for h'is children to come downstairs, he complained loudly about how upset he was that a court order had recently stripped him of custody rights. As a result, Heather quickly called sheriff's deputies to escort him out of the building (without the children). No one was hurt, but after this encounter staff redoubled their efforts to assess the threat of newcomer men.

Simply not being an abuser, however, was not enough. Staff members also could reject men on account of their "questionable" intentions. They feared that some men purposefully sought out victims for romantic relationships. They worried that their clients—having been treated so badly for so long—were especially susceptible to being fooled or tricked by men who showed them the least bit of kindness. They rejected one man for this reason after he approached staff with an offer to give free "self-defense" classes to SAFE clients. Although staff members were initially receptive to the idea of free classes, this man's zealousness worked against him. Lisa commented, "He just seemed to be salivating at the idea of it. He was just too into it." She went on to describe his "wild eyes" and his various "creepy qualities" that staff interpreted as a desire to gain access to vulnerable women. When pressed for his qualifications, it turned out he had none (other than being a manager at a nearby supermarket). Later, when discussing the man's offer, staff reminded each other how important it was to protect their clients from men "too" interested in spending time with victims of DV and SA.

Staff members were not only on guard for questionable men for their clients' sake, they were also on the lookout to protect themselves, too. The advocates and counselors believed that some men feigned being "sensitive" as a way to date women who work at places like SAFE. Staff members believed these men would express their appreciation for SAFE's work as a ploy to distance themselves from other hostile and skeptical men. They described this variation of "creepy" men as hard to ferret out, but not impossible. The most likely telltale sign would be professing an interest in DV and SA, but being unable to articulate anything more than a superficial understanding of the topic. Unknown men who claimed to know everything about SAFE and its mission immediately raised red flags throughout the office.

Staff members were careful to screen for these kinds of duplicitous men—sometimes too careful. I learned this because it almost kept them from interacting with a male colleague of mine, Steve, who had worked in the DV and SA movement for more than a decade. One afternoon, I overheard Lisa talking about an unnerving e-mail she had received unsolicited from a man whose name she recognized from a local feminist Internet discussion group. As it turned out, Steve had sent her an article about the harmful consequences of gendered language (in particular, the use of male generics, like "you guys," to refer to groups including women). Lisa remembered Steve's name from somewhere, but she could not place it at first. This put her on guard.

Although the content of Steve's e-mail was in line with Lisa's general thoughts on gender and culture, she thought the tone and wording of the message was "too familiar . . . like he knew me, or knew about me, more than he did." When I asked Lisa why she was wary about the e-mail, she said that even though she remembered Steve's name from the online feminist discussion group, "a lot of guys join [that group] just so they can meet women." This was ironic. Steve had worked in a rape crisis center in an adjacent county for years and had also organized a campaign for men to speak out against abuse. He was well known in the community for his position regarding violence against women. Yet, his knowledge and implied familiarity with SAFE sent up the wrong signals when Lisa opened her e-mail from him because she did not remember precisely who he was. When I jogged her memory, she quickly put it all together—where he worked, where they had met before—and a wave of relief washed over her: "Oh, okay, that solves that mystery." Over the next few months, Lisa and I would later joke about the e-mail and her initial concerns about Steve. Of all the men in the region, few "got it" when it came to DV and SA better than Steve. However, this case of mistaken identity was directly related to the dilemma faced by advocates and counselors regarding men at work. They wanted—and needed—to keep in touch with men who could act as political allies; however, they were also on the lookout for questionable men who were out to take advantage of SAFE staff members and their clients. Being too lax could put them in danger, but being too restrictive could sever community ties and potential resources for their clients.

Men who could show that they genuinely wanted to help victims of DV and SA still had to pass one final test. They had to articulate the right reasons for wanting to help. Specifically, staff members screened potential male allies to exclude those only interested in threatening and intimidating abusers. The last thing the advocates and counselors needed was men who wanted to help clients get revenge, or to find abusers in order to "teach them a lesson." These overly macho men were barely tolerated—and they most certainly were not awarded progressive merit badges. SAFE advocates and counselors saw their role as "empowering" victims, not lecturing abusers. They tried to avoid men who wanted to do the latter.

This test was most often applied to law enforcement. Staff members paid close attention to the intentions and motivations of sheriff's deputies. In one case, the advocates asked a sheriff's deputy to come to SAFE as a precautionary measure in case of confrontation between a client and her abuser. The abuser was scheduled to drop the client's belongings at the SAFE office, and staff members wanted someone from law enforcement to watch the exchange, but do so from a distance (so as to not to provoke or enrage the man). Because the usual liaison from the Sheriff's Department (Paul) was unavailable, the dispatcher sent a deputy relatively unfamiliar with the agency, Phil. When he arrived, staff members were skeptical. Lisa was especially concerned: "[Phil seemed] excited about working on the case . . . chomping at the bit. . . . I was worried that he could potentially make things worse. To me, he seemed like a guy who is green at this, like he wants to make a speech." At SAFE, "making a speech" was code for guys who wanted to show off in front of women by yelling at or taunting abusers. Before a male deputy could earn SAFE staff members' respect, he had to show them that he understood that confrontation was not helpful. To earn his progressive merit badge, he had to show that he was different from other men.

Once men passed their litmus tests, they gained full acceptance at SAFE. Of course, they could slip up and lose their standing, but this rarely happened. The reason for this was that progressive merit badges became more valuable and durable over time. By simply by doing no wrong, "special" men associated with SAFE earned more and more credit on the basis of their continued presence. Even when these men were not around, they would occasionally come up in conversation as staff members would cite past evidence of their persuasiveness in court or their sensitivity to a client. Without evidence to the contrary, these men's initial investment of goodwill earned interest—bolstering staff members' beliefs that they were not like other men.

Once men's special standing had been established, they could cash in their progressive merit badges. How and how much depended on context. As with all markers of social capital, we never really know their value until they are brought to market. As it turned out, these symbolic credentials came in handy both inside and outside the agency.

The Value of a Progressive Merit Badge

Inside the agency, progressive merit badges came in handy in a number of ways. Men who had earned them were allowed to publicly disagree with the agency's policies. To see this at play, consider the case of Tammy, the difficult client described at length in chapter 4. Tammy was the client who had used her rent allowance to buy drugs. Additionally, she had disregarded SAFE staff members' repeated warnings and moved in with a known abuser. When the advocates mentioned her name to Paul (the sheriff's deputy revered at SAFE) in a court hallway one day, he bluntly stated that he had little sympathy for Tammy. His vocal criticism was surprisingly harsh: "She's in jail, and she deserves to be in jail." The SAFE advocates seemed a little surprised by his remarks, but indicated their silent agreement by nodding their heads. I had never observed them let someone criticize a client like that in court. True, they were at their wits' end with Tammy at the time and were likely thinking the same thing, but they never voiced their concerns in public like that. Yet, Paul was granted this license. And this was not the only time. He had special permission to "tell it like it is" about SAFE clients in ways that staff members could not. Had he been a newcomer, or any other sheriff's deputy, the advocates and counselors would have likely severed ties. However, because Paul had passed SAFE's litmus tests long before, he was allowed.

Paul's progressive merit badge also allowed him to defend men's interests in ways that other men could not. Lisa offered an example of this when she recounted a time that she traveled with Paul and Phil (the deputy whom Lisa initially labeled as "green") to a conference on legal issues around DV and SA. Although most conferences like this are attended almost exclusively by women (as presenters and audience members), some are devoted to criminal justice approaches and subsequently bring out a large number of men from law enforcement backgrounds. Of these, cops and sheriff's deputies are subject to the most scrutiny by advocates and counselors: "I think there is an initial skepticism of men and why they are there." The sessions during these conferences can be contentious if any men in the audience disagree with a speaker or presenter. Lisa recounted a time when one man at a conference rejected a claim that most SAFE staff members took for granted—the general belief that abuse is a way for men to exert power and control over women. At SAFE such a claim would go unquestioned as a matter of fact. When the man at the conference disagreed, the audience was shocked. Lisa chalked up his skepticism as typical among most cops and sheriff's deputies. Men who voiced such skepticism were not offered a progressive merit badge.

Although Lisa believed that Paul (and to a lesser extent, Phil) were different from "most men" on the grounds that they "got it" about DV and SA, their behavior was not perfect, either. Upon Lisa's return from the conference, she complained that they did not take the conference seriously. During her private interview, Lisa told me that Paul and Phil found excuses to sneak away from the conference to go to a bar in town. She also said that during the conference they made more than one comment that SAFE was overly biased against men and that sometimes women were not entirely innocent, either. In short, Lisa was accusing Paul and Phil of the same bad behavior she expected of other unenlightened law enforcement officers. Yet, in the end, she still credited Paul and Phil for their willingness to attend in the first place. They might not have taken the conference as seriously as she would have liked, but their commitment and understanding of issues related to DV and SA were undoubtedly better than the other cops and sheriff's deputies at the conference. In other words, to Lisa, Paul and Phil may not have been perfect, but they were better than the rest; and for that, they were given a pass for their behavior during the trip.

Progressive merit badges shielded men from accountability if their services were not completely in line with SAFE policy. This was the case with Lucas, an independent contractor who served as a facilitator in SAFE's batterer intervention program. Some of the advocates in the office were skeptical of his services—Cathleen once confided to me in court that Lucas was too easy on abusers, vouching for their behavior despite the doubts of other staff members. During one hearing when an abuser sought to get his charges reduced, she leaned over to Lisa and whispered: "He's an alcoholic, and Lucas has said that he isn't." Yet, despite his leniency with abusers, SAFE needed Lucas. Nationwide, batterer intervention programs use mixed-gender teams (one man and one woman) as facilitators. Because SAFE had a hard time recruiting and training male facilitators—partly because of the man-hater stereotype—Lucas was relatively irreplaceable. To maintain his position, he did not have to be flawless; he just had to be the best available.

Outside the agency, progressive merit badges opened doors for men along their current—or desired—career paths. In Lucas's case, he was able to create and promote his own private "men's rehabilitation" consulting business. Men accused of abuse would often be referred to his program to take educational classes on drug abuse and anger management. Because he was affiliated with SAFE, judges trusted him. Lucas needed SAFE, and SAFE needed him; he then leveraged this to refurbish other men's identities before the eyes of the court.

By pointing to their progressive merit badges, some men could establish new careers altogether. One male staff member who worked in SAFE's satellite office used his position as director of the public outreach program to establish and lead a local men's organization to combat family violence. And the assistant district attorney who worked most closely with SAFE advocates and sat on a number of advisory boards with the SAFE codirectors was eventually elected district judge (in chapter 5, I described how—while still an assistant district attorney—he helped me get a protective order signed for a client). His sensitivity to the issue of violence against women was a featured item of his campaign. I voted for him.

Paul's and Phil's progressive merit badges helped smooth their path to promotion through the Sheriff's Department. In Paul's case, during my research he was promoted twice, first to corporal and then to sergeant. To be clear, promotions like these required more than a letter of recommendation from SAFE—they required ability, too. Yet, for men in male-dominated occupations (like law enforcement), seeking advancement by applying for positions devoted to "women's issues" can be a savvy career move. It may not be the most lucrative career path, but it features less competition (among men). Paul characterized many of his male colleagues as uncomfortable with DV and SA assignments. According to him, they would not refuse a DV- or SA-related call or assignment—but they would not volunteer for them, either. Because he did (and had SAFE's blessing), he moved quickly up the ladder, and he could use his special status to bring up other men after him. This is what happened to Phil, who was eventually promoted into a new grant-funded position (mentioned in chapter 5) as the deputy assigned primarily to DV and SA cases. The advocates, especially Lisa, who moved into the new legal advocate position on the same grant, were initially leery of Phil's appointment. However, Paul recommended Phil to the selection committee, and the advocates quickly changed their tune.

For some careers, progressive merit badges are an essential prerequisite. This was true for the "women's self-defense" expert that SAFE invited to train staff members during their annual retreat. The man—who went by the initials TJ—made his living offering "Power of One Self Defense for Women" classes in local gyms in the area. Unlike the "creepy" supermarket manager described earlier who wanted to work with victims on how to protect themselves, TJ's credentials were legitimate. In addition to his many years of experience in the military, he had also worked for the local sheriff's department. He advertised his training as specifically tailored to the needs and abilities of women. In his promotional brochure, he emphasized techniques that did not require a lot of physical strength. Instead, he claimed to teach women how to leverage their "biomechanics" in order to fight back against stronger, heavier men. His website proudly claimed that he "gives the ladies tools to put into their toolbox. He uses natural tools, realistic training, de-escalation and redirection techniques as well as 'pressure point maneuvers.'" These selling points were then backed up with testimonials—exclusively from women—who offered reviews like "I recommend this course for all women!" or another from a self-identified "longtime target of an abuser" who said, "I've been telling every woman I meet to take this course from [TJ]." These comments added value to his services by signaling his sensitivity to women's needs and insecurities; they made TJ different from other "macho" men.

SAFE's annual retreat took place in a small conference facility in a wooded setting about thirty minutes from the main office. After a day of ice breakers, trust falls, and group discussions, staff members gathered on the open lawn to wait for TJ's arrival. Dressed in all black (from combat boots to cargo pants to baseball cap), he outlined how his methodology was particularly well suited to help women. He explained that females—because of their biological instincts—too often fear attack and do not know how to respond to physical aggression. His solution: train females to tap into their mothering instincts to—in his words—"kickstart" their protective impulses (he used the example of a mother hen willing to do anything to protect her chicks). He then walked the staff members through a series of physical maneuvers meant to deflect attempts to grab their arms or pull them into a room or car. During the activities, most staff members treated the lessons with genuine curiosity and interest, earnestly practicing the series of arm movements meant to redirect attackers' momentum by surprise. At the end of the session, TJ offered all staff members one free lesson at a local fitness center and complimented them by telling them that he would feature their abilities in his next press release to the local media. Staff members seemed pleased. After the session had ended, I watched Cathleen stay behind to practice a few moves on Lisa.

Men like TJ can use their progressive merit badges to get invited inside places like SAFE and later point to their interactions with staff members to bolster their sensitive credentials even more. Although I never observed advocates or counselors encourage a client to take self-defense classes, the idea was not entirely outside the realm of their empowerment philosophy. At SAFE, they believed it was their job to equip clients with the tools and resources they needed to improve their lives; if clients asked for self-defense training, it is conceivable that staff members would refer them to men like TJ. During the wrap-up discussion at the end of the retreat, Kelly offered a conditional recommendation: "Maybe this would be right for some clients, if they were ready." As a sociologist, I was put off by TJ's essentialist rhetoric about female instincts, but I was alone in this regard. This kind of talk was not uncommon at SAFE. Staff members believed that women *were* naturally different from men; much of TJ's self-defense theory made sense to them.

To maintain his progressive credentials, TJ did not need to be blindly adored at the SAFE retreat. Some staff members took his characterizations with a grain of salt. Heather, for example, objected to his characterization of abusers as "alpha males" by stating that not all women are submissive: "What about alpha females!" However, for the most part, TJ's rhetoric went unquestioned. The only complaints about the training from staff members were that TJ spent a disproportionate amount of time teaching me specific moves so that we could "spar" as a means to show others what hypothetical attacks look like. I did not ask to be made an example; TJ chose me himself. Slightly confused, I thought the whole episode was slightly ironic: for a class designed to teach women, he spent an awful lot of time working directly with me (the only man in the group). However, most staff members treated the entire class as a novelty experience and enjoyed the time spent outdoors as much as TJ's lessons in biomechanics. TJ did not need glowing feedback to promote his business; simply stating on his website and brochures that he had trained SAFE victim advocates and counselors was enough to further his business interests.

Like most instances of offering this kind of symbolic compensation to men, TJ was not the only one to benefit from the arrangement. For their part, SAFE staff members received a free hour of instruction and by participating in the lesson they could also offer more informed advice to clients who asked them whether they should take such a class themselves. SAFE's budget was limited. Free classes were not something to turn down lightly. They saw an opportunity and took it. In this sense, soliciting TJ's help was strategic.

If one can collect enough progressive merit badges from different causes and organizations, one eventually becomes eligible to give speeches and lead workshops. At SAFE, staff members saw inviting men to facilitate events as a way to increase attendance and media coverage. For example, when Kelly asked the advocates to organize a panel of speakers about DV and SA for a local forum, Heather immediately suggested a man who worked for the Sheriff's Department in a neighboring county: "He is great. He's absolutely amazing . . . and he believes in what he does . . . and he's also in law enforcement, so he can speak to them." To Heather, if men from law enforcement were going to be in the audience, it was better to have a man from their own ranks deliver SAFE's message.

Although staff members appreciated hearing women talking about violence against women, hearing the same ideas from men was considered extra special. I debriefed the advocates and counselors countless times upon their return from various conferences and trainings. The only time any staff member mentioned a speaker by name, it was a man: Lundy Bancroft. Although his name may be unfamiliar to outsiders, Lundy Bancroft is well known among those fighting DV and SA (as well as child abuse) nationwide. He travels the country giving speeches, he has authored numerous books on abuse, and he has served as an expert witness in court cases on the topic. His authority was unquestioned at SAFE, and because the primary theme of his work was making men accountable, he was seen by staff members as an easy to way to garner more publicity and attention to the cause. His is a good example of the progressive merit badge side bet. His pristine antiviolence credentials guaranteed him special status among the women of SAFE; yet, because he worked with SAFE on a contract basis (not a full-time member), he did not have to worry about losing his masculine credentials, either.

The men profiled in this chapter, who help places like SAFE achieve their mission but do so by primarily delivering affiliate "men's" services (law enforcement, protection, men's education), were ideal candidates for cashing in on and receiving privileged status with women's organizations. They could enhance their own careers by helping to clean up the mess caused by other men—and soften SAFE's man-hater image in the process.

SYMBOLIC REWARDS, GENDER, AND INEQUALITY

To be fair, none of the men described in the preceding section moved up the ranks of their careers, or created their own, based solely on their association with SAFE or the special privileges conferred to them by staff members. A progressive merit badge is not *that* valuable. In some circles of men, it may even work against them. But in the career paths of the men who worked with SAFE, the supportive role they played earned them extra credit that served them well. To get these benefits, these men still had to do their jobs—which they all did well—by interacting with women whom outsiders perceive to be hostile to men. Yet, their advancement is a good example of how privilege works. The reputation of the women I studied suffered from SAFE's man-hater stereotype, while it benefited the men described in this chapter (myself included). We were applauded for being able to work—and thrive—in "hostile territory." The dividends we earned were not just for what we did, but for who we were: men.

At SAFE, privileging men associated with the organization served practical ends. It was an effective way to invite and retain men who "got it" about abuse. The advocates and counselors were in no position to turn down help, and when men offered assistance, they gladly accepted (as long as the men passed their litmus tests). This process also helped dismantle the man-hater stereotype they believed hindered their work. The presence of men served as a symbol of moderation by proving that they were not feminazis. Thus, granting some men special status kept them coming back and softened SAFE's image at the same time. From this perspective, recruiting and maintaining male involvement helped everyone involved.

Conducting research at SAFE, I could clearly see how this arrangement was mutually beneficial—but it also came at a cost. Once I assuaged their concerns, I was granted almost unlimited access to collect data; and during public events, I was often cited by staff members as an example that men need not be afraid of their organization. This often took the form of playful sarcasm at my expense during community events or workshops: "See, we treat Ken pretty nice. He's still alive. Just kidding!" This humor pokes fun at the man-hater trope, which can help dismantle it. However, what these jokes fail to mention is that if it were not for the actions of other men—those who take power and control away from the women in their lives—places like SAFE would not even need to exist. Abusive men struck first, and now victim advocates and counselors are belittled as man haters for trying to protect themselves and their clients. All the while, men's participation in the movement receives disproportionate praise. Countless women did more for clients than most men (myself included) ever did, yet none of these women ever received the same amount of applause for simply "being there" or "showing interest."

Despite its short-term benefits, this strategy of privileging men can yield negative consequences in the long term. Although increasing membership and recruiting allies is typically a good thing for any embattled organization, privileging men like me to achieve these ends also (unintentionally) serves to legitimize the notion that women's organizations, without men's participation, can be dismissed as overzealous and biased. Although such a pragmatic decision may help when recruiting and retaining allies, it also contributes to the general devaluation of "women's organizations"—or at least those which do not seek out men's participation.[4]

These costs would not be so daunting if places like SAFE had ample financial reserves and political power. However, they do not. That SAFE relied on symbolic rewards as a means to support the larger mission is not all that surprising. They needed help and were low on resources. Without high pay and prestige to offer, what else did they have to give? For men, it was progressive merit badges. For women, the bargain was a little different: they earned moral wages. However, like privileging male allies, the moral wage bargain has a downside, too.

The drawbacks of relying on symbolic compensation to sustain staff and affiliates are hard to see. Thus far, I have defined moral wages as the positive feelings and sense of satisfaction that comes with seeing oneself as a caring and compassionate person. On its surface, this process is seemingly benign; yet, to confer and accept symbolic rewards in lieu of more tangible compensation can cause people to lose sight of the larger patterns of inequality (across organizations and by gender). This is because when affectual experiences can make up for extrinsic rewards, participants' ability to persevere can be cited as justification for the lack of tangible resources in the first place. When SAFE advocates and counselors put up with their tough working conditions because getting to feel good about doing good makes it all worthwhile, they figuratively lower the heat on policy makers who decide which and how many resources to allocate their way. Ironically, staff members' capacity to make do can be pointed to as evidence that they are satisfied and content with what they have. Thus, the applause they receive for claiming that they are not in it for the money effectively seals off rhetorical strategies for them to ask for more (and still be seen as virtuous).

The function of symbolic rewards to keep unequal arrangements in place is not new. As mentioned in chapter 2, W. E. B. DuBois found that poor whites were willing to put up with meager wages and exploitation by wealthier whites as long as they could reap the "psychological wage" ([1935]1998:700) of feeling superior to blacks. Although less extreme, we see variations on this phenomenon to this day. Recent scholarship offers numerous examples of how some workers will willingly accept unequal arrangements in exchange for the capacity to work in "special" settings.

Sociologist Shamus Khan, in his study of an elite boarding school, found that janitorial and dining hall staff were able to find meaning and value in their menial labor via their interactions with young students. One server in the cafeteria who quit a better-paying job cleaning an office for the opportunity to work at the school explained her reasoning: "I like seeing them. . . . I can tell when they're down and know how to make them smile. That makes it worth it" (Khan 2012:56). Like SAFE staff members, this dining hall worker was able to make sense of her decision to put up with less and see any hardship as worth it. Yet, just because *some* people can consent to—and even like—their lesser position in a given institution or society does not mean we should ignore how symbolic rewards can obscure large-scale inequalities for *all* members of their group (not just those who willingly accept these arrangements).

One reason we should pay attention to these kinds of trade-offs— enduring difficult circumstances for the psychological benefits they offer— is that they all too often serve to preserve existing social hierarchies. In sociologist Sherryl Kleinman's (1996) study of an alternative health organization, the distribution of symbolic rewards effectively rendered gender inequality invisible inside the workplace. All workers (staff members and medical practitioners) in her study saw themselves as doing something different and special for their community. They claimed a moral identity as "alternatives" who offered their clients a different kind of place to seek help and heal. Compared to the cold and sterile environs of hospitals and clinics, they saw themselves as different, better, and more principled. Living up to their moral identity code was not easy, but doing so helped them make sense of their choice to stay during good times and bad. Whenever complaints arose about lack of money or misperceptions of their organization, they reminded each other that what they did was special because it offered their clients an alternative to standard models of medical care where efficiency and profit reigned. From their perspective, the hard parts of their job were worth it because they put their patients' physical and spiritual well-being first. In my terms, the moral wages they earned helped them see the value in their work despite the relative lack of pay, power, or prestige.

However, upon closer inspection, it became clear that the organization's staff members (mostly women) were not only making less money than its professional medical practitioners (mostly men), but were giving up a lot more, too. During a budget crisis, the women on staff willingly gave up their pay in order to keep the organization afloat. Why? Even though the women did not benefit materially from their decision to work for free, they were able to frame their sacrifices for the organization as evidence that they were good people. For the men, even though they made more money in the first place (and were unwilling to give up their pay like the women did), they still believed they were sacrificing the most on the basis of what they *could have earned* elsewhere. They reasoned that simply staying put was indicative of their selflessness: they could have chosen greener pastures elsewhere. Thus, the staff (women) and medical practitioners (men) both saw themselves as making a shared sacrifice even if they gave up unequal amounts. The women surrendered all of their wages, earning nothing to help the organization pay the bills. The men gave up nothing—except the hypothetical higher salaries they might have earned by leaving. In objective terms, the economic inequality in their ranks was stark; however, subjectively, both groups saw the subsequent arrangement and relative sacrifices as fair.[5] How could the women in this organization see it this way? In my terms, the moral wages they earned by seeing themselves as "alternative" made it worthwhile.

The role that moral wages play in helping workers put up with less might be easier to ignore if the patterns were not so clearly gendered. Looking back at the breakdown of "more moral" jobs in chapter 2 (see figure 1), it is no surprise that these jobs are also largely "women's jobs" (with one exception—the clergy—which I address later). The studies cited in chapter 2 about staff and volunteers making sacrifices for others in abortion clinics and a homeless shelter were also stories about women. Conversely, the studies of jobs that actively discouraged workers from caring cited in that chapter (corporate production managers, bill collectors) were also stories about men. Yes, women enter into caring jobs knowingly and willingly, but for them seeking out moral wages is less an option than a gendered expectation. This is because many of the characteristics that define moral work are also built into women's gender identity. Avoiding opportunities to exhibit care and compassion also means disavowing gendered assumptions about women's supposed natural inclinations.

For men, moral wages are more optional. If men abandon opportunities to care, what are the consequences? They are few. In corporate settings, not sympathizing with others is their path of least resistance (Jackall 2010). Because of this, men who can do both—earn money and "do good"—are doubly rewarded. Among the clergy, where men lead 92 percent of all congregations (Chaves, Anderson, and Byasee 2009), the admiration they receive for accepting their "calling" is amplified by popular assumptions that they are also giving up on more lucrative material opportunities elsewhere. Statistically, given the prevailing gender pay gap, these assumptions are largely accurate (England 2010). Women cannot similarly pass up opportunities to which they have relatively less access. For women, opting out of higher-paying career tracks is seen less as a sign of virtuosity than one of pragmatic reality. Thus, for women, working for moral wages is the path of least resistance: women's career options in non-caring occupations are fewer and the negative consequences for eschewing care work are greater. For women, to resist caring is to resist the gendered expectations of womanhood. This is not to say that women cannot make this choice; many do. But for choosing not to care—on the job—women pay a social cost (which men do not).

Focusing on women's disproportionate reliance on moral wages in the workplace also helps us see the extent to which they bear the burden of the physical and emotional caretaking of everyday life.[6] Victims of DV and SA need services. Not everyone wants to do this work, but with enough training and effort almost anyone can. Even men. People in this line of work may disagree, attributing successful advocacy and counseling to the special qualities of women, but sociologists have a different take. We are in the business of demystifying skills that most people think cannot be taught or learned (Chambliss 1989). Some clients were surprised when I (a man) answered the crisis hotline or was present inside the SAFE office. Yet, the skills that make for good victim advocacy and counseling are generic to all humans. Men can listen, explore others' emotions, be diligent with paperwork, and follow up with lawyers and cops; folk wisdom says they cannot, but the effectiveness of male bill collectors at each and every one of these tasks (albeit in different contexts) indicates otherwise (Hochschild 1983; Sutton 1991).

Despite the logical inconsistencies that pervade popular beliefs regarding gender and care work, they are not going anywhere soon. As a result, women currently do the majority of moral dirty work and will continue to do so. Yes, they garner symbolic rewards for their efforts, and those mean a lot, but even then men get the better end of the deal. For men, even the smallest act of selflessness is amplified by virtue of its rarity. Exhibiting care and compassion is not built into men's identity code; thus doing so is seen as special and noteworthy. The pats on the back I received for volunteering and conducting research for this book, for example, were not because others saw my skills as exceptional; I got them mostly for showing up and sticking around. Those with the most privilege (most of the time, men) get credit for giving up some of it, while the fact that they have more at the start goes unexamined. This is the irony of privileging male allies; men get applauded for devoting some of their time and attention to women's issues, while women who do more for the movement earn fewer accolades because this work is expected of them. Yes, some women accept this burden, but as long as their acceptance of this arrangement is seen as indicative of their "natural" inclination to engage in care work, the social costs they would incur if they chose otherwise go unnoticed. Thus, by looking at the ways moral wages and progressive merit badges help the less privileged make sense of their decision to put up with fewer tangible rewards, and the more privileged feel good about giving up a smaller portion of their greater share, we can see with increased clarity how symbolic rewards can serve to obscure inequalities in the workplace.

CONCLUSION

Throughout this chapter, I have tried to analyze the ways that SAFE advocates and counselors managed the dilemma of men at work. On the one hand, they feared that some men posed a clear and dangerous threat to themselves and their clients. On the other hand, they needed men. Because places like SAFE have been subject to an intense political backlash over the past forty years, highlighting their association with some men was an efficient and effective means to combat the man-hater stereotype that impeded their ability to help their clients. As a result, when it came to men, they were torn.

Like the other emotional dilemmas that form the structure of this book, they found a way to manage this one, too. To protect themselves and their clients, they subjected unknown men to a series of litmus tests. Men who made it through these screens were invited to join as helpful allies. These men (myself included) served a dual purpose. They did their jobs (as sheriff's deputies, lawyers, batterer intervention facilitators, self-defense instructors, educators, and so on), yet they also helped soften SAFE's image. In exchange for their help, the advocates and counselors gave them something that was uniquely theirs to give: a progressive merit badge. As I define the process, members of privileged groups can accrue additional privileges by virtue of their affiliate status with organizations or causes devoted to ameliorating inequality or solving social problems. By working with—not for— places like SAFE, men can establish their credentials as men who are sensitive to women's issues, yet as associates only—retaining their primary position with their own "nonfeminist" jobs and careers. On the surface, this arrangement appears mutually beneficial. Yet, as in the other chapters, I analyze the causes and consequences of both this dilemma and the advocates' and counselors' strategy to overcome it.

The women of SAFE earned moral wages in amounts that others envy. This made their work worth it. However, there is more to this bargain than meets the eye. To keep this symbolic compensation flowing, they must continually deal with troubling emotional experiences. Simply *feeling* the wrong way about their clients (anger, frustration, annoyance) could cause them to question their core principles and ideals. Thus, they attended to their doubts and managed them away the best they could. This took a lot of work. They might be able to fool outsiders, but when it comes to subtle emotional displays, other insiders know where to look. And because they were women, the stakes were higher. To turn a cold shoulder to victims would not only put their moral wages in jeopardy, it would call into question their gender identity. As women, they were supposed to care. They accepted this arrangement, and their hard work paid off in symbolic rewards. Yet consenting to this bargain—while entirely understandable—also has implications for the reproduction of gender inequality.

Men are not bound by the same feeling rules as women. Men have other options. I could earn moral wages at SAFE for sympathizing with victims or I could have gone another route. I could have directed my indignation at abusers, sidestepping the victims' feelings altogether. As long as I could control my temper and not appear like a "tough guy," I could earn my progressive merit badge in the process, too. There was a thick strain of this kind of moral identity work among the men who associated with SAFE. Men who facilitated the batterer intervention programs, or represented community groups that held other men accountable, were not engaging in care work in the same way the advocates and counselors were. This phenomenon is not unique to SAFE. National movements like the "Promise Keepers" and the mythopoetic men's movement offer men a way to take a "manly" stand against abuse (Schwalbe 1996). Thus, men have a number of avenues to accrue symbolic compensation for their work in the DV and SA movement. For women, caring is the only path: getting angry—which is an understandable response to abuse and inequality—would only feed the man-hater stereotype.

Although gendered feeling rules are rife with internal contradictions, they still held a lot of weight at SAFE. Staff members did not question their validity. Regardless of what sociologists who study emotions argue, the women of SAFE believed that women were naturally more caring than men.[7] Yet, what they did not see is that these assumptions about "innate" men's and women's emotions ironically make it *harder* for women to be applauded for their capacity to care. Moral wages are reserved for people who exhibit care and compassion above and beyond the expected amount. Clergy earn moral wages because they claim to devote their *whole* lives—not just forty hours a week—to serving a purpose greater than themselves. Volunteers earn moral wages for their work on the weekends or at night *outside* of their everyday duties. This kind of praise is reserved for those who do more than they normally would. Because women are presumed to be innate sympathizers, in order for the advocates and counselors to earn moral wages, they have to show that their emotional response is greater than that of other women. If they cannot frame their caring as extraordinary, then their critics will claim there is nothing special about their advocacy or counseling: they merely do what any woman could do, except that they get paid for it. Men, however, are not bound by these expectations. For them, a mere *willingness* to associate with a place like SAFE is viewed as special—a continued commitment, even more so.

In the next chapter, I conclude the book by summarizing all the various dilemmas outlined in each chapter and offer a few suggestions of my own on how to overcome them. Given that more resources or a cultural sea change regarding DV and SA are not going to come any time soon, my proposals are modest and feasible. I do not set out to tell advocates and counselors what to do; rather I argue that they should institutionalize some of the best and most ingenious practices already in use.

Managing Dilemmas and Retooling

The emotional dilemmas that victim advocates and counselors face are not random. They are not the product of poor coping skills or unpredictable budget cuts. Instead, I argue that these workplace puzzles are structured into their work. People who work in places like SAFE (Stopping Abuse in Family Environments) may interpret their feelings of stress, worry, frustration, as isolated events, but they are not. Staff members' complaints about being misunderstood or underappreciated by outsiders are too predictable to be dismissed as products of chance. Instead, they are constant features of the challenging landscape of victim advocacy and counseling. Their patterned feeling states are indicative of the weak tools afforded to good people trying to tackle a persistent social problem.

Working at a place like SAFE is not easy. Victims of domestic violence and sexual assault (DV and SA) are incredibly vulnerable. Revictimization is a continuous looming threat. This pressure weighed on the advocates and counselors with whom I spent time and interacted. Their troublesome thoughts about what *might* happen to clients did not go away at the end of the day. It lingered. And when they needed to talk about their work, confidentiality constraints and cues of discomfort from friends and family made it hard to share their concerns. For all this, what did they get? If measured in extrinsic rewards (pay, promotion, and prestige), not so much. Most people appreciated them and respected their work, but not all. They did not have to walk too far from the SAFE office to overhear words like *feminazi* that belittled their work and their organizational mission.

Despite the hardships they experienced, there is also a clear upside to victim advocacy and counseling. For all their stress, worry, and frustration, they still liked their work. They liked being around each other; and, except for a few notable "difficult" ones, they liked their clients. They enjoyed being able to finish a day's work knowing that they had done something positive and meaningful. Yet, before they could feel good about their hard work, they had to solve a number of workplace riddles, first.

This book is structured around five primary emotional dilemmas that victim advocates and counselors face on a daily basis. They are specific to places like SAFE, but they are also applicable to other jobs that offer workers limited means to help vulnerable populations. These dilemmas are best categorized by the tough questions they forced staff members to answer: Should they make their workload easier to endure by turning away clients (chapter 2); should they withhold directive advice for clients in the name of empowerment (chapter 3); should they sympathize with the most difficult clients and risk enabling bad behavior (chapter 4); should they embrace the legal work that sometimes ran counter to their organizational principles (chapter 5); and should they openly welcome the assistance of men as a means to help their clients (chapter 6)? All of the answers to these questions entailed risk. If they did any of these things— or none of them—negative consequences would result. So, like savvy operators under trying circumstances, they found the most feasible middle ground.

They managed these dilemmas by making the most of what they had available. When they felt overwhelmed and questioned whether their emotional stress and strain were worth it, they pointed to past and current success stories on the job to make sense of their draining workload. These memories evoked positive feelings and a sense of satisfaction that they were caring and compassionate people. I refer to this form of symbolic compensation as the *moral wages* offered to those who can accomplish a moral identity at work, and I argue that these intrinsic rewards sustained the advocates and counselors in good times and bad. However, their moral wages were contingent upon solving additional riddles, too. In chapters 3 and 4, I show how their work was shaped by their interactions with clients. They wanted to empower the women who sought their help to make their own decisions, but they also feared that their clients sometimes made ill-advised or even dangerous ones. Sometimes they feared for their clients, safety, other times they were bewildered by some clients' refusal to follow the most simple of guidelines. To solve the problem of clients veering toward danger, they found a way to influence their clients in subtle ways—which I call "steering"—to get them back on track, all the while framing their assistance as consistent with their less-directive empowerment ethos. And when clients behaved very badly, advocates and counselors justified withholding their sympathy as in the best interest of clients, the agency, and the wider social movement against abuse.

In chapters 5 and 6, I show how the advocates and counselors approached dilemmas that emerged during their interactions with representatives of other occupations and professions that seek to help victims, too. The advocates were trained to be skeptical of the criminal justice system, but they also found working around its edges to be highly satisfying. By pointing to the "concrete" and "immediate" benefits of using legal remedies to help their clients, they reconciled their legal work with the overall goal of SAFE: to assist victims. Staff members negotiated their institutional identity when working with men, too. They all had stories of angry abusers or otherwise misguided men they wanted to keep out of the building. However, shunning all men was politically unfeasible; to rectify this, they developed a series of tests to which they subjected new men; if the men passed, they were let in. Allowing some—but not just any—men to help their clients served as a protective measure as well as a powerful political relation strategy to show that they were more inclusive and flexible than popular stereotypes would predict.

As with all efforts to combat social problems, even the most well-intentioned solutions can create problems all their own. As a result, I devote time in each chapter to the unintended consequences of staff members' decisions. Although relying on symbolic compensation to make up for meager extrinsic rewards "worked" at SAFE, such workarounds can create new complications. Policy makers and resource allocators can cite victim advocates' and counselors' capacity to make do under challenging circumstances as justification for the meager budgets currently afforded to them. The same goes for their adherence to their empowerment philosophy. Teaching clients how to help themselves is a perfectly reasonable (and affordable) way to help victims. It can be done with or without expensive professional credentials.

Also, by downplaying their influence on clients' decisions, the idea of empowerment helped staff mitigate feelings of guilt should their clients be revictimized. Unfortunately, for perpetually underfunded places like SAFE, their success at squeezing every drop from available resources can be cited as evidence by policy makers that they do not need more. Thus, capitalizing on symbolic compensation and the idea of empowerment can help organizations manage structural deficiencies while also making it harder for them to convince others to grant them the funding necessary to fully overcome them.

Similarly, the strategies they employed to highlight their institutional open-mindedness (embracing the legal system and inviting men into their ranks) can also yield unintended consequences. On the surface, it would seem foolish to avoid using legal remedies like protective orders or criminal charges; these powerful instruments can help their clients. Rigidly adhering to an oppositional stance against the criminal justice system would also mean waiving their right to access considerable state and federal funding opportunities (like those granted via the Violence Against Women Act). Additionally, shunning the help of men would seem to be a particularly bad idea: closing their ranks to all men would only fan the flames of the "man-hater" stereotype that advocates and counselors believed worked against them. However, for advocates and counselors, celebrating the contributions of men and embracing the legal system can have implications for their ability to cast their organization as a true alternative. What makes places like SAFE different are the second-wave feminist ideals upon which they were founded. Without a distinct institutional identity, they risk becoming watered-down versions of the same institutions (legal, medical, and social service) whose shortcomings were the reason that places like SAFE were created in the first place.

Even though I devote space in each chapter to point out some of the potential downsides of their solutions, I am not arguing that the advocates and counselors I studied should have done nothing to manage their dilemmas. That is the nature of dilemmas—there are no perfect options. They were asked to solve problems not of their choosing with tools hardly suited for the job. In the end, they did the best they could.

THE INTERDEPENDENT NATURE OF MORAL IDENTITY WORK

In addition to analyzing the causes and consequences of the emotional dilemmas structured into victim advocacy and counseling, I also try to make some broader theoretical contributions throughout the book. One of which is to underscore the interdependent nature of moral identity work. When staff members were able to manage their dilemmas and feel good about their work, moral wages were theirs to enjoy. However, there was a continuous complication in their efforts to accomplish a moral identity: the behavior of their clients. This thread ran through all the various identity dilemmas discussed throughout the book. Even though difficult clients composed the minority of people they tried to help, these interactions drew disproportionate amounts of time and energy from the advocates and counselors.

Some of staff members' most trying situations on the job arose when clients refused to follow the "victim script." By "going off script," I mean not behaving according to the general conventions of victimhood. Even though staff members were highly critical of what they referred to as the myth of the ideal victim (stoic, innocent, and pure), they still expected their clients to adhere to a basic set of written and unwritten rules on how to behave. Staff members knew that their clients were not perfect, and they did not expect them to mimic the popular depictions of victims on television and in the movies. This open-mindedness was the basis of their moral identity: they were the sympathizers of last resort. Again and again, they reminded themselves that in real life, clients yell at those who try to help them. They told themselves to expect their clients to lie to them, to go back to their abusers, to skip their court hearings, and to refuse to follow up with their social workers at the Department of Social Services. Yet, despite knowing (cognitively) all of these things, they had trouble (affectively) adhering to the feeling rules outlined in their identity code; they still became frustrated when their clients ignored their suggestions or willfully defied their advice. In short, sometimes the behavior of those seeking aid can make it hard for those who help them to feel good about doing good.

To help their clients when they behaved in difficult ways, staff members tried their best to make them feel welcome and appreciated. They forgave them. They generated sympathy for them. If their behavior worsened, staff members tried to steer them back to safety to help them get back on script without directly telling them what to do. If their steering failed, they used sympathy as their tool of last resort: holding out their gifts of sentiment as a means to get clients to change their ways. But redirecting clients to different paths was fraught with consequences, too. What if their steering led clients to even worse outcomes? If that happened, what would keep staff members from blaming themselves? Guilt and regret were occupational hazards at places like SAFE, too. They made it hard to help; and if service providers cannot find meaning and positive value in their work, this has consequences for service recipients. Whether or not advocates and counselors can sustain themselves via moral wages can mean the difference between conveying strength and poise to an unexpected walk-in client or appearing emotionally exhausted.

These struggles with clients are not going away any time soon. Right now, somewhere in an agency like SAFE, a victim is lashing out at the person trying to help her. Victim advocates and counselors know that anger is a natural response to abuse, but that does not make these interactions hurt any less. One moment a shelter resident can be heaping praise on the advocates and counselors for all their help, the next moment she might complain about the curfew. These latter types of interactions, when clients acted in difficult ways, put staff members in a real bind. Feeling angry toward clients can cause them to question the entire nature of their occupation. They want to help clients, not argue with them. How are they supposed to feel when a client ignores their warnings, disregards their advice, and returns weeks later with new needs and no apologies? Sometimes the realities of clients' behavior can make it hard for advocates and counselors to live up to the high standards of their moral identity code.

One important reason why difficult clients pose such a unique challenge to advocates and counselors is that the tools afforded to them to influence their clients' behavior are so weak. They pale in comparison to mechanisms of influence wielded by doctors, police, lawyers, and social workers. Whereas an emergency room physician can dole out expert advice and prescribe precise therapies, SAFE staff members were only able to offer a variety of self-help options from which to choose. A sheriff's deputy can arrest an abuser if he violates the terms of a protective order, but an advocate can only

Chapter Seven

help a client create a "safety plan" for when he comes back. A caseworker in the Department of Social Services can make financial assistance and custody of children contingent upon specific behavioral changes, while SAFE staff members had no similar incentives or penalties for good or bad behavior. In all these examples, we see how agents of other institutions can influence victims' and abusers' decision-making processes in ways that SAFE staff members could not.

That victim advocates and counselors have little power over their clients is not a surprise; this is by design. They are proud of this. They do not want to force clients to obey; doing so would be antithetical to their empowerment philosophy. They saw their job as offering clients options, not mandates. They want clients to make the right choices, but they also want them to make *their own* choices. This indirect approach was their stated goal—and a lofty one. But for empowerment to work, they needed some general cooperation from their clients. The advocates' and counselors' capacity to accomplish their identity as caring and compassionate people depended on their clients' ability stay on script—even if minimally so.

THE LINGERING EFFECTS OF GENDER INEQUALITY

At the opening of the book, I describe a scene during a staff meeting that took an unexpected turn. After a relatively boring series of updates about upcoming events and deadlines, Kelly, a codirector, opened up the discussion to invite suggestions on new ways to keep clients from "falling through the cracks." Although the topic of conversation was supposed to focus on how best to help clients, it quickly became evident that staff members needed help, too. Unbeknownst to everyone but Meg, it was the anniversary of a client's murder. Upon remembering, Jesse and Cathleen began to let loose their fears and frustrations, too. They felt overworked and burdened by the pressure that comes with helping others in such vulnerable positions. Exhausted and near tears, Meg asked Kelly, "Is there a light at the end of the tunnel?" At the time, Kelly's answer was as pessimistic as it was realistic: "Not any time soon." Unfortunately, this assessment is still accurate today. There are no immediate solutions coming any time soon. The general conditions that made it so hard to help Meg's client the year before (imperfect legal remedies, miscommunication between law enforcement agencies, insufficient time in the SAFE office to give clients the attention they deserve) still exist today. If anything, recent budget cuts have made things worse. There is no looming victory in sight, and the reasons why are bigger than anything a SAFE policy can change.

Much of the workplace frustration experienced by advocates and counselors is grounded in their belief that—in the hierarchy of social problems— DV and SA do not get the attention they merit. They are not wrong in this belief. Although legislation like the Violence Against Women Act has meant more resources and support from the criminal justice system to combat abuse, these funds still represent only a fraction of those devoted to other issues (cancer, terrorism, drugs, and others). There are social and political reasons for this: when it comes to SAFE's perspective on abuse, the root cause is not a faceless virus or some "other" enemy; the problem is the entire structure of gender. Victim advocates and counselors indict a culture that raises boys to become men who exert power and control over the other people in their lives. They point the finger at social norms that equate men's success with dominance at work, play, and the home. Their analysis of abuse can be a tough pill to swallow for those unfamiliar with second-wave feminist ways of thinking. As a result, places like SAFE are awarded resources to help victims in need, but not enough to tackle the root causes of abuse as they see them. In other words, they are given enough to treat the symptoms, but not enough to cure the disease.

To their credit, staff members at SAFE make the most of what they have; the cost effectiveness of administering an empowerment philosophy is a testament to their pragmatism. Even during the most trying times, they were still able extract meaningful experiences. It might be tempting at times in this book to see staff members' ingenuity on the job as crass or self-interested. This is not the case. They did not steer clients because they liked to exert power. They did not find ways to manage their guilt because they wanted to evade responsibility. They genuinely wanted to help their clients. However, as a sociologist, it is my job to ask, Under what conditions do workers have to stretch and reach for every opportunity to see their services as worthy and effective?

In chapter 5, I offer a clue to this answer by analyzing the underlying condition that had the greatest effect on their ability to get credit for the quiet ways they helped clients—the devaluation of women's care work. In many ways, legal work in and around courtrooms was everything that care work inside the SAFE office was not. In contrast to the hushed interactions with clients inside the SAFE office, the courtroom was a loud crash of relative excitement. Compared to the ambiguous outcomes of counseling and safety planning sessions, verdicts in court were black and white. On court days, the advocates got a chance to showcase—and sometimes show off—their technical and specialized knowledge in front of people who presumably enjoy more public status and prestige (lawyers and judges). However, readers should not assume that legal work offers more prestige because it is somehow intrinsically more difficult, complicated, or valuable. Helping clients sort through contradictory feelings toward abusers and see the light in seemingly dark times requires an incredible amount of patience and delicacy. Yet, outside of SAFE, legal work trumps care work not because of the techniques involved, but rather because in our current cultural context the legal realm is still men's turf. There, the advocates—as women—were competing on foreign territory. While negotiating with judges, they were defying stereotypes by doing things that presumably were not part of their natural skill set as women. Inside the SAFE office, their sympathizing and nurturing skills could be deflated by essentialist claims that they were doing nothing more than what any woman could do. Inside the courtroom, the same gendered stereotypes made their legal work skills appear special and as something only acquired through training and practice.

Cultural assumptions that cast women as inherently more emotional than men have consequences beyond the devaluation of women's care work, too. These stereotypes are also built into the "man-hater" accusations that I analyze in chapter 6. Women who fight back against DV and SA are often accused of doing so out of spite, or as a way to get back at all men. Women who work at places like SAFE are all too familiar with the presumptions that they are driven by their feelings and not their minds. The mere idea that victim advocates and counselors may choose their line of work for positive reasons (to connect with others, to make a difference in their community) is rendered invisible in the caricatures of hostile skeptics. When outsiders hurl epithets like "bitch," "feminazi," and worse, they are not treating advocates and counselors as rational, thinking beings.

In summary, the underlying root cause of the workplace dilemmas experienced by the SAFE advocates and counselors is the persistent devaluation of women in our culture. This can be seen in the ways that skills associated with women pay less in the marketplace as well as the rates of violence committed against women by men. Unfortunately, the ultimate solutions to these social problems—like stripping dominance, power, and control out of men's socialization practices and debunking gendered essentialist beliefs—are not likely to occur any time soon. The funding provided to places like SAFE is barely enough to enable them to tread water; they cannot afford to staff their ranks with additional experts and professionals or offer victims the economic resources they need to start over. So, advocates do the best they can with what they have. Equipped with such weak tools, they are likely to experience the same emotional and identity dilemmas again and again. So what should they do? Next I offer a few suggestions.

RETOOLING

The irony of a man doling out advice to places like SAFE is not lost on me. However, my suggestions for how managers and directors can help their staff members preempt and manage workplace dilemmas are modest. They do not require radical overhauls of their existing philosophies. Instead, I identify some of the most effective problem-solving strategies I observed during my time at SAFE and describe how they could be institutionalized at other places like it. In other words, my advice is to modify or standardize existing practices and put them into policy. Some may object to these proposals as mere "half-measures"; however, given that major societal and cultural change is beyond the current scope and budget of agencies that assist victims of DV and SA, I think the following five recommendations are achievable.

Stop Privileging Men

Sociologists have developed a rich body of work analyzing a phenomenon we call "subordinate adaptation."[1] Put simply, dominant groups offer subordinate groups (by race, class, gender, sexual orientation, and so on) a limited number of options to improve their group position, all of which typically provoke unintended consequences. For example, consider the phenomenon of women of color taking a supportive role relative to men in their community in the fight against racism. To do this, one tactic they employ is to avoid airing "dirty laundry" about abuse committed by men of color because they do not want outsiders to unfairly label their community as dysfunctional (Cole and Guy-Sheftall 2003). Pragmatically, women of color keep this information under wraps because they know it could be used against them politically. In sociological terms, this is an "adaptive" strategy: they are trying to make the best of a bad situation. It is not their fault that there are few (if any) "good" options. Yet, as a sociopolitical strategy, anthropologist Johnetta Cole and women's studies scholar Beverly Guy-Sheftall argue that when women of color privilege "their" men as a means to combat racism—which they both experience—they exacerbate gender and racial inequalities. Not only is the effectiveness of the movement against racism stifled when it does not tap into the potential contribution of *all* members, the sexism within the community becomes even more entrenched when privileging men is viewed as a legitimate strategy to benefit the group. Thus, the short-term gains achieved via subordinate adaptation can also create long-term problems.

The rationale for why the women of SAFE would be eager to highlight the efforts of men who "get it" about DV and SA also reflect the same basic pattern. As a political move, showcasing men's participation helps deflate the man-hater stereotype. To their credit, the women I studied did not push back against this stereotype by opening their doors to any and all men. The litmus tests they devised showed that they were not willing to sacrifice their clients' safety (or their own) in the name of public relations. Yet, offering disproportionate applause to the few men who passed their tests inadvertently confirmed the cultural assumption that this work does not come instinctively to men. Put another way, metaphorically conferring progressive merit badges to a few special men reinforces the idea that at the end of the day, victim advocacy and counseling is ultimately women's work. It also ignores the fact that if it were not for the actions of other men, SAFE would not need to exist.

To stop privileging men does not mean to exclude them. This would defeat the purpose (and exacerbate the feminazi caricature). Instead, women who work inside places like SAFE can be alerted to the broader social reasons why men who pass their litmus tests seem so special—and the irony of the esteem they enjoy. Instead of patting people like me on the back, our presence should be treated as obligatory, expected, normal. Men are the ones who created the mess; we should not be applauded for helping clean it up. As a society, we do not congratulate people for not robbing banks: obeying the law is what people are supposed to do. Highlighting—and implicitly praising—men's presence at meetings and fund-raisers may send the message that DV and SA agencies are not hostile to men, but it also treats us as exceptions that prove the rule. Instead, men—like me—can be treated with respect and thanked for our work, just like any woman would be.

Create Credentials for Legal Advocates

Rather than redouble efforts to train advocates to value their care work with clients, they should create positions—like the one SAFE did—to create distinct spaces for legal work to occur. Given the current rate of integration between DV and SA agencies and the criminal justice system, the demand for legal work from advocates is likely to increase over time. Offering credentials or certificates to newly created legal advocates would help them signify their skills to skeptical outsiders and create a clearer division of labor between care work and legal work.

Kelly's persistent effort to remind advocates to "go slow" in regard to legal remedies will continue to be a losing battle. No matter how much the advocates respected Kelly, her advice goes against the grain of a much deeper assumption in Western culture. The belief that work involving cognition (the mind) is different and more valuable than work involving feeling (the body) has been around since the time of philosophers like René Descartes. In the eyes of outsiders, logical and rational legal work abilities will almost always trump the emotional skills of care workers. Sociological counterarguments notwithstanding, there is little that places like SAFE can do in the foreseeable future to undo the devaluation of care work or its conflation with "women's work." What they can do, however, is create positions at the boundary of their organizational structure where legal work can be conducted free from the concern that it contradicts their second-wave feminist principles.

To make sure legal advocacy remains effective and consistent with SAFE's core mission, codirectors like Kelly could begin by working with local district attorneys and judges to establish the requirements and powers of legal advocates. For example, credentials could signify how much time legal advocates have spent talking with victims, learning in the classroom, and observing in court. After passing an exam, legal advocates would be able to offer the same services as before—like helping clients fill out protective orders—but with the symbolic resources necessary to get the respect they deserve for their skills and talents. Because these new legal advocates would work as liaisons—with one foot in places like DV and SA agencies and one foot in the criminal justice system—places like SAFE could also lay claim to their core purpose: care work. In the minds of staff members, SAFE was special because it was different. This difference was rooted in its oppositional identity. Credentialing legal advocates and letting them operate on the boundaries of their organizational structure would draw a bright circle around SAFE's primary goals of listening, sympathizing, safety planning, and empowering—thus keeping them from being seen as a subsidiary of the criminal justice system.

Embrace the Latent Function of Empowerment
Sociologists often distinguish between the manifest and latent functions of particular social activities (Merton 1949). The prior refers to the intended purpose of an action, while the latter describes any of its unintended effects. For example, consider a beauty pageant. On its surface, the manifest function of the pageant is to select the most attractive member among a group of contestants. Below the surface, the latent function of such a ceremony is much broader: it feeds into the cultural assumption that women's worth is determined in large part by the care that they direct toward their appearance. The latent function may go unstated—even unrecognized—by audience members and participants alike, but that does not mean that its broader social consequences are any less real.

Using this terminology, we can see that the manifest function of the empowerment philosophy was to help clients. From SAFE's perspective, teaching clients to help themselves was the most sustainable path to recovery. However, as was seen in the aftermath of cases in which clients were revictimized (or even murdered), SAFE's empowerment philosophy also served a latent function: it helped staff members manage away most of their doubts regarding whether or not they were to blame for their clients' suffering. By acknowledging this latent function, places like SAFE can use it to achieve their own ends. Specifically, they can train staff members to look to the empowerment philosophy as a way to ease some of their own emotional burdens.

Instances of revictimization call into question the effectiveness of places like SAFE. If clients come seeking help, and end up getting hurt again after they leave, it is reasonable to expect advocates and counselors to question the degree to which they are responsible for their clients' suffering. By training staff to remind themselves that they are not to blame because their job is to offer clients options and basic advice, not force them to choose one option over the other, places like SAFE can wield the language of empowerment to mitigate their staff members' feelings of self-blame. This is not a cynical ploy to dodge responsibility; this use of empowerment rhetoric is consistent with the philosophical underpinning of their work with victims.

To repurpose empowerment as an emotion management device would be an efficient and effective way to combat the number one occupational hazard of victim services: emotional fatigue. Whether organizations call it "burnout," or "vicarious traumatization," anyone who has helped victims knows that this work takes a toll. One costly solution is to flood places like SAFE with grief counselors in the aftermath of cases like Shelly (the client whose murder was described in chapter 1). However, places like SAFE cannot afford this approach. They hardly have enough counselors for their own clients. Instead, in the future, staff members could be trained to make their empowerment philosophy work not only for their clients, but for themselves, too. If this self-care training could be scheduled in advance—instead of in the aftermath of tragic events—staff members could interpret revictimization through a new lens as it happens rather than be taught ad hoc how to reimagine the past in a different light. This will not solve all their problems. As shown in chapter 3, using the language of empowerment to think through feelings of guilt is not an antidote to emotional suffering, but it can provide a cost-effective buffer when other solutions are too expensive to consider.

Use Higher-Ranking Staff to "Cool Out" the Most Difficult Clients
Instead of asking staff members to sever ties with the most difficult clients, their superiors should do this task for them. Over the course of their careers,

all advocates and counselors eventually encounter some clients who simply cannot abide by the written and unwritten rules of the organization. These cases are few, but they pose a unique challenge to service providers who see saying "no more" as antithetical to their mission and purpose. Thus, staff members need help to metaphorically "break up" with clients who go too far. Soliciting help from someone in another (higher) office could ease the burden.

There was no messier ending at SAFE than with Tammy, the client whose case I described in chapter 4. Privately, in the office, the advocates had become so weary of her actions that they decided that helping her only served to enable her bad behavior. However, they still felt obligated to continue to answer her calls and meet with her in the office. Eventually, they terminated the relationship by not visiting her once they found out she was in jail; however, as a means to symbolically "close" the relationship, this was very unsatisfying. If only staff members and Tammy could both have come to the conclusion that the provider–client relationship was irrevocably damaged. For advice on how to accomplish this, places like SAFE can learn a lot from the teachings of sociologist Erving Goffman (1952) on "cooling out."

Goffman's insight on how best to deliver bad news comes from an unlikely group: con artists. In the parlance of the con, the "mark" is the person who has been swindled out of money. Upon realizing what has happened, the mark becomes "hot" with anger. To keep marks from going to the police, a confederate of the con artist must step in to "cool them out" or otherwise console them. This can be done by convincing them that what just happened is all for the best or by encouraging them to treat the whole episode as a learning experience. If marks can be convinced to see a silver lining in what just occurred, then they are more likely to leave the scene feeling sadder, but "a little wiser" (Goffman 1952:451).

To be clear, I am not implying that advocates and counselors are con artists and victims are marks. However, staff members can still learn from Goffman's analysis into how to end a relationship. Telling someone that they can no longer be a SAFE client or a shelter resident follows the same generic social process as asking for a divorce or telling a student they have failed out of school (Clark 1960). These are weighty interactions. Effectively, they entail one person telling another that they "can no longer sustain one of [their] social roles and is about to be removed from it" (Goffman 1952:462). This can be heartbreaking for both the recipient and deliverer of bad news.

One of Goffman's explicit strategies on how to do this is to ask someone a few levels up in the chain of command to deliver the message (1952:457).[2] This could help the disengagement process with clients like Tammy in two ways. One, it would signal to the client that their status vis-à-vis the agency had clearly changed. Having a new face of the organization—and a more senior one at that—enter the room would immediately send the message that the familiar appeals for extra chances would no longer work. A calm and careful explanation that the agency could no longer offer services would convey more finality if it came from a director or manager of higher rank instead of the same advocate or counselor whose warnings had not materialized before. Two, asking directors and higher-ranking staff to cool out clients would distribute the emotional risks of victim services more equitably throughout the office. As shown in chapter 5, the codirectors were not exposed to the same day-to-day trauma as the rest of the staff. Their job as the face of the organization was to tout its accomplishments, impress outsiders, and solicit donations. They had greater emotional reserves to withstand these troubling interactions. Thus, to help their staff members the most when telling clients good-bye, those in charge should do the talking. These ceremonies would be undoubtedly unpleasant, but they would offer a better chance for all parties to part ways on better terms.

Acknowledge Microhierarchies

My last suggestion is likely the most controversial: Give clients directions. This may upset some because it goes against the first rule of DV and SA victim services: Do not take power and control away from victims. In theory, SAFE advocates were trained to adopt an egalitarian stance of a peer or an ally with clients. In practice, this often made their job more difficult: they wanted to keep their clients free from harm, while also not influencing them too much or admitting their private thoughts about what they should do. This was why their moral identity code was such a high standard to achieve. To help someone without being able to voice explicit instruction or disagreement is incredibly hard, but this is the bar that they set for themselves. However, taking a purely nondirective position and casting themselves as equals with victims causes problems, too—which can be eased by establishing some degree of microhierarchy during clients' sessions.

Although the advocates believed in SAFE's nondirective style, some clients were skeptical. Some clients suspected that their service provider had a secret agenda. These clients presumed the advocates wanted them to do one thing or another but kept their true wishes secret. In some ways, these clients were right. In private, the advocates often articulated what they wanted particular clients to do; however, they kept their ideas from these clients so as to not "disempower" them by dictating specific courses of action. This caused the most problems in cases involving difficult clients. These clients became surprised and upset when the advocates finally drew a line in the sand regarding how much they were willing to tolerate. When I asked the advocates to explain why they eventually set such limits—given their empowerment philosophy—the advocates explained that letting a client go too far could harm the reputation of the agency and its ability to help other victims as a result. One way they resolved this dilemma was to either steer clients or use sympathy as a means to influence them. They were not alone in drawing on such strategies; indeed, subtly nudging and prodding clients in various directions is a common—albeit seldom acknowledged—tactic in most DV and SA agencies.

The general finding that advocates try to influence clients' behavior will not surprise anyone who has worked in a similar agency. In a recent study, sociologist Amanda Gengler also found that shelter advocates often engaged in indirect (and sometimes direct) techniques to coerce residents to see some options as more desirable than others (2012:502). Empirically, steering happens. Everyone at SAFE had seen it take place, and most everyone had admitted to doing it on some level. For some positions in the agency, in some circumstances, telling clients what to do was allowed. The counselors at SAFE enacted a more prescriptive approach on the grounds that they were professionals who could offer expert advice. They believed this was their therapeutic duty. The shelter staff could be directive, too. They had residents sign contracts on what they could or could not do. Breaking these rules could mean expulsion. However, the victim advocates were unique in that they had no such credentials nor explicit rule-making authority. But they still had opinions about what could keep their clients out of danger. They kept these private thoughts hidden from clients. If they were allowed to embrace a microhierarchical relationship with their clients, they might be able to preempt some of the problems their secrecy caused—especially with difficult and skeptical clients.

When people need help, they are already in a position of subordination. If they cannot overcome their problems themselves, they need some type of intervention. This does not require oppressing them or establishing dominance over them (that is why I borrow Candace Clark's [1997] term *microhierarchy*), but it does mean finding a soft middle ground between peer and expert.[3] When we seek out advice from others, we do so with the understanding that they are more informed than us. They can offer us direction without dominating us. We can accept their suggestions without holding them responsible for every possible outcome. Of course, victims are in a much more fragile state: mimicking the actions of abusers—even in "softer" ways—could turn them away. However, if advocates have clear evidence that one option is safer for their clients based on their training, experience, and access to information, giving their clients clear guidance should not be seen as disempowering.

At SAFE, advocates were trained that clients were "the expert of their situation." In many cases, that may be true. But it is unreasonable to assume that is always the case. And by pretending otherwise—keeping advice hidden that could keep clients safe—is to create a veneer of equality in an inherently unequal relationship. By virtue of asking for help, clients are signaling that they want some direction. They do not want to be told where they absolutely must go, but they do want their map annotated with warning signs and short cuts. If advocates know which path they should follow, or at least what potential pitfalls certain paths may offer, they should tell them.

Fieldwork Methods

To become more acquainted with the work of victim advocates and counselors—and to facilitate my entry into the field site—I first trained to become a volunteer. This was at a nearby but different agency than SAFE (for reasons I explain later in this appendix). This training totaled thirty-five hours during nights and weekends, over a period of four weeks. Through seminars and group discussions, we were taught "Domestic Violence 101" (their term). Trainers highlighted common patterns and misperceptions regarding domestic violence (DV) and sexual assault (SA). As aspiring volunteers, we were taught to help clients "tell their story" through "active listening" techniques. By asking open-ended questions, we practiced ways to help clients develop their own strategy for improving their situations. We were not supposed to tell clients what to do. This strategy—what the trainers called the "empowerment model"—was the core message.

As trainees, we participated in role-playing exercises to practice interacting with mock clients. Sitting back to back, one trainee would read from a scripted scenario while the other would ask the "client" questions to learn about her situation and offer options. As the training progressed, past and current clients of the agency were invited to speak to the volunteers, share their stories, and answer questions. After we had completed the thirty-five hours of classroom training, each of us "shadowed" an experienced volunteer for four-hour shifts on at least two occasions.

Once I finished the training and shadow period, I worked as a volunteer. I worked my own shifts, answered the crisis hotline, and conducted client intake interviews once a week, four hours a day, for three months.

ENTRY INTO SAFE
I had hoped that the agency where I trained to be a volunteer would become the setting for my research, but, over time, funding cutbacks and reduced staff

capacity made this untenable. Given the limited time and energy staff members had to spend with clients, the agency decided it could not spare any of the advocates' or counselors' time to participate in my research project. At the time, DV and SA agencies statewide had experienced budget shortfalls because of a reduction in funding from a previously reliable governmental agency.

Unbeknownst to me at the time, another member of my volunteer training group had become the volunteer coordinator at a similar agency in a neighboring city. Sharing the same emphasis on empowerment, this agency—SAFE (Stopping Abuse in Family Environments)—had more staff, less turnover, a larger budget, and served more clients. When I called to ask about studying their agency, my former training partner answered the phone. We quickly touched base, and she became instrumental in helping me gain access to my new setting.

Entry into SAFE was relatively easy. The codirectors of SAFE (Kelly and Liz) were accustomed to hosting graduate students in social work and counseling as interns who needed to fulfill curriculum requirements. As a researcher, my role would be different, yet familiar. Also, my past training and volunteer experience (as well as having an ally on staff who could vouch for me) enabled me to convince staff that my objectives were sincere. In exchange, I offered to share findings with them at the completion of the project. Staff members were receptive and enthusiastic about my fairly broad request: to conduct participant observation and in-depth interviews as a means to learn how SAFE staff managed their emotions and identities in the face of challenging work.

DATA COLLECTION

I visited the SAFE main office over a period of fourteen months about once a week (except on holidays) to conduct fieldwork or in-depth interviews. Fieldwork visits lasted roughly seven hours each visit. Although I focused my research on the main office, I also visited the shelter once a month and attended staff meetings at the satellite office. In addition, I accompanied the advocates as they worked with clients in court on twelve different occasions (court sessions usually lasted three to four hours).

Staff granted me nearly unlimited access to client consultations and private meetings. They also allowed me to roam about the office and ask questions during spare moments. I also helped out around the office occasionally by answering crisis calls, conducting client in-take, and a wide variety of other tasks—from photocopying to delivering furniture to helping clients get protective orders signed by judges.

I made my research objectives known to all the staff and took notes openly. At first, they repeatedly glanced at my notepad. However, as weeks and months passed, they seemed to take my presence for granted. Lisa was the most aware of my note taking. She once said: "We must have just given you some juicy quotes right then." In her interview, I asked her what she thought of my presence: "I think you've blended in really fine. In fact [laughs], Cathleen and I were just talking yesterday about how we feel funny because we vent whenever you're around. All the stuff that is bothering us, we tell you about it. And it is probably because of how free we feel in telling you stuff that we won't tell each other." Consistent with Lisa's statement, staff members often told me that they enjoyed having someone ask questions about their work. For SAFE staff, a sympathetic audience was not a guarantee; outsiders were often uncomfortable discussing the topics of DV or SA.

One of the refrains of staff members who dealt directly with clients was that their workload limited the time they had to "process" (think about and manage their work-related stress). For example, Cathleen, an advocate in her second year at SAFE, voted to minimize any talk about clients during a staff retreat because "there isn't time to think about taking care of yourself." In other words, she wanted staff members to spend more time on themselves—not just on their clients. This appetite for self-reflection helped me as a researcher. By asking the advocates and counselors how they dealt with their emotions, I gave them an opportunity to focus (even if briefly) on themselves. To counteract the possibility that staff would only vent their frustrations with me, I made a concerted effort to seek out examples of staff satisfaction and optimistic feelings about their work, especially during their in-depth interviews.

I closely observed interactions among staff and asked questions grounded in the immediate context. I asked staff to provide specific examples whenever they described client cases or their own interactions. When respondents replied with "generalized accounts," I probed for more specificity and detail (Weiss 1994:72–73).

When staff members were busy preparing documents or talking with clients, I observed their interactions and tried not to interfere with their work. Afterward, when they had a quiet moment, I asked them about what had just occurred and how they understood it. Staff introduced me to clients as someone who was researching the agency and shadowing staff around the office; then they would ask the client whether she felt comfortable with me in the room. Clients often seemed surprised to see me—a man—in the SAFE office, but after being introduced by a staff member, they permitted me to observe their sessions on every occasion. If I was not entirely convinced that a client wanted me to be there, I voluntarily declined to observe her session. This happened fewer than five times over the course of fourteen months. As a researcher, I wanted to observe as much as possible; but as a person sensitive to the needs of victims, I tried to err on the side of caution. And when I did observe a client's session, I focused my attention on the actions and reaction of the advocate or counselor. Although I did record the general outline of clients' cases, I did so only to better gauge how staff members understood and responded to their clients' questions and concerns. I did not interview clients or ask them questions. Some may view this as a weakness of my book, but I see it as what makes my project unique. There are ample studies on victims and abusers, but my study offers the reader a sustained focus on the service providers in the middle.

Once I returned from the field, I typed the field notes as soon as possible, while they were still fresh in my mind. On average, seven hours in the field yielded eight thousand to nine thousand words of notes (roughly twenty-five double-spaced pages). In total, I collected forty-three sets of field notes (one for each visit to the field). In addition to field notes, I digitally recorded and transcribed interviews with all staff members who had direct contact with clients (fourteen in total). In total, to conduct fieldwork or interviews, I visited the field fifty-seven times after my volunteer training.

In-depth interviews lasted from seventy-five to ninety minutes each and were based on a semi-structured interview guide prepared in advance. Questions covered topics both specific (How long have you worked at SAFE? How many clients do you interact with on a daily basis?) and open-ended (What does "empowerment" mean to you? How did you feel the last time a client returned to her abuser?). On average, the transcripts yielded about thirteen thousand words (or forty double-spaced pages).

All field notes and interview transcripts were entered into Atlas.ti, a qualitative data analysis program, to facilitate coding. My coding strategy consisted of three stages: identification, conceptualization, and refinement. First, I identified and coded all persons, places, and topics of discussion. For example, if Heather and Meg were talking in the district court's hallway about Kelly's training policies, I would code this passage as "Heather," "Meg," "district court," "Kelly," "training." The next stage of coding consisted of labeling conceptual codes as they emerged. For example, any discussion related to empowering clients and domestic violence protective orders would be coded "empowerment model" and "protective order."

Finally, after identifying conceptual codes that became lasting issues, I refined them into subcategories. For example, staff discussed protective orders with each other, or clients, on 141 different occasions. Of these times, twenty-two different issues emerged. These ranged from discussions about the inability of protective orders to fully protect clients (23 times), to the difficulty staff had convincing judges to sign them (16 times). After completing all three coding stages, if I wanted to know how many times Cathleen discussed protective orders, I could simply use Atlas.ti's "co-occurrence" query tool to locate the 55 different occasions of overlap between the codes "Cathleen" (frequency 322) and "protective orders" (frequency 141). If I wanted more specific information, such as direct quotes from all the times Cathleen not only discussed protective orders but worried about the possibility that protective orders might cause violence, I narrowed my search to see the co-occurrence among the codes "Cathleen" (frequency 322) and "protective orders—can cause violence" (frequency 16) to find those specific passages (there were 6 such instances).

It was during the refinement of conceptual codes that themes began to emerge from the data. As I saw trends and patterns accumulate, I used the Atlas .ti "memo" feature to build my analysis. Because Atlas.ti memos are anchored to specific passages of data, a brief one-paragraph memo could grow to multiple pages over the course of a year. When one is searching back for the original passage that started the memo, Atlas.ti shows the memo in its entirety, not just the nascent paragraph. Using this approach, I could reinterpret initial observations with insight gathered months later.

The strategy allowed me to cover topics I did not expect to study when I entered the field (that is, the role of the empowerment model in helping staff cope, and the complex ways staff struggled to cultivate sympathy for their clients). Although this method involved uncertainty at the outset, its flexibility allowed for a deeper investigation into the issues that concerned the research subjects and not just the researcher.

CHAPTER ONE. EMOTIONAL DILEMMAS

1. I use the label *victim* throughout the book. However, there is a debate among domestic violence and sexual abuse agencies about this term and whether to use an alternative, like *survivor*. Staff members almost always used the term *client* when referring to people who sought services, but they usually used the term *victims* to refer to all people who suffer abuse (whether or not they sought out SAFE services). Staff members used "survivor" on occasion, but usually to refer to a former client who had succeeded in achieving her goals. Staff also used "survivor" to disassociate their clients from the stigma associated with "victim" (Dunn 2005). However, staff members typically used "survivor" during abstract or theoretical discussions about violence against women, but not about specific clients.

Like the staff, I use "client" to describe people who sought services from SAFE, and "victim" to refer to people who (staff believed) suffered abuse. To complicate matters, the advocates and counselors were willing to accept anyone as a client; yet, in order to consider someone a victim, staff members had to believe the person had experienced abuse.

Also, when referring to victims and clients, I use the female pronoun. This usage not only reflects the empirical reality of SAFE clients (98 percent were women), but also the way staff referred to "clients" and "victims" as women during hypothetical discussions. They knew men could be abused by other men, and occasionally by women, but they believed it was easier (and more accurate) for them to refer to victims and clients as women.

2. I use the label *abuser* rather than *batterer* to refer to those who exercise power and control and outright physical and/or sexual violence. This term allows for a more comprehensive depiction of people who control, oppress, and hurt

others. However, some at SAFE used the term *batterer*. This term was also common in the training literature and educational materials they offered to clients. I argue, however, that *batterer* connotes physical abuse, with the expectation of markings, bruising, and swelling. Emotional abuse, on the other hand, leaves no visible scars.

Staff members consistently used "batterers" and "abusers" in conjunction with the male pronoun. Staff members were quick to point out to me that this was because 98 percent of their clients were women. Had the percentage been different, it is possible that they might have adopted more gender-neutral pronouns. Their "power and control" theory of abuse implies that anyone can be an abuser. For example, lesbians can abuse one another, physically or nonphysically. Staff members believed strongly that because abuse is rooted in a culture that promotes domination, no one is immune to its effects (Pence and Paymar 1993).

3. All names and places in this book are pseudonyms. For a more detailed description of my fieldwork methods, see the appendix.

4. For a description of batterers' intervention programs, see Schrock and Padavic (2007).

5. Some clients called the hotline repeatedly—any time they needed help after hours. This explains why staff members spent so much time on the hotline even though the frequency of *new* hotline callers per year (see table 1, chapter 1) appears relatively low compared to the other points of contact with SAFE staff members.

6. Although these titles and responsibilities may differ in other places like SAFE, it is important to note the distinctions within any workplace that outsiders may not be familiar with. As I have argued elsewhere (Kolb 2011a), different roles within an organization can offer different pathways to overcoming workplace dilemmas.

7. For a clear and concise overview of the frequency of DV and SA in the United States, see also the fact sheet produced by the National Coalition Against Domestic Violence (2007).

8. Part of the difficulty in determining how many of these agencies exist is that some organizations are exclusively devoted to helping victims of sexual assault (most commonly known as "rape crisis centers"), while others offer refuge only to women escaping abusive partners (initially referred to as "battered women's shelters"). Some—like SAFE—offer both. Typically, tallying the number of these organizations is done by consulting the directories of regional umbrella organizations that seek to organize and facilitate communication among organizations at the state, regional, and national levels. Thus, agencies like SAFE may be counted twice—as both a shelter and a rape crisis center—or, not counted at all

if they do not pay (or cannot afford) the dues that some regional associations charge.

9. For an overview of DV and SA agencies, definition of abuse, see Pence and Paymar 1993.

10. The exception to SAFE's nearly all-white staff could be found in one of their satellite offices that served a predominately Latino population. However, the data for my research come primarily from the main office and the shelter, not the outreach programs.

11. For more on how the emergence of empowerment philosophies signaled a change in focus away from structural inequalities and toward the "neo-liberal individual as the locus of change" among agencies that assisted victims of DV and SA, see Morgan and Coombes 2013:531.

12. For more on moral identities, see also Katz 1975; Hardy and Carlo 2011.

CHAPTER TWO. MORAL WAGES

1. Deeb-Sossa (2013) argues a similar point in her work on community clinic workers. I thank her for crediting me in her earlier work (2006:128) with the term *moral wages* and the reference to DuBois.

2. Carol Joffe (1978) used the concept of "dirty work" to describe jobs in an abortion clinic. Abortion clinic staff can be classified as "medical assistants"— who make an average of $28,650 a year according to U.S. Department of Labor, Bureau of Labor Statistics (2012).

3. Of course, moral wages are never guaranteed. As shown in chapter 4, workers felt frustrated by "difficult" clients who lied and broke SAFE rules, and experiencing these feelings made it hard for them to see their work as an indicator of their moral worth. But when interactions with clients went as they expected, they took great pride in their work.

4. To make things more complicated for clients, there were additional distinctions in the office. SAFE employed between twenty-five and thirty people, half of whom provided administrative support (fund-raising, payroll, volunteer coordination, and program management). The other half, the advocates and counselors—and the focus of this book—interacted directly with clients.

5. These figures are relatively consistent with the regional and national averages for social and human service assistants, mental health counselors, and social workers (U.S. Department of Labor, Bureau of Labor Statistics, 2012).

6. See Irvine (2000) for more on how institutions—such as that of clinical counseling—offer members discursive tools to convince themselves and others that they belong.

7. Elsewhere, I have argued that the different ways of talking about clients and their problems constituted a "division of discourse" within SAFE (Kolb 2011b).

8. I discuss how and why Lisa moved into the "legal advocate" position in chapter 5.

9. Arlie Hochschild (1983) used the example of bill collectors to show that not all jobs that require emotional labor ask workers to be happy and nurturing to others. Using Hochschild's terminology, if jobs that call upon workers to smile and express happiness are the "toe" of emotional labor, then bill collectors represent the "heel."

10. Collins (2010) also offers an interesting analysis of the unintended consequences of relying on unpaid labor to cure social problems.

11. For more on how Americans often believe in a mixture of relativistic and traditional religious beliefs, see Smith and Denton's (2005) discussion of "therapeutic deism."

12. Erving Goffman's (1959) dramaturgical analysis of "frontstage" and "backstage" highlights how identity work is usually tailored to the types of audiences with which one is faced.

CHAPTER THREE. EMPOWERMENT IN PRACTICE

1. According to the *Oxford English Dictionary* online, to empower is "To invest legally or formally with power or authority; to authorize, license," or "To impart or bestow power to an end or for a purpose; to enable, permit" (OED online 2012).

2. Political scientist and legal scholar Rose Corrigan reported similar findings in her book, *Up Against a Wall: Rape Reform and the Failure of Success* (2013). According to the 170 different rape victim advocates she interviewed across six different states, she found that "almost every one of [them] described respect for client wishes (often described as an 'empowerment philosophy') as an absolutely fundamental, core value of their practice with victims" (Corrigan 2013:266).

3. Kasturirangan (2008) also offers an exhaustive overview of the varying definitions, applications, and critiques of "empowerment" in victim services today.

4. For a more detailed critique of "mandatory arrest" and "no-drop" policies, see Bumiller 2009:11–13.

5. Although the counselors relied heavily on their prior professional training when assisting clients, they became acquainted with SAFE's particular policies and procedures through the same "shadowing" method as the advocates.

6. For an overview of the "safety planning" process, see Davies, Lyon, and Monti-Catania 1998.

7. I outline the entire protective order process in more detail in chapter 5.

8. These "backstage" debates about how much to "empower" or "steer" clients are not unique to SAFE. Legal and social work scholar Corey Shdaimah, in

her book, *Negotiating Justice: Progressive Lawyering, Low-Income Clients, and the Quest for Social Change* (2009) outlines the ways that "progressive" lawyers are also conflicted about the degree to which their status as expert relative to that of their clients can inadvertently serve to marginalize even more those they are trying to help.

9. SAFE clients staying in the shelter were referred to as "residents."

10. In her groundbreaking book, *The Battered Woman and Shelters: The Social Construction of Wife Abuse*, sociologist Donileen Loseke (1992) outlined the interpersonal conflicts that can emerge between shelter staff and residents in more detail.

11. Although seemingly benign, Bumiller argues that these requirements to meet with social workers "and apply for all appropriate state benefits as part of a process of showing that they are taking all necessary steps to gain self-sufficiency" (Bumiller 2009:5) should be viewed in light of neoliberal welfare reforms that enhance the power of the state to regulate and control women's behavior.

12. SAFE staff members may disagree with my interpretation of some of their steering practices. This is a difficult position for a sympathetic researcher to take, but a necessary one. For more on how sympathy can shape fieldwork analysis, especially my ability to analyze a value-laden concept like "empowerment," see Kleinman and Kolb 2011.

13. Again, my study analyzes the ways that staff members were able to construct an interpretive frame whereby they could see their actions as empowering, whether they were steering clients or not. I do not know whether this client, after talking with Cathleen, the sheriff's deputy, or the hospital nurses, was actually empowered by this interaction. Instead, I argue that Cathleen was able to use the others in the room to get the client to do what she secretly believed was best. By framing the encounter as "empowering," she maintained access to moral wages and the guilt-relieving emotion management strategies that come with this approach.

14. Even though they framed their empowerment philosophy as a better way to help victims—because of its emphasis on peer relationships—this did not keep them from sending their clients to seek explicit, directive advice elsewhere. When their clients were injured, they sent them to hospitals. When they had complex legal questions, they set up appointments with pro bono lawyers. When they needed long-term social support for a given problem, they arranged for them to visit the DSS to speak with a caseworker to identify a solution. Thus, the advocates and counselors facilitated the delivery of expertise to their clients all the time, yet were careful to point out to me that these interactions took place outside the domain of SAFE's typical services. This preserved the meaning of SAFE as a space for egalitarian and nonhierarchical relationships.

1. As Norwegian criminologist Nils Christie argues, in his piece entitled "The Ideal Victim": "Being a victim is not a thing, an objective phenomenon. It will not be the same to all people in situations externally described as being the 'same.' *It has to do with the participants' definition of the situation*" (emphasis in original) (1986:18).

2. My extended analysis of "difficult" clients may leave readers with the impression that such cases were the norm. They were not. These cases represented between 5 and 10 percent of staff members' workload. However, even though they were few in number, these clients drew a disproportionate share of staff members' time and energy; and the effects of the emotional dilemma they provoked were felt for weeks and months afterward.

3. During my time at SAFE, only one resident per month left because of conflict over shelter rules. In some cases, residents were explicitly asked to leave. But in most cases, clients could see that expulsion was likely and left voluntarily. Although these extreme cases represented only about 5 percent of shelter clientele, they also weighed heavily on staff members and were a frequent subject of discussion.

4. See Loseke's 1992 work, *The Battered Woman and Shelters*, for similar findings.

5. Residents often had to leave their clothes and belongings behind before fleeing to the shelter. As a result, buying clothes from local thrift stores was a common expense.

6. Counselor "shopping" (looking for a more lenient service provider) was not as much of a problem. Compared to the advocates' clients, the counselors' clients were required to make their appointments with the same counselor so as to build a "therapeutic relationship."

7. I have argued this point more extensively elsewhere (Kolb 2011b).

8. For more detailed descriptions of contemporary victim "myths," see Lamb 1999:108; Altheide 2002:97.

9. Marilyn Frye uses the concept of a birdcage to describe how the various "double binds" that women face are systematically related to one another—creating an oppressive social space from which they cannot escape (1983).

10. Sociologist Candace Clark (1987; 1997) outlined unwritten "rules" that govern these exchanges of sympathy as part of a wider "socio-emotional economy." They are (1) Do not ask for sympathy you do not deserve. (2) If you deserve some, do not ask for too much. (3) If sympathy is offered to you, be sure to accept at least some. (4) Once you accept sympathy, reciprocate later.

11. Clark refers to this "balance" as one's "sympathy margin" (1987).

12. Clients' ability to refuse staff members' requests or suggestions looks, on the surface, to be indicative of their greater position in "microhierarchical"

terms; however, to agree with that assumption would be to ignore the multitude of other ways staff members could exert control over clients. The advocates and counselors were in control of scheduling appointments, decided whom to refer clients to, and could limit the amount of time they consulted with them when other clients were waiting.

13. This myth of "eternal" suffering applies to victims of offenses other than DV and SA, too. For more see Best 1997.

14. Scholar and therapist Sharon Lamb argues that this myth also "robs victims of agency" and portrays them as "reactors rather than actors" (1999:109).

CHAPTER FIVE. THE ALLURE OF LEGAL WORK

1. No one argued this point more strongly than Heather. Before working as an advocate for SAFE, she worked in a similar capacity at a different agency when she was abused by her (now) ex-husband. Instead of receiving sympathy from her employer—the director of a DV and SA agency, no less—she was scolded for not pressing charges. Her boss knew about the risks involved with criminal justice solutions, but told Heather that the agency's reputation could suffer if its own staff did not take advantage of the agency's own services. Heather described this explanation as the most "disempowering" thing anyone could do. Heather quit her job at the agency and was relieved to hear that SAFE took empowerment more seriously. Upon arrival, Heather became a strong proponent of empowerment in the SAFE office, often citing this example as a reason not to push clients to go the legal route.

2. For additional evidence of this phenomenon, a recent journal article that conducted a meta-analysis of recent research on the topic was titled, "More Than a Piece of Paper? Protection Orders as a Resource for Battered Women" (Fleury-Steiner, Fleury-Steiner, and Miller 2011).

3. The focus of this chapter is on the advocates. The counselors at SAFE did not spend as much time in and around courtrooms as the advocates did. If the counselors were in court, it was usually to testify as an expert on behalf of a client.

4. Given my analysis of steering practices in chapter 3, and the use of sympathy to redirect clients away from harm in chapter 4, readers may also wonder if there were times when the advocates "pushed" clients into contacting law enforcement or filing for a protective order. I can say with confidence that I never witnessed anyone at SAFE force a client into such a decision. Although I do argue that the energy they derived from court was satisfying to them in ways that their everyday care work with clients could not match, I do not claim that they would purposefully push a client toward legal work just so they could experience the excitement of making backroom plea deals with lawyers, for example. The appeal

of legal work was not enough to put clients in jeopardy. However, its attractiveness was a surprising finding—especially considering their training and policies—and thus worthy of analysis.

5. As a reminder, my study is focused on the experience of service providers, not clients. Thus, while readers may want to know more about what clients thought and felt during the protective order process, I did not collect this data.

6. In chapter 2, I compare and contrast advocates and paralegals in more detail. For two rich investigations into the experiences of paralegals, see Lively 2001, and Pierce 1995.

7. I analyze the implications of confidentiality constraints on staff members in places like SAFE in more detail elsewhere (Kolb 2011c).

8. The SAFE main office did not handle many Spanish-speaking clients, but the satellite office managed by the other SAFE codirector, Liz, did.

9. Kelly and Liz, the SAFE codirectors, maintained in private and to the rest of the staff that they took a number of factors into consideration when deciding to hire Lisa, not Meg. They stressed that language skills were not the only reason Lisa got the job.

10. As I explain in chapter 3, "no-drop" policies—although a political achievement for the movement—are also not without critique among victim advocates and counselors on the grounds that they restrict victims' "power and control" over their cases (Ford 2003).

11. For more, on how essentialist beliefs regarding women's capacity to nurture others serves to devalue their caring labor, see England 2010; England, Herbert, Kilbourne, Reid, and Megdal 1994; Kilbourne, Farkas, Beron, Weir, and England 1994; Reskin 1988. Conversely, men can benefit from not expressing emotions at work. As Sattel (1976) argues, men use "inexpressiveness" as an instrument of power.

12. The SAFE counselors were confident that outsiders perceived their care as specialized and skillful, but that was because their professional credentials indicated that they had received training to hone their abilities beyond their "natural" level. I explore this point in more detail elsewhere (Kolb 2011a).

CHAPTER SIX. MEN AT WORK

1. I thank Martha Copp for suggesting this term during an e-mail correspondence.

2. For men, progressive merit badges afforded privileges similar to those included within the "patriarchal dividend" (Connell 2005). However, unlike the patriarchal dividend, progressive merit badges are not exclusive to men and are not granted automatically.

3. Men can also earn progressive merit badges by working full time (exclusively) for women's causes or organizations. However, if they do so, the value of their special privileges might be offset by the taunts and hostility aimed at men who work only on women's issues. For more on the content and delivery of these taunts, see C. J. Pascoe's (2007) work on men's use of gay slurs to police gender performance in other men. Additionally, she also cites the ways that male athletes acquire "jock insurance" that shields them against accusations of being "fags."

4. I argue a similar point elsewhere regarding the reproduction of male privilege (Kolb 2007).

5. For a counterexample of how less powerful workers can highlight inequality in the workplace and leverage all available resources to their advantage, see the example of wait-staff leveraging power from managers in Paules (1991).

6. Arlie Hochschild (1997) refers to the time spent by women on the emotional needs of the family as their "third shift."

7. Sociologists have argued that men and women follow cultural scripts on how they should feel—and to what extent—in different contexts. Hochschild (1983) coined the term "feeling rules" to dissociate them from natural, innate, genetic, behavioristic responses to stimuli. The primary evidence to support her conceptualization was the capacity of people to manage and change their emotions, suggesting that people have much more control over their feeling states than behavioristic theories would presume. Also, because "feeling rules" vary across time, culture, and place, their "fixed-ness" becomes less certain and more of a social construction. Yet, independent of sociologists' arguments, the women of SAFE perceived their caring capacities to be natural, and these perceptions guided their actions.

CHAPTER SEVEN. MANAGING DILEMMAS AND RETOOLING

1. For a longer description of "subordinate adaptation," see Schwalbe et al. 2000:426–30.

2. For more ways to "cool out the mark," see Goffman 1952:457–62.

3. For an overview of Candace Clark's conceptualization of microhierarchies, see Clark 1997:229–36.

Adams, Jill. 2009. "The Civil Restraining Order Application Process." *Ethnography* 10(2):185–211.

Altheide, David L. 2002. *Creating Fear: News and the Construction of Crisis.* New Brunswick, NJ: Transaction.

Andersen, Margaret L., and Claire Renzetti. 1980. "Rape Crisis Counseling and the Culture of Individualism." *Contemporary Crises* 4(3):323–39.

Anderson, Kristin J., Melinda Kanner, and Nisreen Elsayegh. 2009. "Are Feminists Man Haters? Feminists' and Nonfeminists' Attitudes toward Men." *Psychology of Women Quarterly* 33(2):216–24.

Barner, John, and Michelle Carney. 2011. "Interventions for Intimate Partner Violence: A Historical Review." *Journal of Family Violence* 26(3):235–44.

Becker, Howard S. 1960. "Notes on the Concept of Commitment." *American Journal of Sociology* 66(1):32–40.

———. 1970. *Sociological Work: Method and Substance.* New Brunswick, NJ: Transaction.

Bell, Margret E., Sara Perez, Lisa A. Goodman, and Mary Ann Dutton. 2011. "Battered Women's Perceptions of Civil and Criminal Court Helpfulness: The Role of Court Outcome and Process." *Violence Against Women* 17(1):71–88.

Bemiller, Michelle. 2008. "When Battered Mothers Lose Custody: A Qualitative Study of Abuse at Home and in the Courts." *Journal of Child Custody* 5(3–4):228–55.

Bemiller, Michelle, and L. Susan Williams. 2011. "The Role of Adaptation in Advocate Burnout: A Case of Good Soldiering." *Violence Against Women* 17(1):89–110.

Bennett, Larry, Stephanie Riger, Paul Schewe, April Howard, and Sharon Wasco. 2004. "Effectiveness of Hotline, Advocacy, Counseling, and Shelter Services for Victims of Domestic Violence: A Statewide Evaluation." *Journal of Interpersonal Violence* 19(7):815–29.

Best, Joel. 1997. "Victimization and the Victim Industry." *Society* 34(4):9–17.

Bevacqua, Maria. 2000. *Rape on the Public Agenda: Feminism and the Politics of Sexual Assault*. Boston: Northeastern University Press.

Black, Michele C., Kathleen C. Basile, Matthew J. Breiding, Sharon G. Smith, Mikel L. Walters, Melissa T. Merrick, Jieru Chen, and Mark R. Stevens. 2011. *National Intimate Partner and Sexual Violence Survey (NISVS): 2010 Summary Report*. Atlanta: National Center for Injury Prevention and Control, Centers for Disease Control and Prevention.

Blumer, Herbert. 1969. *Symbolic Interactionism: Perspective and Method*. Berkeley: University of California Press.

Bumiller, Kristin. 2009. *In an Abusive State: How Neoliberalism Appropriated the Feminist Movement Against Sexual Violence*. Durham, NC: Duke University Press.

Burawoy, Michael. 1979. *Manufacturing Consent: Changes in the Labor Process under Monopoly Capitalism*. Chicago: University of Chicago Press.

Buzawa, Eve S., and Carl G. Buzawa. 1996. *Do Arrests and Restraining Orders Work?* Thousand Oaks, CA: Sage.

———. 2003. *Domestic Violence: The Criminal Justice Response*. Thousand Oaks, CA: Sage.

Campbell, Rebecca. 1998. "The Community Response to Rape: Victims' Experiences with the Legal, Medical, and Mental Health Systems." *American Journal of Community Psychology* 26(3):355–79.

Catalano, Shannon. 2007. *Intimate Partner Violence in the U.S.* Washington, DC: US Department of Justice. http://bjs.ojp.usdoj.gov/content/intimate/ipv.cfm.

———. 2012. *Intimate Partner Violence, 1993–2010*. Washington, DC: US Department of Justice: Bureau of Justice Statistics. http://www.bjs.gov/content/pub/pdf/ipv9310.pdf.

Chambliss, Daniel F. 1989. "The Mundanity of Excellence: An Ethnographic Report on Stratification and Olympic Swimmers." *Sociological Theory* 7(1):70–86.

Chaves, Mark, Shawna Anderson, and Jason Byassee. 2009. *American Congregations at the Beginning of the Twenty-First Century*. Durham, NC: Duke University, National Congregations Study.

Christie, Nils. 1986. "The Ideal Victim." In *From Crime Policy to Victim Policy: Reorienting the Justice System*, ed. Ezzat A. Fattah, 17–30. New York: St. Martin's Press.

Clark, Burton R. 1960. "The 'Cooling-Out' Function in Higher Education." *American Journal of Sociology* 65(6):569–76.

Clark, Candace. 1987. "Sympathy Biography and Sympathy Margin." *American Journal of Sociology* 93(2):290–321.

———. 1997. *Misery and Company: Sympathy in Everyday Life*. Chicago: University Of Chicago Press.

Cohen, Philip N., Matt L. Huffman, and Stefanie Knauer. 2009. "Stalled Progress? Gender Segregation and Wage Inequality among Managers, 1980–2000." *Work and Occupations* 36(4):318–42.

Cole, Johnnetta B., and Beverly Guy-Sheftall. 2003. *Gender Talk: The Struggle for Women's Equality in African American Communities*. New York: One World/Ballantine.

Collins, Patricia Hill. 2010. "The New Politics of Community." *American Sociological Review* 75(1):7–30.

Connell, R. W. 2005. *Masculinities*. Berkeley: University of California Press.

Cooley, Charles Horton. 1902. *Human Nature and the Social Order*. New York: Charles Scribner's Sons.

Corrigan, Rose. 2013. *Up against a Wall: Rape Reform and the Failure of Success*. New York: New York University Press.

Danis, Fran S. 2003. "Social Work Response to Domestic Violence: Encouraging News from a New Look." *Affilia* 18(2):177–91.

Davidson, Howard A. 1995. "Child Abuse and Domestic Violence: Legal Connections and Controversies." *Family Law Quarterly* 29(2):357–73.

Davies, Jill M., Eleanor Lyon, and Diane Monti-Catania. 1998. *Safety Planning with Battered Women: Complex Lives/Difficult Choices*. Thousand Oaks, CA: Sage.

Deeb-Sossa, Natalia. 2006. "Inequalities at Work: Health Care Workers and Clients in a Community Clinic." PhD dissertation, Department of Sociology, University of North Carolina, Chapel Hill.

———. 2013. *Doing Good: Racial Tensions and Workplace Inequalities at a Community Clinic in El Nuevo South*. Tucson: University of Arizona Press.

DeVault, Marjorie L. 1991. *Feeding the Family: The Social Organization of Caring as Gendered Work*. Chicago: University of Chicago Press.

DuBois, W. E. B. 1935[1998]. *Black Reconstruction in America 1860–1880*. New York: Free Press.

Dunn, Jennifer L. 2002. *Courting Disaster: Intimate Stalking, Culture, and Criminal Justice*. New Brunswick, NJ: Transaction.

———. 2005. "'Victims' and 'Survivors': Emerging Vocabularies of Motive for 'Battered Women Who Stay.'" *Sociological Inquiry* 75(1):1–30.

Dunn, Jennifer L., and Melissa Powell-Williams. 2007. "'Everybody Makes Choices': Victim Advocates and the Social Construction of Battered Women's Victimization and Agency." *Violence Against Women* 13(10):977–1001.

England, Paula. 2010. "The Gender Revolution: Uneven and Stalled." *Gender & Society* 24(2):149-66.

England, Paula, Melissa S. Herbert, Barbara S. Kilbourne, Lori L. Reid, and Lori M. Megdal. 1994. "The Gendered Valuation of Occupations and Skills: Earnings in 1980 Census Occupations." *Social Forces* 73(1):65-99.

Ezzell, Matthew B. 2012. "'I'm in Control': Compensatory Manhood in a Therapeutic Community." *Gender & Society* 26(2):190-215.

Fleury-Steiner, Ruth E., Benjamin D. Fleury-Steiner, and Susan L. Miller. 2011. "More Than a Piece of Paper? Protection Orders as a Resource for Battered Women." *Sociology Compass* 5(7):512-24.

Ford, David A. 2003. "Coercing Victim Participation in Domestic Violence Prosecutions." *Journal of Interpersonal Violence* 18(6):669-84.

Freire, Paulo. 2009. *Pedagogy of the Oppressed: Thirtieth Anniversary Edition*. New York: Continuum.

Frye, Marilyn. 1983. *Politics of Reality: Essays in Feminist Theory*. Freedom, CA: Crossing Press.

Gengler, Amanda M. 2012. "Defying (Dis)Empowerment in a Battered Women's Shelter: Moral Rhetorics, Intersectionality, and Processes of Control and Resistance." *Social Problems* 59(4):501-21.

Goffman, Erving. 1952. "On Cooling the Mark Out: Some Aspects of Adaptation to Failure." *Psychiatry: Journal of Interpersonal Relations* 15(4):451-63.

——. 1959. *The Presentation of Self in Everyday Life*. New York: Anchor.

——. 1963. *Stigma: Notes on the Management of Spoiled Identity*. New York: Simon and Schuster.

Gutiérrez, Lorraine M., Kathryn A. DeLois, and Linnea GlenMaye. 1995. "Understanding Empowerment Practice: Building on Practitioner-based Knowledge." *Families in Society* 76:534-42.

Hackett, Conrad, and D. Michael Lindsay. 2008. "Measuring Evangelicalism: Consequences of Different Operationalization Strategies." *Journal for the Scientific Study of Religion* 47(3):499-514.

Hardy, Sam A., and Gustavo Carlo. 2011. "Moral Identity." In *Handbook of Identity Theory and Research*, ed. Seth J. Schwartz, Koen Luyckx, and Vivian L. Vignoles, 495-513. New York: Springer.

Hochschild, Arlie Russell. 1983. *The Managed Heart: Commercialization of Human Feeling*. Berkeley: University of California Press.

——. 1997. *The Time Bind: When Work Becomes Home and Home Becomes Work*. New York: Holt Paperbacks.

Holden, Daphne. 1997. "'On Equal Ground': Sustaining Virtue among Volunteers in a Homeless Shelter." *Journal of Contemporary Ethnography* 26(2):117-45.

Hughes, Everett C. 1971. *The Sociological Eye: Selected Papers.* New Brunswick, NJ: Transaction.

Huisman, Kimberly, Jeri Martinez, and Cathleen Wilson. 2005. "Training Police Officers on Domestic Violence and Racism Challenges and Strategies." *Violence Against Women* 11(6):792–821.

Iovanni, LeeAnn, and Susan L. Miller. 2001. "Criminal Justice System Responses to Domestic Violence." In *Sourcebook on Violence Against Women*, ed. Claire M. Renzetti, Jeff L. Edleson, and Raquel K. Bergen, 303–27. Thousand Oaks, CA: Sage.

Irvine, Leslie. 2000. "'Even Better Than the Real Thing': Narratives of the Self in Codependency." *Qualitative Sociology* 23(1):9–28.

Jackall, Robert. 2010. *Moral Mazes: The World of Corporate Managers: Twentieth Anniversary Edition.* New York: Oxford University Press.

Joffe, Carole. 1978. "What Abortion Counselors Want from Their Clients." *Social Problems* 26(1):112–21.

Jordan, Carol E., Adam J. Pritchard, Danielle Duckett, and Richard Charnigo. 2010. "Criminal Offending among Respondents to Protective Orders: Crime Types and Patterns That Predict Victim Risk." *Violence Against Women* 16(12):1396–1411.

Kanter, Rosabeth M. 1977. *Men and Women of the Corporation.* New York: Basic Books.

Kasturirangan, Aarati. 2008. "Empowerment and Programs Designed to Address Domestic Violence." *Violence Against Women* 14(12):1465–75.

Katz, Jack. 1975. "Essences as Moral Identities: Verifiability and Responsibility in Imputations of Deviance and Charisma." *American Journal of Sociology* 80(6):1369–90.

Khan, Shamus R. 2012. *Privilege: The Making of an Adolescent Elite at St. Paul's School.* Princeton, NJ: Princeton University Press.

Kilbourne, Barbara S., George Farkas, Kurt Beron, Dorothea Weir, and Paula England. 1994. "Returns to Skill, Compensating Differentials, and Gender Bias: Effects of Occupational Characteristics on the Wages of White Women and Men." *American Journal of Sociology* 100(3):689–719.

Kleinman, Sherryl. 1984. *Equals before God: Seminarians as Humanistic Professionals.* Chicago: University of Chicago Press.

———. 1996. *Opposing Ambitions: Gender and Identity in an Alternative Organization.* Chicago: University of Chicago Press.

Kleinman, Sherryl, and Kenneth H. Kolb. 2011. "Traps on the Path of Analysis." *Symbolic Interaction* 34(4):425–46.

Kolb, Kenneth H. 2007. "'Supporting Our Black Men': Reproducing Male Privilege in a Black Student Political Organization." *Sociological Spectrum* 27(3):257–74.

———. 2011a. "Claiming Competence: Biographical Work among Victim-Advocates and Counselors." *Symbolic Interaction* 34(1):86–107.

———. 2011b. "Sympathy Work: Identity and Emotion Management among Victim-Advocates and Counselors." *Qualitative Sociology* 34(1):101–19.

———. 2011c. "Victim Advocates' Perceptions of Legal Work." *Violence Against Women* 17(12):1559–75.

Konradi, Amanda. 1996. "Preparing to Testify: Rape Survivors Negotiating the Criminal Justice Process." *Gender and Society* 10(4):404–32.

Koss, Mary P., Karen J. Bachar, C. Quince Hopkins, and Carolyn Carlson. 2004. "Expanding a Community's Justice Response to Sex Crimes through Advocacy, Prosecutorial, and Public Health Collaboration: Introducing the RESTORE Program." *Journal of Interpersonal Violence* 19(12):1435–63.

Lamb, Sharon. 1999. "Constructing the Victim: Popular Images and Lasting Labels." In *New Versions of Victims: Feminists Struggle with the Concept*, edited by Sharon Lamb, 108–38. New York: New York University Press.

Larcombe, Wendy. 2002. "The 'Ideal' Victim v Successful Rape Complainants: Not What You Might Expect." *Feminist Legal Studies* 10(2):131–48.

Lehman, Edward C. 1993. *Gender and Work: The Case of the Clergy*. Albany, NY: State University of New York Press.

Lipsky, Michael. 1980. *Street-level Bureaucracy: Dilemmas of the Individual in Public Services*. New York: Russell Sage Foundation.

Lively, Kathryn J. 2001. "Occupational Claims to Professionalism: The Case of Paralegals." *Symbolic Interaction* 24(3):343–66.

Loseke, Donileen R. 1992. *The Battered Woman and Shelters: The Social Construction of Wife Abuse*. Albany, NY: State University of New York Press.

Maier, Shana L. 2008a. "Are Rape Crisis Centers Feminist Organizations?" *Feminist Criminology* 3(2):82–100.

———. 2008b. "'I Have Heard Horrible Stories . . . ': Rape Victim Advocates' Perceptions of the Revictimization of Rape Victims by the Police and Medical System." *Violence Against Women* 14(7):786–808.

Martin, Patricia Y. 2005. *Rape Work: Victims, Gender and Emotions in Organization and Community Context*. New York: Routledge.

Matthews, Nancy A. 1989. "Surmounting a Legacy: The Expansion of Racial Diversity in a Local Anti-Rape Movement." *Gender & Society* 3(4): 518–32.

———. 1994. *Confronting Rape: The Feminist Anti-Rape Movement and the State*. New York: Routledge.

McQueeney, Krista. 2009. "'We Are God's Children, Y'All': Race, Gender, and Sexuality in Lesbian- and Gay-Affirming Congregations." *Social Problems* 56(1):151–73.

Mears, Ashley. 2011. *Pricing Beauty: The Making of a Fashion Model*. Berkeley: University of California Press.

Mellow, Muriel. 2006. *Defining Work: Gender, Professional Work, and the Case of Rural Clergy*. Montreal, Canada: McGill-Queen's University Press.

Merton, Robert K. 1949. *Social Theory and Social Structure*. New York: Free Press.

Moracco, Kathryn E., Kathryn Andersen, Rebecca M. Buchanan, Christina Espersen, Michael J. Bowling, and Courtney Duffy. 2010. "Who Are the Defendants in Domestic Violence Protection Order Cases?" *Violence Against Women* 16(11):1201–23.

Morgan, Mandy, and Leigh Coombes. 2013. "Empowerment and Advocacy for Domestic Violence Victims." *Social and Personality Psychology Compass* 7(8):526–36.

Murray, Susan B. 2000. "Getting Paid in Smiles: The Gendering of Child Care Work." *Symbolic Interaction* 23(2):135–60.

National Coalition Against Domestic Violence. 2007. "Domestic Violence Facts." http://www.ncadv.org/files/DomesticViolenceFactSheet(National).pdf.

———. 2008. *National Directory of Domestic Violence Programs*. http://www.ncadv.org/resources/NCADVResources.php.

OED Online. 2012. "Empower, V." New York: Oxford University Press. http://www.oed.com/view/Entry/61399?redirectedFrom = empower.

Pascoe, C. J. 2007. *Dude, You're a Fag: Masculinity and Sexuality in High School*. Berkeley: University of California Press.

Paules, Greta. 1991. *Dishing It Out: Power and Resistance among Waitresses in a New Jersey Restaurant*. Philadelphia: Temple University Press.

Pence, Ellen, and Michael Paymar. 1993. *Education Groups for Men Who Batter: The Duluth Model*. New York: Springer.

Pierce, Jennifer L. 1995. *Gender Trials: Emotional Lives in Contemporary Law Firms*. Berkeley: University of California Press.

Powell-Williams, Melissa, S. Dale White, and Todd Powell-Williams. 2013. "'I Help the Ones That Want Help': Emotion Work and the Victim Advocate Role." *Sociological Spectrum* 33(3):258–75.

Randall, Melanie. 2010. "Sexual Assault Law, Credibility, and 'Ideal Victims': Consent, Resistance, and Victim Blaming." *Canadian Journal of Women & the Law* 22(2):397–433.

Rappaport, Julian. 1987. "Terms of Empowerment/Exemplars of Prevention: Toward a Theory for Community Psychology." *American Journal of Community Psychology* 15(2):121–48.

Reskin, Barbara F. 1988. "Bringing the Men Back In: Sex Differentiation and the Devaluation of Women's Work." *Gender & Society* 2(1):58–81.

Sanders, Clinton R. 2010. "Working Out Back: The Veterinary Technician and 'Dirty Work.'" *Journal of Contemporary Ethnography* 39(3):243–72.

Sattel, Jack W. 1976. "The Inexpressive Male: Tragedy or Sexual Politics?" *Social Problems* 23(4):469–77.

Schechter, Susan. 1982. *Women and Male Violence*. Cambridge, MA: South End Press.

Schrock, Douglas P., and Irene Padavic. 2007. "Negotiating Hegemonic Masculinity in a Batterer Intervention Program." *Gender & Society* 21(5):625–49.

Schrock, Douglas, and Michael Schwalbe. 2009. "Men, Masculinity, and Manhood Acts." *Annual Review of Sociology* 35(1):277–95.

Schwalbe, Michael. 1996. *Unlocking the Iron Cage: The Men's Movement, Gender Politics, and American Culture*. New York: Oxford University Press.

Schwalbe, Michael, Sandra Godwin, Daphne Holden, Douglas Schrock, Shealy Thompson, and Michele Wolkomir. 2000. "Generic Processes in the Reproduction of Inequality: An Interactionist Analysis." *Social Forces* 79(2):419–52.

Schwalbe, Michael, and Douglas Mason-Schrock. 1996. "Identity Work as Group Process." *Advances in Group Processes* 13:113–47.

Shdaimah, Corey. 2009. *Negotiating Justice: Progressive Lawyering, Low-Income Clients, and the Quest for Social Change*. New York: New York University Press.

Shibutani, Tamotsu. 1955. "Reference Groups as Perspectives." *American Journal of Sociology* 60(6):562–69.

Simon, Rita J., and Pamela S. Nadell. 1995. "In the Same Voice or Is It Different? Gender and the Clergy." *Sociology of Religion* 56(1):63–70.

Smith, Christian, and Melina Lundquist Denton. 2005. *Soul Searching: The Religious and Spiritual Lives of American Teenagers*. New York: Oxford University Press.

Smith, Dorothy E. 1993. "The Standard North American Family: SNAF as an Ideological Code." *Journal of Family Issues* 14(1):50–65.

Snow, David A., and Leon Anderson. 1987. "Identity Work among the Homeless: The Verbal Construction and Avowal of Personal Identities." *American Journal of Sociology* 92(6):1336–71.

Steen, Julie A. 2009. "The Perceived Impact of a Child Maltreatment Report from the Perspective of the Domestic Violence Shelter Worker." *Journal of Interpersonal Violence* 24(11):1906–18.

Stein, Karen. 2011. "Getting Away from It All: The Construction and Management of Temporary Identities on Vacation." *Symbolic Interaction* 34(2):290–308.

Sutton, Robert I. 1991. "Maintaining Norms about Expressed Emotions: The Case of Bill Collectors." *Administrative Science Quarterly* 36(2):245–68.

Tierney, Kathleen J. 1982. "The Battered Women Movement and the Creation of the Wife Beating Problem." *Social Problems* 29(3):207–20.

Tjaden, Patricia, and Nancy Thoennes. 2000. *Extent, Nature, and Consequences of Intimate Partner Violence: Findings from the National Violence Against Women Survey*. Washington, DC: US Department of Justice.

U.S. Department of Labor. Bureau of Labor Statistics. 2012. *Occupational Outlook Handbook*. http://www.bls.gov/ooh.

Weiss, Robert S. 1994. "Interviewing." In *Learning from Strangers: The Art and Method of Qualitative Interview Studies*, 61–99. New York: Free Press.

Whittier, Nancy. 1995. *Feminist Generations: The Persistence of the Radical Women's Movement*. Philadelphia: Temple University Press.

Williams, Christine L. 1992. "The Glass Escalator: Hidden Advantages for Men in the 'Female' Professions." *Social Problems* 39(3):253–67.

Wolkomir, Michelle, and Jennifer Powers. 2007. "Helping Women and Protecting the Self: The Challenge of Emotional Labor in an Abortion Clinic." *Qualitative Sociology* 30(2):153–69.

911 (emergency response line), 38, 63, 113

"abuse 101," 49, 187
abortion clinics, 31–32, 163, 195n2
abuse: rates of, 10, 149, 194n2; as a social
    problem, 10–11, 34, 56, 67–68, 78,
    108, 143–44, 148, 174, 176
academic credentials, 13, 23–24, 35–45,
    50, 58, 83, 127. *See also* professional
    credentials
active listening techniques, 38, 42, 187
Adams, Jill, 116
advisory boards, 155
advocate shopping, 94, 198n6
advocates and counselors: backstage talk,
    53, 65, 68; clients confused by their
    job titles, 35; communication with
    shelter staff, 3; differences between,
    5, 9, 35–45, 47, 93; different from bill
    collectors, 24, 35, 45–47, 50; different
    from clergy, 24, 35, 47–50; different
    from corporate managers, 24, 35,
    46–47, 50; different from paralegals,
    24, 35, 41–43, 45, 47, 50; different
    from volunteers, 24, 35, 47–48, 50;
    disagreements between, 69;
    interacting with abusers, 69; earn
    ample respect, 142; keep thoughts
    private from clients, 66–69, 77–79,
    90, 185–86; professional credentials
    of, 23, 35–45, 50; share common

identity, 6; sympathetic stance
    towards clients, 31, 45–49, 50; take
    pride in difficulty of job, 39–40; why
    study them, 6, 21, 132
advocates: career aspirations, 43;
    different job than counselors, 5, 9,
    35–45, 47, 93, 119, 131, 185–86; found
    legal work exciting, 116–32, 139–41;
    similar skills as bill collectors, 46;
    similar skills as paralegals, 43; take
    pride in nonprofessional status,
    35–45
affective solutions: different from
    cognitive solutions, 24, 82, 173, 180
agencies that assist victims of domestic
    violence and sexual assault: as
    alternative organizations, 15, 54, 58,
    72, 80, 133–34, 197n14; census of, 11;
    evolution of, 10–11, 15; help victims
    in different ways, 12, 68, 80, 108, 172;
    underfunded, 13, 80–81, 84
aggravated assault, 10, 129
airing dirty laundry, 179
allies, 80, 133, 146–47, 151, 160
alpha males, 158
alternative health organization, 162
anger management, 155
anniversary of a client's murder, 4. *See
    also* Shelly
anti-feminist backlash, 143, 165
anti-racism, 61, 147, 179

anti-rape movement, 10, 14, 57
appointments, 9, 26, 69
arrest warrants, 29, 113, 118, 132, 135, 149, 172, 174
arson, 66
assistant district attorneys. *See* district attorney
Atlas.ti, 190–91
audiologist, 46

babies, newborn, 76–77
bachelor's degree, 42. *See also* academic credentials
backstage versus frontstage, 49, 65, 196n12
bailiffs, 115, 117, 120, 122–24, 126, 129
bake sales, 14
Bancroft, Lundy, 159
banks, 180
bars, 154
battered women's movement, 55–57
battered women's shelters. *See* shelters
batterer intervention programs, 8–9, 12, 124, 154–55, 166–67
bench, judge's, 115, 122, 124, 126
Bible, 121
bill collectors, 24, 163–64; different from advocates and counselors, 24, 35, 45–47, 50
biomechanics, 156, 158
birth certificates, 63
blue jeans, 125
boots, snakeskin, 2
bragging, 27
breadwinner identity, 18
breakfast, 119
broadswords, 113
bruises, 44, 67, 103, 130
budget cuts, 8, 10, 21, 24, 80–81, 158, 161, 182, 187–88. *See also* funding
Bureau of Labor Statistics, 42
burnout, 182. *See also* emotional experiences of staff

cable news, 33
cafeterias, 162
Canada, 116

candles, 92
candy, 122
car trips, 8
care work, 114, 118, 128, 130, 134–37, 180–81; devaluation of women's, 19–20, 112, 118, 136–39, 160, 177–78, 200n11; difficult to measure, 134; *See also* "sit and listen" approach
carpet, 126
case files, 25, 95
cereal, 91
charitable organizations, 50, 99
chickens, 109
child abuse, 159
child care providers, 22
Child Protective Services, 15, 58, 77
children, 26, 77, 79, 88, 107, 128
children's toys, 29
Christian identity, 18
Christie, Nils, 198n1
cigarettes, 70, 78, 92
civil documents, 124
civil rights movement, 12
civil versus criminal law, 124
Civil War, 22
Clark, Candace, 87, 106–7, 186
classmates, 99
clergy, 24, 48–50, 164, 167; called to service, 48; different from advocates and counselors, 24, 35, 47–50; fostering community, 48
clerk of court, 65, 115, 119–23, 126, 128
clients' cases, specific: decided to divorce abuser, 63; died in fire, 66–67, 75, 79, 82; found a job, 25; learned how to walk again, 27; overly difficult, 86, 97, 183 (*see also* Tammy); quickly recovered, 109–10; reunited with her children, 29–30; sought after at SAFE by abuser, 150; underwent rape kit exam, 33; was murdered, 1–4, 132, 140, 175 (*see also* Shelly)
clients, SAFE: ask for explicit advice, 37–38; break rules, 19, 84; cry for help in subtle ways, 5; demographics of, 72, 195n10; do not return to SAFE, 28, 84; do not return staff's calls, 28; lie,

19, 84; return to abusers, 62–63,
73–74, 84; success stories of, 26–30;
are unpredictable, 20; yell at staff,
19, 84
clinical license, 13, 36, 58, 96. *See also*
professional credentials
clipboards, 64
clothes, 33, 93, 198n5
clothes, stylish, 110
coding strategies, 190
codirectors, SAFE, 1, 4–5, 13, 29–30, 36,
43, 61, 73, 93, 114–15, 119, 131, 135,
175, 180, 184, 188; sooth staff, 4; years
of experience, 5, 30
coffee shops, 8
cognitive solutions, 6, 173; different from
affective solutions, 24, 82, 173, 180
Cole, Johnetta, 179
college students, 120
combat boots, 157
community college, 98
community events, 160
community members, 29
compassion fatigue, 182. *See also*
emotional experiences of staff
complaints, 25, 43, 45, 51, 58, 69, 104,
132, 158, 162, 169
con artists, 183–84
conferences on domestic violence and
sexual assault, 99, 153–54, 159. *See
also* training, staff
confidentiality requirements, 117, 127
contact hours with clients, 96. *See also*
professional credentials
Cooley, Charles Horton, 17
cooling out, 182–84
Coombes, Leigh, 59
coordinated community response, 11, 57,
133. *See also* Duluth Model
coping strategies, 7, 191. *See also* affective
solutions; cognitive solutions
Copp, Martha, 200n1
cops. *See* law enforcement
corporate managers, 24, 163; different
from advocates and counselors, 24,
35, 46–47, 50
Corrigan, Rose, 196n2

counselors: critical of colleagues in
private practice, 43–44, 50; different
job than advocates, 5, 9, 35–45–47,
93, 119, 131, 185–86
counselors' professional training, 35–36,
39–45. *See also* academic credentials;
professional credentials
country club set, 44
court: building, 89, 94–95, 97 103, 108–9,
128, 153, 181, 188; docket, 116;
hallways, 125–26; hearings, 2–3,
102–3, 115–19, 129–30, 134, 155, 177;
recess, 33, 65, 116; symbolic architecture of, 117, 125–28; system, 35
credential divide 35–45. *See also* academic
credentials; professional credentials
credentials: indicators of expertise, 39;
See also academic credentials;
professional credentials
creepy men, 14, 143, 150, 156
criminal justice system, 12, 19; advocates
and counselors trained to be
skeptical of, 2, 5, 19, 58, 62, 64, 77,
112–19, 128, 133, 139–41, 171–72, 176;
can fail victims, 3; confusing to
navigate, 88, 115–16, 121; evolving
relationship between places like
SAFE and, 13–14, 118, 131–35, 140,
180–81; *See also* legal remedies
criminals, 107
crisis, clients in, 36, 93, 100
crisis hotline, 4, 32–33, 35, 82, 88, 142;
author's experiences with, 37–39,
164, 187–88
crying, 1, 4, 103
cubicles, 121, 123
cultural capital, 127
curfews, 93, 174
custody battles, 23, 29, 59, 69, 78–79, 118,
134, 150, 175

defendants, 121, 126
defense attorneys, 115, 130
Department of Social Services (DSS),
11–12, 15, 54, 58, 69, 72, 80, 89–90,
173, 197
Descartes, René, 180

difficult clients: break rules 85, 91-93, 173; express anger, 85, 93-94, 99-100, 173-74; hard to change behavior of, 86; lie, 85, 88-89, 173; negative consequences of, 85; return to abusers, 85, 89-91, 173; skip appointments, 85, 94-96, 173; staff want to forgive, 85-97, 106-8, 173; sympathy can enable behavior of, 86, 173

dirty work, 30-31, 35, 142

disability checks, 2

discussions of violence, 33

disempowerment, staff's concerns about, 52, 59, 93, 104, 185

disharmony at work, conditions that foster, 43, 94

dishes, 91

dispatchers, 144, 152

district attorney: assistants, 4, 58, 77, 80, 113, 122, 126, 128-30, 155, 181; office, 131, 140

divorce, 183

Doctors Without Borders, 50

doctors, 12, 15, 54, 72, 80, 83, 107, 174

domestic violence and sexual assault: frequency of, 10, 134, 149, 178; means of calculating rate of, 149

domination, 11, 14, 34, 186, 194n2

donors, 110-11

doorbell, 9

driving clients, 26, 73

drug abuse, 89, 92, 98, 101, 103, 108, 153, 155

DuBois, W.E.B., 22-23, 161; See also psychological wage

Duluth Model, 11, 57, 133. See also coordinated community response

Dunn, Jennifer, 102

e-mail, 151

egalitarian workplaces, 12, 40, 197n14

elementary school teaching, 147

elite boarding schools, 161

embosser, notary, 122

emergency cell phones, 38, 63

emergency rooms, 12, 80, 174

emotional abuse, 9, 28, 194n2

emotional costs of advocacy and counseling, 24, 30, 104, 174, 182, 184

emotional dilemmas: efforts to solve, 49, 71, 79, 144, 165-66; specific descriptions of, 85-6, 106, 117, 139, 141, 144, 165; structured into staff's work, 7, 20, 24, 50; summary of, 19, 20, 170-71; unintended consequences of efforts to solve, 50-51, 80-84, 171-72

emotional experiences of staff: compassion, 4; satisfaction, 4, 25-30, 49, 116, 128-32, 136, 139, 170; exhausting all sympathy, 19, 97 101; fear of abusers, 143-44, 149-51, 171; fear of giving bad advice, 38-39; fearful for clients' safety, 4, 37, 52, 54-55, 62, 81-83, 107-8, 137, 169, 172; frustration, 4, 38, 79, 86, 111, 128, 130-31, 166, 169, 173; grief, 1, 4-5, 19, 21-22, 25, 49, 66-67, 81-83, 169, 189; guilt, 4, 66-67, 81-83, 172, 174, 182; sympathy, 4, 19, 54, 86, 94, 138, 166, 171, 181

emotional investments, 28

emotional labor, 45-47, 91, 138

emotional memory, 74

emotional reserves, 26, 101, 105, 184

emotional solutions to problems. See affective solutions

emotional strain, 34

emotional subcultures, 136

emotions, sociology of, 20, 105, 167, 180

empowerment philosophy, 5, 19, 26-27, 52-55, 158; and ambiguity, 55, 59-60, 69, 104-05; application of, 62-67; clients leery of, 37-38, 62-71, 185-86; clients' resistance toward, 94; as critical of "expert" advice, 35, 58, 62, 83-84, 171, 175, 185-86, 197n14; definitions of, 53, 59-62, 181-82; framing steering as, 65, 71-72, 76; historical origins of, 56-59; and looking for signs of empowerment in clients, 23, 75, 93, 100; and not being directive, 3, 19, 26-27, 40, 54-55, 62, 64, 75, 80-84, 91, 94, 99, 114, 136, 171, 175, 184-86; as found in popular discourse, 61

enabling bad behavior, concerns about, 86, 97, 100–1, 104, 183

enraged abusers, 2, 77, 114, 152

essentialist beliefs, 118, 132, 137–38; assume men are aggressive, 138, 157; assume men are non-caring, 164–65; assume women are caregivers, 145, 157, 163–67, 179–81

evidence based prosecution, 133

ex parte, 123

experts of their situations, treating clients as, 38, 52, 63, 83, 186

explaining victims' behaviors to outsiders, 49, 56, 102, 104, 111

extrinsic rewards, 16, 24, 30, 47–48, 50, 127, 169

feeling rules, 167, 173 201n7

feminazi stereotype, 4, 20, 34, 97, 108, 140–46 159–60, 165, 167, 169, 171–72, 177, 179

feminism: critiques of, 12–13; declining influence on places like SAFE, 14–15, 134, 140, 143, 172; and identity of activists, 14, 18; rhetoric of, 14–15; second-wave, 7, 10, 13–14, 56, 140, 176, 180–81

fieldnotes, 126, 190

fleeing abusers, 59, 62–63, 66

forensic examinations, 32–33

forgotten memories, 74

Freire, Paulo, 61

frontstage versus backstage, 49, 65, 196n12

Frye, Marilyn, 198n9

funding: governmental, 13, 84; insufficient, 1, 4, 6, 19, 35, 51, 83–84, 171–72; opportunities, 13, 51, 110, 118, 134, 138. *See also* budget cuts

fundraising, 10, 14, 110–11, 160, 180, 184

furniture, 120, 126, 188

gas stations, 108

gender identity, 163, 166

gender inequality and violence, relationship between, 11, 15, 34, 56, 127, 149, 176

gender pay gap, 137–39, 164, 178

gender violence, 33–34, 56, 109, 118, 127, 133, 143, 193n1

generalized accounts, 189

Gengler, Amanda, 15, 54, 185

glass escalator, 147

Goffman, Erving, 183

graduate program requirements, 36, 96

grass-roots organizations, 13

greener pastures, 44, 50, 163

grocery stores, 49, 108, 150

guns, 3, 124, 133

Guy-Sheftall, Beverly, 179

gyms, 156

hair follicles, 33

handouts, 37, 53, 57, 63, 68, 89, 105, 125

Haven House, 10

hens, 157

hiding thoughts from clients, 3, 38, 66, 68, 75–80, 90, 184–86

Hochschild, Arlie, 45, 196n9

Holden, Daphne, 47

holidays, 91, 188

homeless shelters, 48, 163; comparisons with SAFE, 47–48

homelessness, 103

honoring clients' wishes, 74, 77

hospitals, 8, 11–12, 15, 32, 58, 76, 162, 197

housing, 26, 59, 69, 99–100, 113

Hughes, Everett C., 30

ice cream, 29

ice-breakers, 156–57

identities: as accomplishments 15–18; as dynamic and fluid 14; as symbols, 15–18; social function of, 18; sociological approach to understanding, 16–18, 20

identity work, 16–18, 109, 167, 173–75, 196n12

ideological codes, 127

imams, 48

"imminent danger," 54, 78–79, 88, 121

immunization records, 63

impression management, 18, 80, 109. *See also* frontstage versus backstage

in-home family counseling program,
8, 36
individualistic perspectives, 7, 11, 56,
105, 133
industrial managers. *See* corporate
managers
institutions that also serve victims (legal,
medical, social service), 5, 7,11–12,
15, 26, 54, 57, 80, 111, 133, 145, 172
Internet discussion groups, 151
intervening because of imminent danger,
54, 66–67, 71. *See also* rescuing
clients, temptation to
intimate partner violence, 10, 67, 149
intrinsic rewards. *See* moral wages
intuition, 40

Jackall, Robert, 46
jail, 88, 98–99, 101, 108, 113, 134, 153, 183
jobs: and expressing sympathy, 45–47;
good versus bad, 23, 30; workers'
motivations towards, 23–24, 30;
jock insurance, 201n3
Joffe, Carol, 195n2
"journey to recovery," clients', 28
judge's bench, 115, 122–24, 126
judge's chambers, 126
judges, 2, 12, 14, 64–65, 77–78, 80, 85, 88,
97, 102–3, 109, 114–15, 117–21, 122–24,
129, 133, 135, 144, 155, 177, 181, 188
juries, 72, 103, 109

Khan, Shamus, 161
kindergarten classroom, 147
kindled flame, 27
"kiss my ass" (KMA), 41
kitchens, 27, 91, 118, 146
Kleinman, Sherryl, 18, 162
Konradi, Amanda, 103

LA Law, 127
Lamb, Sharron, 199n14
Larcombe, Wendy, 102
latent functions, 181–82. *See also* manifest
functions
Latino population, 13, 131, 195n10
laughter, 24, 41, 48, 129

Law and Order, 127
law enforcement (cops, police officers,
sheriff's deputies), 3, 8, 15, 54, 68, 72,
77, 80, 88–89, 97–98, 101–3, 107,
113–15, 124, 126, 128, 131, 140,
154–55, 158, 159, 164, 166, 174
law firms, 41–45, 127
lawbreakers, 14
lawyers, 12, 14–15, 35, 42–43, 53, 69, 72,
78, 80, 83, 97–98, 101, 103, 117–24,
126–29, 133, 144, 164, 166, 174
legal advocate position, 40, 128, 131, 155,
180–81; establishing credentials
for, 181
legal expenses, 43, 78
legal jargon, 2, 64, 78
legal notepads, 125, 132–33
legal reforms, 11, 15, 58, 134–35
legal remedies, 113–36, 138–41, 154, 172;
can create more risks for victims, 88,
132, 174–75; effectiveness of, 134–35
legal system: confusing to clients, 64,
115–16, 121, 124; did not always keep
clients safe, 114–15, 140. *See also*
criminal justice system
legal victories, 117, 128–32
legal work, 19, 94, 112; different than care
work, 117, 119, 128, 177, 180–81; easier
to explain than care work, 127–28,
137; greater social value than care
work, 127–31, 135–38, 177; seen as
"concrete and tangible," 117–19, 125,
130–31, 135, 139, 171
legislators, 14
librarianship, 147
litmus tests, 143, 149–53, 166, 171, 180.
little victories, importance of, 23, 26, 28,
136, 139
Lively, Kathryn, 41
looking glass self, 17
Loseke, Donileen, 197n10
lunch breaks, 33

macho guys, 143–44, 156, 166. *See also*
litmus tests
macro level analysis, 8, 132, 145
magistrates, 117

"making a speech," 152
making calls for clients, 26, 69, 94
male generic pronouns, 151
man-hater stereotype, 4, 20, 34, 97, 108, 140–46 159–60, 165, 167, 169, 171–72, 177, 179
mandatory arrest policies, 58, 88, 133, 196n4
manhood acts, 148
manifest functions, 181–82. *See also* latent functions
manila folders, 25, 130
marks, 183–84
Martin Luther King day, 146
masters in social work degree (MSW), 36, 41, 43
McQueeney, Krista, 48
Mears, Ashley, 137
media coverage, 85, 137, 157–58
medical practitioners, 162–63
men, leery of, 5–6, 20, 37, 141–46, 149–53, 171, 179
men's education about abuse, 159
men's rehabilitation consulting businesses, 155
metal detectors, 122
micro level analysis, 8. *See also* research methods
middle class status, 12, 48, 120
military, 156
misconceptions about abuse, 11, 51, 67, 87, 99, 108, 111, 169
misperceptions: of SAFE's mission 117, 142: of SAFE's clients 49, 102–5, 109–11, 173–75
moral "dirty work," 23–24, 30–35, 44–45, 50, 164
moral entrepreneurs, 112
moral identity code, 18–19, 54, 73, 80, 136, 162, 173–75; hard standard to achieve, 18–19, 54, 72, 79, 94, 140, 184; *See also* identities
moral identity, 18, 22, 28, 30, 46, 48, 86, 109, 162, 173
moral rhetoric, 24, 48
moral wages, 86–87, 94, 106, 112, 136, 138, 140, 146, 162–67; definition of,

16, 22, 25, 49; experienced in slow doses, 28; downsides of, 51; earned in different amounts in office, 29–30, 35–45; impediments to earning, 45–48; pathways to earning, 30, 35–49; vary by occupation, 47; what it felt like to earn, 24–30; workplace conditions that foster, 35–51, 80–81; and workplace sacrifices, 18–19
moral worth, 27, 48, 195n3
Morgan, Mandy, 59
movement against domestic violence and sexual assault, 14, 86, 97, 101, 145, 171
movies, 102
MSW (masters in social work degree), 36, 41, 43
music, 92
mythopoetic men's movement, 167

National Center for Injury and Prevention Control, 10
National Coalition Against Domestic Violence, 194n7
National Directory of Domestic Violence Programs, 11
National Organization for Women, 10
neoliberal reforms, 13, 84, 197n11
newsletters, 111
nightmares, 1
"no drop" policies, 58, 133, 196n4, 200n10
nonfeminist jobs, 166
nonprofit organizations, 43, 84, 97, 110, 162–63
nurses, 15, 33, 58, 77, 197n13. *See also* sexual assault nurse examiners
nursing, 147

office harmony, conditions that foster, 37, 40–41, 43
office space, SAFE's, 5, 25, 79, 88, 115, 120; kitchen, 118; upstairs versus downstairs, 9, 29, 35–37, 40, 43, 149
old guard, 9
organizational efficiency, 13
Oxford English Dictionary, 196n1

paralegals, 24, 35, 42–43, 45, 127; different from advocates and counselors, 24, 35, 41–43, 45, 47, 50

Pascoe, C.J., 201n3

pastors, 48

patients, 107

patios, 92

patriarchal dividend, 200n2

patriarchy, 11, 34, 56, 127, 149, 176

pay, power, and prestige, 16, 24, 30, 47–48, 50, 127, 169. See also extrinsic rewards

penal system, 13–14

Perry Mason, 127

petechiae, 98, 106

pets, 99, 109

pews, 122

photos of victims, 98, 106

physical abuse, 9–10, 28, 33, 57, 103, 109, 135, 149, 193n2

physical therapy, 27

pick-up trucks, 120

Pierce, Jennifer, 41

plants, 92

plea bargains, 126, 128

police cruisers, 98

police officers. See law enforcement

policy makers, 14, 161, 171–72

political allies, 147, 133, 151

politicians, 110, 133

politics, 9, 144; of law and order, 14

post-traumatic stress disorder, 101

posture, 103

power and control, 12, 14, 57, 82, 89, 114, 134, 160, 176, 178, 184–85

Power and Control Wheel, 57, 61, 67, 89

practitioners, suggestions for, 20, 168, 178–86

preachers, 48

premature euphoria, 74, 90–91

pressing charges, 37, 54, 62, 77, 114

pride parades, 146

priests, 48

principal's office, 147

privileging male allies, 159–60, 165, 179–80

pro bono lawyers, 2, 100, 120, 123, 125, 197n14

probation officers, 126, 128

prodding clients, 27, 84, 185. See also steering

professional colleagues, 29, 43–44, 60

professional credentials, 13, 23–24, 35–45, 50, 58, 83, 127, 180–81, 185, 200n12. See also academic credentials

progressive causes, 146–47

progressive merit badges, 145–53, 179; value of, 153–59

Promise Keepers, 167

protective orders, 2–3, 37, 43, 64–65, 78–79, 85, 88–89, 114–15, 129, 135, 172, 174, 181; application process, 119–24; and author's experiences, 119–24, 140, 188; and how they work, 123; "only a piece of paper," 114, 132, 134, 199n2; advocates cannot fill out, 2, 64

psychological wage, 22–23, 161; See also W.E.B. Dubois

psychological wounds, 31. See also emotional abuse

public funding regulations, 13, 134–35, 172

public officials, 29

public prestige, 24

public sentiment, 30, 97, 109–12

questions asked of victims: "what was she wearing?", 32; "why doesn't she call the cops?", 49; "why doesn't she leave?", 32, 89; "why does she go back?", 89

rabbis, 48

racial diversity, 12

racial inequality, 61, 147, 179

Randall, Melanie, 102

rape crisis centers, 11, 14–15, 143, 151, 194n8

rape kits, 32–33

rape, 6, 10, 14, 26, 32–33, 58, 103, 115, 149

Reader's Guide to Periodical Literature, 10

Reconstruction, post Civil War period of, 23

"red flags," 150–51

reflected appraisals, 17

regional awards, 10

religious institutions, 48

rent payments, 88, 100

reputation, SAFE's: in community, 20, 85, 143, 101, 185; in court, 20, 79, 97

rescuing clients, temptation to, 19, 26, 65–66, 71

research methods, 8, 60, 126, 142–43, 160, 187–91. *See also* coding strategies; fieldnotes

research on victim service providers, 6, 21, 118

restaurants, 8, 110, 128

restraining orders. *See* protective orders

retreats, 156–58, 189

rewards, 29. *See also* workplace motivations.

risky behavior, 19, 52, 71, 82, 87, 103, 170

robbery, 10

rookies, 107

SAFE: and alternative theories of abuse, 7, 11–12, 34, 56; board of trustees, 14; database, 25; interacting with community, 9–10, 184; promotional materials, 125; salaries of staff, 21, 24, 31, 36, 38–39, 42–43, 110, 127; similarities with other organizations, 8

safety planning, 63, 119, 175, 181

salaries, SAFE staff's, 21, 24, 31, 36, 38–39, 42–43, 110, 127

saving face, 63, 81

scalpels, 113

scars, 67, 115, 194n2

schadenfreude, 129

scholarship of domestic violence and sexual assault, 6, 11, 21, 118, 190

school enrollment requirements, 63

school system, local, 8

school, 122, 128

scratches, 67

self-blame, 82, 181–82

self-defense training, 150, 156–58, 166

self-help discourse, 61

selflessness, 27, 32, 43, 147, 163, 165

service gaps, 1, 5

services at SAFE, 8–9, 35–36; brainstorming with clients, 76; community outreach, 8–10; client contacts, 125; counseling, individual, 8–9; counseling, in-home, 8, 36; counseling, support groups, 8–9; court advocacy, 8–9, 68; driving clients, 69–70; education, youth, 8–9; educational outreach, 28, 155; effectiveness of, 6

sexual assault nurse examiners, 33, 58

sexual assault and domestic violence: frequency of, 10, 134, 149, 178; means of calculating rate of, 149

shadow training, 37, 60, 187, 189, 196n5

Shelly, 1–4, 132, 140, 175.

shelters, 11, 14, 15, 54, 143, 186; SAFE's, 3, 8, 68, 70, 91; behavioral contracts with clients, 70, 91; and communication with SAFE advocates and counselors, 3; concerns about clients leaving, 75–76; expulsion from, 91–92; secret location of, 3, 8, 143; staff, 3, 27, 40, 70, 73, 75, 81, 91–92, 99, 136, 185

sheriff's department, 149, 155, 158

sheriff's deputies. *See* law enforcement

shoes, 33

side bets, 148

"sit and listen" approach, 58, 114, 118, 128, 130, 134–37, 139, 180–81. *See also* care work

simple assault, 10

smile, 103

smoking, 70, 78, 92

sneers, 103

social capital, 153

social change, versus individual, 15

social control, 101

Social Security cards, 63

social service agencies, SAFE's coordination with, 9, 13, 26, 70, 90, 173

social service caseworkers, 15, 54, 58–59, 70, 72, 80, 173–75

social status, 41–42, 88, 106–8, 120, 127, 159
social work, 36, 43, 96, 147, 188, 196n8
sociological perspectives, 6, 33, 55, 86–87, 101, 105–8, 132, 176
soup kitchens, 146
Spanish language, 131
sparring, 158
spirituality, 61
sports, 33
staff meetings, 1, 4–5, 33, 175
stalking, 102, 133
steering, 55, 71, 87, 99, 171, 174–78; and planting seeds of doubt, 72–74; and relying on authority of others, 76–79; and speculating about brighter futures, 75–76; staff admit to, 71, 75, 77, 79
Stein, Karen, 17
stigma, 32, 45, 141, 193n1
strangulation, 76, 98, 101
strategic friendliness, 72
street level bureaucrats, 59
subordinate adaptation, 178–80
suicidal, abusers who are, 3–4
sunglasses, 102
supermarkets. See grocery stores
Sutton, Robert, 46
symbolic compensation in lieu of extrinsic rewards, 22–24, 30, 35, 44, 50–51, 106, 140, 161–64, 172; and reproduction of inequality, 16, 159–65; See also moral wages
symbolic interactionism, 17
sympathizers of last resort, 86, 96, 103, 111, 173
sympathy: generating more, 105; limits of, 101–8; mechanism of control, 87, 174; and microhierarchies, 107–8, 184–86; micropolitics of, 87–88, 106; reserves, 105; and workplace stance toward clients, 23–24, 35

talking about work with outsiders, 10, 19, 32–34, 44, 129, 137, 184, 189
Tammy, 98–101, 103–5, 107, 111–12, 153
tax returns, 35

teachers, 99, 107, 147
television sets, 46
ten day hearings, 123, 125
terminology: "abusers" versus "batterers," 193–94n1; "victims" versus "survivors," 193n1
testing stage of victim services, 68
textile manufacturing, 46
"thank yous," 28
theoretical contributions, 173–78
therapeutic jargon, 42
therapeutic terminology, 39
time spent in field, 8. See also research methods
tissue boxes, 4
T.J., 156–58. See also self-defense training
To Kill a Mockingbird, 127
tokens at work, 147
tough guys. See macho guys; litmus tests
"tough on crime" policies, 14, 133
trailer, 75
training, SAFE staff, 35–37, 60, 83, 114, 117, 131, 135, 153–54, 159, 182; and advocates taking pride in nonprofessional aspects, 41; experienced as "sink or swim," 39; materials, 125; and shadowing more experienced staff, 37, 60, 189, 196n5; staff retreats, 156–58, 189
transplants, 9
tricks of the trade, 20
tropes, cultural, 87, 102, 144, 160
trust falls, 157
tuition scholarships, 98
turning away clients, 5, 18–19, 21, 30, 170
TV remote controls, 2

undesirable men, screening. See litmus tests
United Way, 50
utilities, 100

veterans, 107
veterinary technicians, 22
vicarious traumatization, 182. See also emotional experiences of staff

victim blaming, 31, 50–52, 109

victim myths, 102–5, 109–11, 173–75; "perfect victim," 85–87; perpetual victimhood 109–12; domestic violence and sexual assault agencies rely on, 109–11

victim scripts, 173–75

victim stereotypes, 97, 102–5, 109–11, 173–75

victimhood, 85, 87, 90, 97, 102–4, 109–12

Violence Against Women Act, 133, 140, 172, 176

volunteering, 24, 35, 110, 163, 167; author experiences with, 8, 82, 102, 111, 117, 119–24, 142, 146, 148, 165, 187–88, training, 37–38, 82

volunteers, different from advocates and counselors, 24, 35, 47–48, 50

"wait-and-see" approach, 12, 95. *See also* care work

walk-in clients, 1, 4, 88, 174, 187

war, 33

welfare, 13

wife abuse, 10

Williams, Christine, 147

women's movement, 12–13. *See also* feminism

work schedules, 21, 9, 36, 40, 45, 119

working-class whites, 22

workload, heavy, 1, 5, 20–21, 25, 30, 33, 49, 106

workplace motivations, 23–24, 30

"worried well," 44, 50